ALIENATION

RICHARD SCHACHT is Associate Professor of Philosophy at the University of Illinois (Urbana-Champaign Campus). He has studied at Tübingen University (in Germany), and received his Ph.D. from Princeton University in 1967. His area of special interest is nineteenth- and twentieth-century Continental philosophy. Among his other writings are essays on "Hegel on Freedom" and "Husserlian and Heideggerian Phenomenology."

WALTER KAUFMANN is Professor of Philosophy at Princeton and has written, among other books, *Faith of a Heretic*, *From Shakespeare to Existentialism*, *Hegel: A Reinterpretation*, and *Tragedy and Philosophy*.

To my father and mother,
Robert H. and Alice M. Schacht

CONTENTS

ACKNOWLEDGMENTS   xiii

INTRODUCTORY ESSAY *by Walter Kaufmann*   xv

INTRODUCTION   1

1. THE LINGUISTIC AND INTELLECTUAL BACKGROUND   9

TRADITIONAL USES OF "Alienation" AND *Entfremdung*   9

    I. The Term "Alienation"   9
    II. The Term *Entfremdung*   13

HEGEL'S PREDECESSORS AND CONTEMPORARIES   15

    I. Alienation in Earlier Theology   15
    II. Alienation in Social Contract Theory   16
    III. Hegel's Contemporaries: Fichte and Schiller   21

HEGEL'S EARLY VIEWS   25

    I. The "Early Theological Writings"   26
    II. The Essay on Fichte and Schelling   30
    III. Early Political Essays   33

2. HEGEL'S *PHENOMENOLOGY OF SPIRIT*   38

   I. Introduction   38
   II. First Sense of "Alienation" (as Separation)   45
   III. Second Sense of "Alienation" (as Surrender)   54
   IV. Alienation, Objectification, and Otherness   62
   V. The Overcoming of Alienation$_1$ 65
   VI. Evaluation   68

3. MARX'S EARLY WRITINGS   73

   I. Introduction   73
   II. Man and Labor   81
   III. The Alienation of One's Product   92
   IV. The Alienation of Labor   96
   V. Alienation from Other Men   102
   VI. Self-alienation   108
   VII. The Origin and Overcoming of Alienation   114
   VIII. Concluding Remarks   119

4. ERICH FROMM AND KAREN HORNEY   123

ERICH FROMM   124

   I. Introduction   124
   II. Man's Relation to Nature   126
   III. Man's Relation to Others   130
   IV. Man's Relation to Society   135
   V. Man's Relation to Himself   138
   VI. "Alienation" in Other Contexts   144
   VII. Concluding Remarks   147

KAREN HORNEY   148

   I. *New Ways in Psychoanalysis*   148

II. *Our Inner Conflicts*   151
III. *Neurosis and Human Growth*   153

5. THE SOCIOLOGICAL LITERATURE   161

   I. Introduction   161
   II. Alienation and Others   164
   III. Alienation and Work   168
   IV. Alienation, Events, and Structures   173
   V. Alienation, Culture, and Society   183
   VI. Conclusion   200

6. EXISTENTIAL PHILOSOPHY AND
   THEOLOGY   205

   I. Introduction   205
   II. *Entfremdung* in Heidegger's *Being and
      Time*   208
   III. Estrangement in Tillich's *Systematic
      Theology*   213
   IV. *Aliénation* in Sartre's Major Works 226
   ADDENDUM. Philosophical Anthropology: Arnold
   Gehlen and Helmuth Plessner   240

7. ALIENATION: A GENERAL
   CONSIDERATION   245

   I. Introduction   245
   II. A Systematic Attempt at Generalization 249
   III. Proposed Restrictions   256
   IV. Basic Issues   267

REFERENCES   275

INDEX   287

ACKNOWLEDGMENTS

I should like to acknowledge a great debt of gratitude to Professor Walter Kaufmann, of the Department of Philosophy of Princeton University, both for contributing his fine introductory essay to this volume, and for the many ways in which he has been helpful to me. His interest in alienation long preceded mine; and it was he who first suggested to me, when I was a graduate student at Princeton, that the literature on alienation was badly in need of a systematic critical analysis, and that I might find it interesting to undertake such an analysis in my doctoral dissertation, which he offered to supervise. He was quite right on both counts; and the guidance and assistance he gave me, and the interest he took in my work, far exceeded anything ordinarily expected of a dissertation supervisor. He continued to be most helpful after the dissertation was completed, as it was revised and revised again in preparation for publication; so that his contributions extend from the original idea of this study to its present form. He thus is partly responsible for its existence, and deserves credit for a considerable part of whatever merit it may have as well.

Many others have been helpful in a variety of more specific ways. I should like to single out my father-in-law, Professor Marshall Clinard, of the Department of Sociology of the University of Wisconsin, for his suggestions relating to my discussion of conceptions of alienation in recent sociological literature, and for his many other helpful suggestions and general encouragement; and Drs. Helmut Fahrenbach and

Frithjof Rodi, of the Philosophische Seminar of Tübingen University (West Germany), for their suggestions in connection with my discussions of Marx and recent Continental philosophers.

I would also like to thank my original and present editors at Doubleday, Mr. Orde Coombs and Mr. William Whitehead, respectively, for their helpful suggestions in the course of my successive revisions of my original discussion. I also am grateful to Miss Judith Checker, who checked many of my references for me. And finally, I would like to thank my wife Marsha for her patience and understanding throughout the long five years during which I worked on this study.

WALTER KAUFMANN

The Inevitability of Alienation

The analysis of confused concepts has been one of the central functions of philosophy since Socrates. But how can one analyze "alienation"? If we concentrate on one person to prove that he does not know what he thinks he knows and that he contradicts himself, we leave the impression that one hapless victim was in a bad way while dozens of reputable writers know perfectly well what they are talking about. Thus Socrates' method fails us.

What is needed is a careful, critical survey of the ways in which many of the most influential writers have used the term. That, of course, is a difficult undertaking and requires considerable scholarship. But short of that, we shall always be reduced to confusion when we read about alienation. And if we simply do not care how other men have used the word and say, in effect, "This is how I shall use it," we are quite apt to be told that the term really means something else and that we ought to read this writer or that.

Richard Schacht has written a badly needed book. He tells us briefly how "alienation" was used before 1800; he shows how Hegel, the father of the contemporary discussion, spoke of alienation in two diametrically opposed senses, and how Marx's uses of the term, which are analyzed at length, are still different. Anyone interested in Hegel and Marx will find these chapters fascinating, and all who are concerned with alienation will find them immensely helpful and illuminating. Schacht goes on to give us a detailed critique of the many senses in which Erich Fromm has used the term, a briefer discussion of Karen Horney, an extremely interesting survey of recent sociological literature on alienation, and finally some discussion of Heidegger, Tillich, and Sartre.

Henceforth, nobody should write about alienation without first reading Schacht's book. Others have had doubts whether the word had not been used so promiscuously that its usefulness had been seriously impaired. But what was needed was not a blanket resolve to abandon the term or to use it in some clearly specified way. What was needed was clarification.

Nor is this all Schacht offers us. He shows that there is no single general meaning of "alienation" of which different writers could be said to have discussed different aspects. But it does not follow that the conditions to which the term has been applied do not deserve serious study. On the contrary, it is high time to reconsider them. But anyone who wishes to do that—as I do, for example—will also be in Schacht's debt for having brought together in a single volume the major claims that have been made about these phenomena.

Schacht has given us a prolegomena to any future study of alienation. This introductory essay gives me an opportunity to suggest where we might go from here.

My central interest is not in the concept but in the conditions to which it has been applied. These are widely held to be specifically modern, but I hope to show that they were common to most, if not all, of the great philosophers of the past. I shall deal similarly with literature and art—not only with a few major poets of the past but also with Oedipus and Hamlet and with the public's relation to literature, art, and music. Whether we choose to speak of alienation or not, the experiences widely associated with that term are often held to be distinctive characteristics of our time, or of capitalistic societies; but we shall see that they are actually encountered in abundance in past ages and in noncapitalistic societies.

Then I shall criticize Marx's dream of an unalienated society as well as the fashionable notion that things have never been worse than they are now. Marx's vastly influential restriction of our term to destructive conditions will be seen to be open to serious objections. Neither will it do to restrict the term to fruitful estrangement. Alienation is neither a disease nor a blessing but, for better or worse, a central fea-ture of human existence.

1. Historical Perspective

"Alienation" came into its own during the Cold War, as a meeting place for East and West, for Marxism and existen-tialism. In *Escape from Freedom* (1941), Erich Fromm, who later did as much as anyone to popularize the term, used it a couple of times (pp. 119, 151), and some of the phenomena to which he later applied it are discussed at some length (117 ff.), but the word was not considered worth listing in the index. And it was only during the 1960s that the term gained entrance into philosophical dictionaries.

This is odd because Hegel used the term frequently, and in his first book, *Phenomenology of the Spirit* (1807), one whole chapter, over a hundred pages in length, bore the title "Spirit *alienated from itself.* Culture." This was followed by a chapter on "Spirit *certain of itself.* Morality." That aliena-tion was not discussed in the English-speaking world even during the heyday of Anglo-American Idealism is not sur-prising, because the Idealists concentrated on Hegel's later works and generally paid little attention to the *Phenomenol-ogy.* It is not so easy to explain why the German Hegel litera-ture also neglected this theme. Hermann Glockner did not list the two German words for alienation, *Entfremdung* and *Entäusserung,* in his four-volume *Hegel-Lexikon* (1935–39), and Johannes Hoffmeister did not include them either in the index of his scholarly edition of the *Phänomenologie* (1952) or in his immensely learned *Wörterbuch der philosophischen Begriffe* (2d ed., 1955). That Hegel used two terms and that both were colored strongly by his conception of the develop-ment of spirit, does not really explain why this whole com-plex of ideas received so little attention for so long. It was the case of an idea whose time had not come.

The one great exception confirms this view. Karl Marx, who was thirteen years old when Hegel died in 1831, was fasci-nated by this aspect of Hegel's philosophy when he came to study it twelve years later. In his "Philosophical Manuscripts" of 1844 we encounter long discussions of *Entfremdung* and *Entäusserung*, but most of this material was not published until 1932, and in *The Communist Manifesto* (1848) Marx specifically denounced talk of alienation as "philosophical nonsense."[1]

Even in 1932 the time was not yet ripe for "alienation." Less than a year after the publication of Marx's early manuscripts the Nazis came to power in Germany and put an end to scholarly discussions of Marx's thought. And the Soviet hierarchy accepted the view of "alienation" put forth in *The Communist Manifesto*. (The ideas of the young Marx will be considered briefly below.)

Martin Buber had spoken of *Verfremdung* in his long discussion of "the proliferation of the It-world" in Part Two of *Ich und Du* (1923). In retrospect, we can even say that most of Part Two deals with alienation; but the term was not and did not become a slogan; neither did the book trigger any widespread discussion of alienation. For a quarter of a century the influence of the book was confined largely to Protestant theologians.

Later, Bertolt Brecht developed an anti-Aristotelian poetics and spoke of a *Verfremdungseffekt* or, for short, *V-Effekt*. He meant that the audience should not be taken in by an illusion: Dramatists should go out of their way to remind the audience that it is in a theater, watching a play. In this sense, the playwright should alienate the audience or keep it detached: He should forestall emotional identification.

Others, too, had spoken of *Entfremdung* and *Verfremdung*, but before World War II these terms did not catch on any more than "alienation" did in the English-speaking world. It was only when the world was divided into two camps that Marxism and existentialism sought common ground in discussions of alienation.

---

[1] In section III.1.c: *"Die deutschen Literaten* [a disparaging term for writers] *. . . schrieben ihren philosophischen Unsinn hinter das französische Original. Zum Beispiel hinter die französische Kritik der Geldverhältnisse schrieben sie 'Entäusserung des menschlichen Wesens' . . ."*

To begin with Marxism, the publication of Marx's early manuscripts was a godsend for Georg Lukács, the Hungarian critic who in the fifties and sixties came to be more widely admired in the West than any other Marxist theoretician. In the twenties the Communist Party in the Soviet Union had vilified him for his Hegelian deviations from true Marxism. When the Nazis came to power, he fled to the Soviet Union, abjured his heresies, abased himself, and paid ample tribute to Stalin. At the same time, he went to work on a long German book, which was finished substantially in 1938 and published after thorough revision in 1948: *Der junge Hegel* (The Young Hegel). The final section of this volume bore the title: "*Entäusserung* as the [or: a] central philosophical concept of the *Phenomenology of the Spirit*."

In these final thirty-five pages Lukács made the stone that the builders had rejected for one hundred and forty years the chief cornerstone of Hegel's first book, which by that time had come to be widely considered Hegel's most original and brilliant work. But of the forty footnotes that support Lukács' argument in this section, only six refer to Hegel's writings, while two refer to Lenin, two to Engels—and twenty-one to Karl Marx.

The modern interest in Hegel's and Marx's discussions of alienation seems to date from this book. This is rather odd, because the final section of the volume obviously has to be understood in the context of Lukács' troubled career—as an elaborate attempt at self-justification. His own Hegelianism was not to be considered a deviation, after all; Hegel had been misunderstood; "alienation" was central in his thought—no less than in Marx's. Of course, "alienation" was not to be found in the books Marx himself published—except where he expressly condemned those who used the term—but it was central in his early manuscripts, and these in turn provided the key for the correct interpretation of his mature thought.

The strategy is transparent, and Stalin's functionaries were not persuaded. It seems scarcely credible that the modern vogue of "alienation" should derive from such an unpromising beginning. It seems even less likely when one considers that Lukács stressed *Entäusserung* rather than *Entfremdung*, although, like Hegel and Marx, he used both terms.

As long as we see Lukács' predicament as entirely personal, it does not seem possible to make sense of the development that actually followed in the fifties and sixties. But what had prompted his deviationism in the first place was his humanist background and his early affinity to existentialism. It has even been suggested that some of Heidegger's most characteristic concerns, including the distinction between authentic and inauthentic existence, were derived from Lukács' early work, although Lukács himself has said, more plausibly, that "the problem was in the air." And he himself has said that "Kierkegaard played a considerable role in my early development; in the last years before the War [i.e., before 1914] in Heidelberg I even planned to write a monograph on his critique of Hegel."[2] Lukács was also strongly influenced by Georg Simmel and by Max Weber; and Weber, though remembered chiefly as a sociologist of genius, also exerted a formative influence on Karl Jaspers. Lukács had never wanted to renounce his roots, and the humanism of the young Marx provided, at long last, a desperately needed bridge for some rapprochement between Marxism on the one hand and existentialism and humanism on the other.

Meanwhile, some Western writers who were more or less close to existentialism were looking for ways to effect a rapprochement with Marxism, and they, too, seized on the manuscripts of the young Marx and "alienation."

Herbert Marcuse, who had dedicated his first book to Heidegger, under whom he had studied, actually beat Lukács to the punch. Lukács, writing in German, could not publish his Hegel book until 1948, while Marcuse, writing in English in the United States, published *Reason and Revolution: Hegel and the Rise of Social Theory* in 1941, making ample use of Marx's early manuscripts and devoting a good deal of attention to alienation. This may actually be the first book whose index includes "Alienation (*Entfremdung*)," although it should be noted that the index in John Baillie's English version of Hegel's *Phenomenology* lists "Alienation from self (spiritual)," followed by a reference to Hegel's discussion of

[2] *Geschichte und Klassenbewusstsein*, preface to the 1968 edition (*Werke*, vol. II), pp. 24 and 11.

the "unhappy consciousness," and "Estrangement (self)," followed by two references to the chapter mentioned above.

Karl Löwith, who had also studied with Heidegger, included some discussion of alienation in his *Von Hegel bis Nietzsche* (1941), written in exile in Japan and published in German in New York and Zürich. Here the concept was not central, as in Lukács and Marcuse; but the chapter on *Arbeit* (work or labor) included two *Referate* (reports alternating between paraphrase and quotation) on "Hegel: labor as self-alienation [*Entäusserung seiner selbst*] in the forming of the world" and on "Marx: labor as self-estrangement [*Selbstentfremdung*] of man in a world he does not own." Löwith's book contained a great many chapters that were easily as important as the one on labor, and the whole volume was studded with reports on the views not only of Hegel, Marx, Kierkegaard, and Nietzsche but also of a great many lesser writers. It could hardly have served to attract attention to alienation. But Marcuse's book might have—and did not: The time was not yet ripe.

Although Marcuse did not publish another book for the next fourteen years and went to work for the O.S.S. and the U.S. Department of State from 1941 till 1950, the discussion of Marx followed his lead and Lukács'. Sidney Hook's *From Hegel to Marx* suddenly belonged to a bygone era, although it had been published only five years earlier, in 1936; for it made no mention of alienation.

In the fifties a few refugees from Germany and Austria naturalized "alienation" in the United States. Marcuse's *Eros and Civilization* (1955), Erich Fromm's *The Sane Society* (1955), Erich Kahler's *The Tower and the Abyss* (1957), and Hannah Arendt's *The Human Condition* (1958) made constant mention of it—and the indices of these books include numerous references to it. That in Fromm's *Sane Society*, for example, includes, *inter alia*, pages 111–70 and 170–84 (of the paperback edition).

Hannah Arendt, like Marcuse, had long been under the spell of Heidegger, although she is widely associated with Karl Jaspers, to whom she was close personally. Paul Tillich, who also contributed to the vogue of "alienation," frequently

stressed his affinity with existentialism. Kahler and Fromm
lacked any distinctly existentialist background: They were,
in different ways, humanists.

This sudden explosion of interest in estrangement was
preceded by the appearance of a paperback edition of *The
Stranger* in 1954. Camus had published *L'Étranger* in 1942,
and Stuart Gilbert's translation had come out in 1946, but
it was only the paperback edition that made this short novel
one of the most influential books of the mid-century: The
protagonist became one of the heroes of a new generation.

In Germany the concept of alienation began to attract a
great deal of popular attention after Marx's early writings
appeared in a popular edition in 1953 (*Die Frühschriften*,
ed. Siegfried Landshut). But it is noteworthy that one of
Jaspers' students had been one of the very few who had ad-
dressed themselves to this problem before: Heinrich Popitz,
whose dissertation *Der entfremdete Mensch* (subtitled "The
Young Marx's Critique of the Age and Philosophy of History") appeared the same year.

It was Fromm who introduced Marx's early manuscripts to
the American public. The way in which he did this, in 1961,
speaks volumes about the transformation of the American
scene in the course of the sixties.

Marx's early manuscripts were published under Fromm's
name, not Marx's: Erich Fromm, *Marx's Concept of Man*.
The book's title was also the title of Fromm's introductory
essay, which was followed by a selection from the manuscripts
themselves. Perhaps this was not merely a reflection of
Fromm's ego; it may also have been a symptom of the after-
math of the McCarthy period. A publisher could still be
persuaded that Fromm's name would have a far wider appeal
than Marx's. It was also symptomatic that Fromm said at the
outset: "Marx's philosophy, like much of existentialist thinking, represents a protest against man's alienation, his loss of
himself and his transformation into a thing; it is a movement
against the dehumanization and automatization of man inherent in the development of Western industrialism."

Lukács had tried to make his early existentialist leanings
respectable by appealing to the young Marx. In the United

States Marx was made more appealing by attempts to show that he had much in common with existentialism.

Lukács' approach no longer seemed self-serving. Before the discovery of the "Philosophical Manuscripts," it had been hard to find much philosophy in Marx, and writers of an earlier generation had often found themselves compelled to turn to Engels instead. It was even harder to find much concern for the individual human being in countries with Communist governments. For all who felt distressed on either or both of these counts, the *young* Marx spelled salvation. In his manuscripts one found detailed criticisms of Hegel along with attempts to work out a different philosophy; and now it became a commonplace that these early writings and not Engels' later works revealed Marx's true philosophy. But, above all, one could now quote Marx himself in support of protests that would previously have suggested Western bourgeois influences. In France and Germany, in Poland and Yugoslavia, "alienation" became central in the discussion of Marxism; and in the United States the word became so ubiquitous that it was no longer clear whether the myriad uses to which it was put allowed for any single definition.

Fromm used the term in as many different senses as anyone. At one point in his essay "Marx's Concept of Man" he says: "the concept of alienation is, in nontheistic language, the equivalent of what in theistic language would be called 'sin'" (p. 46); and the one common denominator of virtually all of Fromm's uses of the word is that he is against alienation. Most, but not all, writers agree in deploring alienation and in considering it a distinctively modern phenomenon. When it is admitted that alienation can be found in the past, too, this concession is generally followed by the claim that in our time it is much more extreme or even "total."

The diagnoses of the ills of our time that were put forward in the seminal books of the fifties seemed wrong to me, but I felt that a new analysis ought to be coupled with a detailed critical survey of the literature on alienation. Now that Schacht has provided the critical review, the time has come to reconsider the phenomena to which the term has been applied.

2. Analysis

The verb "alienate" is transitive like its two German equivalents, and its literal meaning is "to make strange, to make another's." But the noun "alienation," like the German *Entfremdung* and unlike *Entäusserung*, does not usually bring to mind an activity, except in special contexts where it functions as a technical term. Our primary association with "alienation" and *Entfremdung* is a human state of being—the state of *being* alienated or estranged from something or somebody. And it is phenomena of this sort that I propose to discuss now.

We are concerned with a relationship between A and B. A is a person or a group of persons: an individual, a social class, a whole generation, a people, or perhaps a smaller group. A is usually specified, and if there is any great vagueness, it rarely results from failure to indicate who A is. But B also needs to be specified, and confusion frequently and typically results from the failure to specify from whom or what A is supposed to be alienated. "Alienation" is an elliptical term that requires completion in *two* directions.

What might B be? An individual (for example, one's father, wife, or child); a group (perhaps one's family, fellow employees, fellow students, teachers, employers, colleagues, or neighbors); other people in general; the society in which one lives (for example, American or Soviet society); oneself (perhaps especially one's body or some particular aspect of one's character or of one's past); nature (hardly a univocal term, but possibly in the sense in which we speak of nature lovers); or, finally, the universe.

This is not an exhaustive list. One can also be alienated from what one does (from one's activity, work, or labor) or from things (such as the products of one's labor). The young Marx stressed both of these forms of alienation along with man's alienation from his essence or true nature—a concept that was central in his thought in 1844. While Marx uses "alienation" in several different senses, the phenomenon that concerns him most is the dehumanization of man. Man's loss of independence, his impoverishment, his estrangement from his fellow men, and his involvement in labor that is devoid of any originality, spontaneity, or creativity are so many aspects of man's estrangement from his true nature. Whether man has an essence is, of course, questionable; and seeing how Marx's early manuscripts have been used to bring him closer to existentialism, it is ironical that nobody has argued more passionately that man has no essence than has Jean-Paul Sartre.

Yet the young Marx and the early Sartre are not by any means diametrically opposed. In his early existentialist phase Sartre made much of his distinction between the being of things (*en soi*) and the human mode of being (*pour soi*). Man, he said, lacked the solidity of things; man was condemned to be free. He showed in detail, not only in his philosophical works but also in his short stories, novels, and plays, how men constantly succumb to bad faith, hiding their freedom from themselves and seeing themselves as if they were things. His extravagant emphasis on man's complete freedom was certainly at odds not only with Marxism but also with the facts of life; and, more than any other single factor, it was his growing awareness of the hollowness of this rhetoric and of the ways in which the oppressed and starving are not completely free—his social conscience, in brief—that led him to his later rapprochement with Marxism. But even his earlier philosophy could have been formulated in terms of a concept of human nature. The main difference between the young Marx and the early Sartre is not that one has such a concept while the other rejects it; it is rather that Sartre concentrates on the psychological processes that lead men to see themselves as objects, as things, as unfree, while Marx concerns himself with the economic processes that lead to much the same result. Both are concerned with man's loss of his freedom, but Marx sees the unfree as victims while the early Sartre insists that we are our own victims, that we really are free, and that we are at fault for not realizing it.

Thus one could also speak of alienation from freedom. And for those who believe in God or gods there may also be alienation from God or gods. But to speak of alienation without making clear who is held to be alienated from whom or from what is hardly fruitful, and talk of the "total" alienation of modern man is as nonsensical as talk of the total absence of alienation.

What comes to mind most often when we hear of alienation is estrangement from other men—usually from one's society. If anything at all could be said to be alienation *par excellence*, this would be it. We shall therefore use this kind of experience as an example to make a more general point about alienation.

We must ask not only from whom or what a person or group is supposed to be alienated but also what would constitute the absence of this alienation. Would a nonalienated person find no group of people, no individuals, nothing about the society in which he lived strange in any way at all? If so, could one really call him a person? And if one did, would one not have to add that his condition was severely pathological and bordered on idiocy?

Self-consciousness involves a sense of what is other—*alienum* in Latin. If anyone literally found nothing human alien to himself, he would be totally lacking in any sense of selfhood. (Terence's beautiful line, *Homo sum; humani nil a me alienum puto*[3]—I am a man, and I hold nothing human strange to me—refers not to the total absence but to the overcoming of a sense of strangeness: a triumph that involves imagination and understanding, not imbecility.) If anyone could not tell a strange hand from his own and actually experienced the one just as he did the other, we might as well say that he experienced his own hand as strange and was alienated from himself and, more specifically, from his own body.

Have we illicitly confounded otherhood and strangeness? A person whom I know to be other than myself need not seem strange to me. He may be a familiar sight—always at the same street corner at 9 A.M., or a waiter I usually see when I go to a certain restaurant, or a well-known actor, politician, or other public personage. He is no stranger nor strange to me: I know him. But how well do I know him? I simply do not care enough to think about the 99 percent of

[3] *Heauton Timorumenos* (163 B.C.), I.1.25.

him that is for me *terra incognita*. We are strangers but not
sufficiently interested to realize it or be bothered by it, and
one might well hesitate to speak of alienation or estrangement
in such cases lest one be taken to imply that there was a prior
state of closer rapport.

Now suppose I am suddenly struck by the fact that I
hardly know this person. This could happen as we began to
talk to each other. I might never have hesitated to say, "I
know him"; but now that I know him a little better, I might
come to feel that I really do not know him at all and that he
is quite strange.

This paradox may seem to be reducible to the double
meanings of "know" and "strange." As Hegel pointed out,
what is *bekannt*, or known by acquaintance and hence familiar, is not necessarily *erkannt*, or known in the sense of being
comprehended. But that is not all. Familiarity actually ob-
structs knowledge, and comprehension involves the overcoming of a sense of strangeness. This point, too, is central in
Hegel's thought.

Another image may make it clearer. It is hard to see in
perspective and comprehend what is very close to us: Comprehension requires some distance and consists in a triumph
over distance. Thus Oedipus, who solved the riddle of the
Sphinx about the human condition, did not recognize his
father and mother and did not grasp his relation to his wife
and children. And Freud failed to perceive the psychological
problems of his favorite disciples, Sandor Ferenczi and Otto
Rank. Similarly, it is often easier to understand other people's problems than our own. In these cases, of course, emotional involvement may blind us. But the same phenomenon
can be observed when a play, a painting, or a piece of music
is exceedingly familiar to us: We lack distance and must
become alienated if we would comprehend it.

Plato and Aristotle remarked that philosophy begins in
wonder or perplexity. We could also say that it begins when
something suddenly strikes us as strange—or that philosophy
is born of estrangement. It need not be alienation from other
human beings; it could be estrangement from oneself or the
universe. Or a belief or system of beliefs, a moral conviction
or a code that we had taken for granted may suddenly seem

strange to us. Such alienation need not be a merely intellectual event; it may involve a deep estrangement from the faith and morals of our society.

It may seem a *reductio ad absurdum* to speak of alienation when a child begins to ask questions about all sorts of things that but a few months earlier had not struck him as at all strange and that most Philistines would not dream of questioning. For it is clearly the child who does *not* ask questions that one has to worry about; and alienation of this type is a symptom of mental health, while lack of it is pathological. Those who assume that alienation is by definition regrettable would not think of applying the term to a healthy child. But adolescence is our second childhood; and when students start asking questions about their schools and the societies in which they live, it is often said that they are alienated. A healthy child ought not to be satisfied with the reply that this is simply how things are. Should an adolescent be content with such an answer?

Some people, no doubt, would apply the term to adolescents only by way of registering regret or disapproval. But in purely descriptive terms, the adolescent who gains a sense of distance experiences a gulf between himself and all sorts of things and people, and he feels estranged. The curiosity of the small child who asks questions is not so regularly accompanied by a deep sense of alienation.

Most writers who make much of alienation consider it a distinctively modern phenomenon—and deplore it. We have suggested, in effect, that they are wrong on both counts. Later we shall return to the question whether the term ought to be restricted to destructive conditions. But let us first examine with some care whether alienation is, after all, a distinguishing feature of our times, and perhaps, as many writers would have it, confined to capitalistic societies.

At this point we must not stretch the meaning of the term. The question is whether the conditions that loom so large in the contemporary literature on alienation and in the seminal books published in the fifties can be found in earlier periods and in noncapitalistic societies. One might suppose that those who deplore alienation and blame it on modernity or, more specifically, on our economic system, would have considered these matters with some care. After all, there is no other way of establishing that their diagnoses are right; and if they are wrong, their prescriptions would scarcely merit much attention.

What is needed is historical perspective. But although the vogue of "alienation" has its roots in the early writings of the founder of so-called historical materialism, one of the most striking features of the vast literature on alienation is its historical blindness. That class alienation is to be found in former ages, that we encounter slavery, slave rebellions, and revolutions, is so obvious—and was so plain to Marx—that the point does not need laboring. But we have argued that philosophy is born of alienation. Let us begin our historical reflections with philosophy and then turn to literature.

3. Alienated Philosophers

Plato is the first philosopher known to us by complete works and not mere fragments. He is also widely considered the greatest philosopher of all time, and his dialogues are in a very substantial sense the foundation of all subsequent Western philosophy. Was he "alienated"?

His alienation from society does not have to be inferred from our reflections on the origin of philosophy, nor need we rely on scattered quotations from his writings. Consider his major work on social and political philosophy, *The Republic*, which is generally held to be his *magnum opus*. It is the work of a man estranged from Athenian society and from the politics and morals of his time. He is disaffected, disillusioned, and convinced that it would be utterly pointless for him to try to participate in the public life of his city. What is required, he thinks, is not a series of changes that might be brought about within the existing system, nor even a reform of the system. Either kings have to become philosophers, or philosophers, kings: Until "the motley horde of those who at present pursue either [politics or philosophy] apart from the other are excluded by force, there can be no cessation of troubles" for our states or for the human race. Meanwhile Plato describes a city that "can be found nowhere on earth. . . . But it makes no difference whether it exists now or ever will come into being. The politics of this city only" deserves a philosopher's attention.[4]

Whether Plato was also alienated from himself is more difficult to decide because the notion of alienation from oneself is less clear. But more than once Plato cites approvingly an ancient play on words that was dear to the Orphic sect: The body (*soma*) is the soul's tomb (*sema*). This means that the soul is buried in the body, that life is one long exile, and that salvation is to be found only in death. To be a self is to be a stranger.

Plato does not merely divide man into body and soul; he further divides the soul into three parts, and he argues for the existence of the three parts by calling attention to instances in which they are at odds with each other and pull us in different directions. Thus Plato also knew the experience of the divided self. He felt at home neither in his body nor with his appetites.

These references to self-alienation are crucial for Plato's position. He offers a path to salvation and tells us how such alienation could ultimately be overcome. But it remains doubtful at best whether it can ever be overcome in this life. Perhaps Socrates overcame it in the hour of his death, described at the end of the *Phaedo*. But it is clearly part of the point of *The Republic* that in the kind of society then existing anywhere a triumph over self-alienation could not be expected by many, if any.

What about alienation from nature? This notion is far from clear. But if we assume, however naïvely, that some peasants or primitive peoples are in tune with nature, at home in it, close to the earth, and not alienated, then it must be said that Plato, like Socrates, his master, *was* alienated from nature. At the beginning of the *Phaedrus* Plato has Socrates admit that he hardly ever leaves the city to walk in the countryside: "I am a lover of learning, and trees and countryside won't teach me anything, while men in the city do." Socrates compares himself to an animal that can be led

[4] *The Republic* 473 and 592. I have slightly modified Paul Shorey's translation.

if you dangle a carrot in front of it: He can be got out of the
city if you dangle a book in front of him.

There is no evidence that Plato felt more intimate with
nature than did Socrates. His path to salvation required men
to regard their senses as deceivers, sense experience as an
illusion, and nature as unreal. To be saved, we must turn our
backs upon nature and attune our minds first to mathematical
concepts and then, eventually, to dialectic. We must not seek
to feel at home in *this* world; we have to become convinced
of its unreality and place our trust in another world that lies
beyond all sense experience, beyond change and time.

The point here is not that "alienation" is the *mot juste* for
Plato's attitudes or condition, but rather that phenomena
now frequently subsumed under this concept by writers who
consider them distinctively modern, were, in fact, eminently
characteristic of Plato.

We know more about Plato than about any of his philosophic predecessors. At most, we have fragments of their
works, and it is hazardous to venture opinions about their
personal condition. None of them comes to life for us as a
personality as does Heraclitus of Ephesus. And he said of his
fellow citizens: "The Ephesians would do well to hang themselves, every adult man, and leave their city to adolescents,
since they expelled Hermodorus, the worthiest man among
them, saying: 'Let us have not even one worthy man; but if
we do, let him go elsewhere and live among others!'" (fragment 121). How is that for estrangement from the popular
culture of his day and an expression of despair of all but the
young? (In the nineteen sixties we got the cliché of trusting
"no one over thirty.")

Heraclitus' remarks about the culture heroes of his time—
Homer and Hesiod, Pythagoras and Xenophanes—evince
quite as much bitterness. Of course, we need not label these
attitudes as alienation from society; but if that term is used
for modern attitudes of this kind and it is assumed that
alienation from society must be prompted by specifically
modern causes, then the case of Heraclitus becomes relevant.

Few modern writers are as dear to those who consider
themselves alienated as Hermann Hesse. The novel that

marked Hesse's breakthrough to his own distinctive voice was *Demian*, published over a pseudonym in 1919 and not recognized at first as being by him. Its epigraph was a variation on one of Heraclitus' best-known aphorisms, "I sought myself": "I did not want anything but to try to live what wanted all on its own to come out of myself. Why was that so very difficult?" This is also the theme of Hesse's later novels—and a way of saying that alienation from oneself is hard to overcome.

Not all of the pre-Socratics were loners like Heraclitus. Pythagoras, in the late sixth century B.C., may have been a solitary figure, but his followers, the Pythagoreans, formed a sect. During the fifth century B.C., when Athens became a great power and produced the temples on the Acropolis before she was plunged into the Peloponnesian War; during the whole age of Aeschylus, Sophocles, and Euripides—the Pythagoreans lived their withdrawn life in a commune in southern Italy. It was probably from them that Plato received the Orphic notion of the body as the tomb of the soul along with their doctrine of the transmigration of souls, the notion that a philosophic life is required for salvation, and that the right kind of society can be a vehicle of redemption. Plato was also influenced by their admission of women to their society, by their practice of holding all property in common, and by their division of mankind into three basic types—with tradesmen the lowest class; those in whom the desire to excel is highly developed, superior; and those who prefer contemplation, the best.

It would be tedious to go through the whole history of philosophy to assemble an imposing array of illustrations of alienation. One final example may suffice, so long as we choose the man most widely regarded as the greatest non-Greek philosopher, Kant.

Like Socrates, he did not care to leave his city and wander in the country. He was totally alienated from nature. And, like Plato, he considered it not ultimately real. He, too, believed that there were two worlds, and he sought freedom and immortality—and God, if any—in the other world.

Such otherworldliness is usually a sign of alienation from this world, from concrete human society, and from one's empirical self. This self is not ultimately real; my freedom and unique worth depend on another dimension, which Kant called *noumenal*.

As in Plato, the self encountered in moral experience is divided against itself. One of Kant's greatest admirers, Friedrich Schiller, aptly parodied this aspect of Kant's moral philosophy in two distichs:

CONSCIENTIOUS SCRUPLE

Gladly I serve my friends, but alas out of inclination;
And though this pains me oft, virtuous I am not.

DECISION

There is no other counsel, but you have to try to despise it
And with abhorrence do that which your duty commands.

One need not speak of self-alienation when discussing Kant's ethics, but it is essential to recognize that this Kantian division of the self—this sense of estrangement from one's own natural inclinations—was precisely what first Schiller and then Hegel tried to overcome by developing a different ethic. In fact, Hegel went on to develop a different conception of man and his place in the world, of spirit, and of the nature of reality. This is the context in which Hegel's discussion of alienation has its place.

An altogether different approach also suggests that the great philosophers were deeply "alienated" in an important sense. Who were the greatest philosophers of modern times? There is a surprising consensus about the answer: Descartes, Spinoza, and Leibniz; Pascal and Hume; Rousseau and Kant; Hegel and Nietzsche; Russell and Sartre. No doubt, many people would want to add three or four men to this list, but few indeed would deny that these philosophers are among the most interesting and influential.

Descartes lost his mother when he was one year old; Spinoza was six when his mother died, and Leibniz six when his father died. Pascal's mother died when he was three; Hume's father, when he was three. Rousseau's mother died soon after his birth, and when he was ten his father left him. Both Kant and Hegel lost their mothers at thirteen. Nietzsche was four when he lost his father. Russell's mother died when he was two; his father, two years later. And Sartre lost his father at two.[5]

In his first *Duino Elegy* Rilke says that "we are not very reliably at home in the interpreted world." This has often been taken for a formulation of a very modern *malaise*. But our data create a strong presumption that this feeling was shared by the major philosophers since Descartes; and their works bear this out—most obviously in the cases of Descartes, Pascal, and Hume; Rousseau, Kant, and Nietzsche; Russell and Sartre. Spinoza, Leibniz, and Hegel seem much less skeptical. But closer study of Hegel reveals that what he sought and eventually found in philosophy was a triumph over an unbearable sense of alienation. Having decided in his twenties that religion could not grant him such salvation, he turned to philosophy and, after years of struggle, obtained through it a sense of reconciliation. One might hesitate to speak of alienation in this context, had not Hegel bequeathed this term to us precisely in this context. I suspect that the cases of Spinoza and Leibniz are essentially similar.

4. Literature and Art

Great philosophers are by definition unrepresentative men. But those we have considered have been very widely read and acclaimed, and generations of students have immersed themselves in their books. Great writers are also atypical men; yet it is a commonplace that contemporary writers are alienated, and "alienation" looms large in book reviews and literary criticism. Usually the word is used so loosely that it seems best, if one takes such writing seriously at all, to point out how vague and ambiguous the term is, and in how many different senses it has been and is used. But it may also prove illuminating if we show, at least very briefly, how central some of the phenomena in question have been in the works

[5] My friend Ben-Ami Scharfstein, Chairman of the Department of Philosophy at Tel-Aviv University, called most of these data to my attention in another context.

of some great writers of the past. As in the case of the philosophers, we shall confine our attention to men and works of the very first rank, and we shall eschew such obvious outsiders as Euripides and Villon, Poe and Baudelaire.

Goethe may serve as our first example. If rebellion against the establishment were a sign of alienation, we should have to consider the young Goethe a paradigm of alienation. Werther, the hero of his first novel, committed suicide—and all over Europe large numbers of young people committed suicide with a copy of the book clutched in their hands or buried in a pocket. Goetz, the hero of Goethe's storm-and-stress play, uttered the most celebrated obscenity in German literature, showing the poet's contempt for convention. Both works were antiestablishmentarian—and became instant successes that made the author the hero of the younger generation.

Does it make sense to consider Faust's wholehearted disgust with academic learning proof of his—or the poet's—alienation? Hardly. But that is how our contemporaries frequently use the term. Or consider Faust's famous outcry, quoted and discussed at length in Hermann Hesse's *Steppenwolf*:

> Two souls, alas, are dwelling in my breast,
> And one is striving to forsake its brother.

Is this division of the self a sign of alienation? It certainly prevents one from feeling at home with oneself, as each soul eyes the other as a stranger. But if that is alienation, who is *not* alienated? Surely, this goes with having any spiritual depth at all, or any spirit.

If we associate alienation primarily with a deep sense of estrangement from one's fellow men and from society, then the stage in life at which Goethe became a paradigm of alienation coincides precisely with the period of his greatest fame, when he is widely held to have been a pillar of the establishment. From the start, *Faust* had been written with an utter disregard for the possibility of performance on the stage. When Goethe became director of the theater in Weimar, a great variety of plays and operas were performed, but never *Faust*. Goethe had started writing the play in the 1770s; he had published a fragment in 1790; and the whole of Part One appeared in 1808. But Part One was never staged in public until 1829, when Goethe turned eighty and people wanted to honor him, and even then the play was cut severely. The first performance of nearly the whole of Part One took place in 1876.

The Second Part was not intended to be staged at all. And when it was finished, not long before Goethe died—sixty years after he had begun the project—he tied up the manuscript and sealed it, refusing to divulge the conclusion even to old and trusted friends. He had no wish to see his *magnum opus* performed; he did not want to have it published until after he was dead; and he had no desire to share it with anyone. If that is not alienation from society, what is?

"Ah," some people may retort, "the *modern* writer's alienation is far more profound. Although James Joyce, for example, published what he wrote, he was so alienated that he might just as well not have, because there simply was no public for him until after he was dead." But this simply is not true in the case of *Ulysses* (1922), which came to be admired internationally long before the author's death in 1941; nor did *Finnegans Wake* (1939) have to wait long for commentaries and a great deal of critical attention. Samuel Beckett's *Waiting for Godot* (1954), widely hailed as a landmark of alienation, became an almost instant classic, read and seen on the stage, uncut, by large numbers of people in a great many different countries. Goethe, on the other hand, knew well that *Faust II* could never become popular, and that he would be much happier not reading what scholars and critics would write about it. In fact, the work was much farther ahead of its time than were Joyce's and Beckett's masterpieces: roughly, a hundred years.

Goethe lived at least on the threshold of modernity. Let us take as our second literary example the greatest poet of the Middle Ages: Dante. After all, the Middle Ages are often viewed nostalgically as a happier time when all was harmony and integration. There is no need here to dwell on the dark side of that period, its superstition and inhumanity, as evidenced, for example, in the persecution of Jews and heretics. Dante was a paradigm of alienation. His *Vita Nuova* is a case study of self-alienation—of viewing oneself as a stranger. And his *Divina Commedia* is the work of an outsider, literally an exile, consumed by bitterness. He creates a vast hell to people it with his fellow men, including members of the Establishment.

If alienation is associated rather more with being artistically out of touch with one's time, and what is meant is inaccessibility, the description also fits Dante perfectly. How many of his contemporaries could possibly have fathomed his work? And how many, since his time?

Those who look back nostalgically to some past period generally single out either Dante's age or fifth-century Athens. Let us therefore choose our next example from the great period of Greek literature: Sophocles' *Oedipus Tyrannus*.

Sophocles appears to be the archetype of the nonalienated poet: He was vastly appreciated by his contemporaries, and his tragedies usually won first prize, often second, and never placed third. He also held important offices and was highly respected as a man. *Oedipus Tyrannus* was soon accepted as a masterpiece, and Aristotle admired it as perhaps the best tragedy ever written. That estimate still stands. At the same time, it is plain that the continued appeal of the play is due not only to Sophocles' superb craftsmanship and plot construction but also to the central figure of the play, who, particularly as conceived by Sophocles, continues to haunt men's minds. We feel that in some sense he represents us; that his tragedy, though larger than life, is ours—but not necessarily in the way Freud suggested.

Oedipus is alienation incarnate. His father was warned by the gods not to have children, and Oedipus came into the world unwanted. Hence his ankles were pierced and he was cast out into hostile nature to perish. Saved by a shepherd, he was brought up in Corinth, a stranger without realizing it. To avoid defiling nature and violating the most sacred harmonies of the universe, he left Corinth to go into voluntary exile. Nevertheless he committed what the Greeks—and not only the Greeks—considered the most unnatural acts, outraging nature as well as society.

In Thebes, of which he was a native, he assumed that he was an alien. And when he discovered who he was, what he had done, and that he was not a stranger at all, he asked to be thrown out of the city.

Can we consider such an imperious and proud man alienated from himself? If one were to seek an epigraph for Sophocles' play, one could not do better than quote Heraclitus: "I sought myself." Oedipus is a stranger to himself; and when he discovers who he is, he is filled with such loathing that he destroys his own eyes. He even says that he wishes he could destroy his hearing, too, cutting his last bonds to the world and to his fellow men.

Whoever wants to understand alienation or wonders whether it is an essentially modern phenomenon, should reflect on the perennial fascination of this tragedy. Would it have haunted men so much if alienation from the universe, society, and oneself had been foreign to most men until recently?

If there is another play that has fascinated men as much as *Oedipus Tyrannus*, it is surely *Hamlet*. And if there is another hero who totally dominates a drama with his pervasive sense of alienation, it is Hamlet.

Perhaps all tragedies deal with alienation in some way: It is impossible to decide that without a clear idea of what precisely counts or does not count as alienation. But Hamlet displays almost every conceivable form of alienation. He views himself, his fellow men, and the society in which he lives with loathing. And generations of readers have identified with him. If they have included a high percentage of young people, writers, and artists, it is worth asking whether these groups have not always been prone to feel rather intensely what is nowadays called alienation.

It may be objected that formerly relatively few writers and artists felt deeply alienated, while in our century many do. This question is complicated by the fact that today there are so many more writers and artists than there have ever been before. Also, we lack detailed information about the lives and personalities of writers and artists of past ages, especially about the multitude of those who were not of the first rank. This makes comparisons difficult. But it seems that examples both of deeply alienated and of not so deeply alienated artists and writers can be found in former ages as well as in the twentieth century. Thus, Leonardo and Michelangelo seem to have felt much more profoundly alienated than, say, Rodin and Renoir. But such comparisons of exceptional and, hence, unrepresentative men are hardly to the point. Those who make much of alienation usually have in mind large groups of people.

It may therefore be more relevant to ask whether alienation does not characterize the modern public's attitude rather than the artist's. It is often suggested that the public no longer sees works of art as paintings or sculptures; instead, the works are seen as marketable commodities, investments, or status symbols. Thus modern man is estranged from art. This is the line taken by many critics of capitalistic society.

It sounds plausible—unless one has seen, for example, a traveling Van Gogh exhibition both in Warsaw and in Tel-Aviv (in 1962–63). In Warsaw it was scarcely attended at all, and the intellectual community took no notice of it, while in Tel-Aviv the doors had to be kept open till midnight and the crowds were immense. Many people came again and again; many a visitor contemplated the same picture for a long time. Of course, none of the paintings was for sale.

It is easy to find instances of alienation in modern capitalistic societies, but there is no evidence that people in Communist countries have a more intimate relationship to art. Nor is it at all clear that the attitude toward art which is so often characterized as alienated and modern is particularly modern. Did not the pharaohs of Egypt and the kings of Europe, the Renaissance patrons and popes, and the wealthy citizens of northern Europe look on paintings and sculptures as status symbols?

Beethoven made a great point of seeing his art, himself, and artists in general, in a new light. Of course, this does not mean that he felt less alienated than did his predecessors.

On the contrary, he felt almost unbearably alienated; and his Heiligenstadt Testament bears eloquent witness to the way in which his deafness contributed to his profound sense of estrangement from other men. One could argue that those who had treated artists in the manner against which Beethoven protested so successfully, had been less alienated from art than were the public of the late nineteenth century and our own contemporaries. Today, the artist is a person apart, and art and music are no longer amenities.

The term "alienation" has been used so indiscriminately that it is not clear who is supposed to be alienated: the minority who read Kafka and Euripides with understanding, or those who consider Edward Albee and Andy Warhol great, or perhaps the vast majority who read *Reader's Digest* and an occasional best seller. If the last group, what are we to say of the overwhelming majority of Rembrandt's and Mozart's contemporaries, who never so much as heard of them?

Who is more alienated—a writer in America who in 1970 does not have a television set, or one who spends much of his leisure time watching television? The nonconformist is obviously alienated from his society, but perhaps those who conform are alienated from themselves.

For those who operate with a conception of man's true nature and assume that man is essentially creative, as the young Marx did, it is clear that one who watches television in his spare time is self-alienated—and alienation from oneself is the most basic form of alienation. It is hardly an exaggeration to say that, according to this view, all other evils derive from this.

5. Marx's Dream

The humanism of the young Marx is attractive, and his conviction that the worst feature of modern life is that it dehumanizes man has very wide appeal. But his reasoning is open to several objections.

First, as our examples show, it is naïve to assume that all forms of alienation issue from one root form, and that the person who is liberated from this type of self-alienation will no longer suffer from any alienation. On the contrary, the creative person is, perhaps even by definition, a nonconformist who questions or deviates from tradition. The more profoundly original he is, the more profoundly is he bound to become alienated from his society.

Secondly, there is a widespread tendency to assume that in preindustrial society men were much less alienated—perhaps not at all—and that they were not only happier and more intimate with nature but also more humane. Those who take this for granted should come to grips with the abundant evidence to the contrary, ranging from the Mayas and the Aztecs to the Cretans of Nikos Kazantzakis' *Zorba the Greek* and the Indian village of Khushwant Singh's *Train to Pakistan*. And in *The Painted Bird* Jerzy Kosinski has given us not only a shattering picture of a peasant society but also one of the greatest symbols of alienation to be found in world literature. He tells—and this is no invention—of the bird catcher who now and then chose the strongest bird from his cages, painted it in rainbow hues, squeezed it to make it twitter and attract a flock of its own species, and set it free. One after another, the drab birds would attack the painted bird until he dropped to the ground, soaked in blood. The whole book develops this theme.

Finally, consider Marx's famous words from the *German Ideology*: "As soon as the division of labor sets in, everybody has a determinate and exclusive sphere of activity that is imposed on him and from which he cannot escape. He is hunter, fisherman, or shepherd, or critical critic, and must remain that if he does not want to lose his means of livelihood—while in Communist society, where Everybody does not have an exclusive sphere of activity but can train himself in any branch whatever, society regulates general production and thus makes it possible for me to do this today and that tomorrow, to hunt in the morning, to fish in the afternoon, to rear cattle in the evening, and to criticize after dinner, as I please, without ever becoming hunter, fisherman, shepherd, or critic. This fixation of social activity, this consolidation of our own product into an objective power over us that outgrows our control, crosses our expectations, and nullifies our calculations, is one of the main features in the development of history so far . . ."[6]

Marx's dream has not come true in any Communist society, but to a significant degree it is realized in the United States of America. It is not in the least unusual for the same person to have many different jobs before he is thirty. College students, in particular, support themselves in a variety of ways during the academic year, and then, during the summers, work in factories and freight yards, on construction jobs and in offices, doing one sort of thing one summer and another the next. Moreover, it is not at all uncommon for men with all kinds of jobs to find the time to hunt or fish occasionally, and criticism is one of the most popular American sports and undoubtedly indulged in with greater frequency and less inhibitions than in any Communist country. While it is doubtful that many people manage "to rear cattle in the evening,"[7] this part of Marx's vision only shows how an inveterate city-dweller imagines bucolic bliss. It might even be taken as evidence of his alienation from nature.

Even if one associates the condition Marx indicts with alienation, it is far from clear what it has to do with capitalism. The division of labor is, as he says, "one of the main features of the development of history so far"; and most of the advances we take for granted depend on it. When we have acute appendicitis, few of us would care to seek help from a man who had not specialized in medicine, and specifically in surgery. And it is not only in medicine that progress depends on specialization and the expertise that goes with that.

What makes it possible for laborers as well as doctors and students to go hunting and fishing is a high standard of living coupled with a short work week—say, five eight-hour days and an annual vacation. Moreover, Social Security and all kinds of pension plans make it possible for large numbers of people to retire early enough in life to spend the rest of their years doing what they please.

[6] Karl Marx, Friedrich Engels, *Die deutsche Ideologie* . . . 1845–1846, im Auftrage des Marx-Engels-Lenin Instituts Moskau herausgegeben von V. Adoratskij, Wien/Berlin, 1932, 22 f.

[7] *"abends Viehzucht zu treiben."*

Of course, there are large areas of poverty in the United States, and it remains to be seen whether the Government, as presently constituted, will muster the determination to deal with this crucial problem. But whether American society is more of a class society than is Soviet or Polish society, for example, is an altogether different question—not to speak of "third world" countries in which, by and large, the masses live in poverty and Marx's dream still seems utopian. Above all, it is not at all obvious that alienation is greatest in capitalist countries. It seems that the only way to achieve a sufficiently high standard of living to permit the realization of Marx's dream leads through the division of labor and the development of a large class of highly skilled experts of various kinds.

Yet the division of labor need not be accompanied by the imposition of rigid roles that dehumanize men. One of the results of the social mobility in the United States—lateral as well as upward—is that a waiter, for example, is much less likely to feel, or to make those on whom he waits feel, that his role defines him, freezes him, and determines his relation to others. For all we know, he may be a college student; and even if he is too old for college, it would be rash to presume that he will still be a waiter a year hence. Moreover, we may have waited on table ourselves, and we may have children who have a similar job right now. Thus the alienation implicit in the division of labor is diminished significantly. Men are much less likely to forget their own humanity and that of others. Clearly, this is only a tendency, and it is possible and highly desirable to go much further in this direction than the United States has yet gone.

There is no evidence that in the Soviet Union or China or any other country that tries to achieve rapid industrialization most jobs are more interesting than in the United States. How many hours a week people must spend on dull jobs to support a family and have the means to go fishing if they please, is an altogether different question; and capitalism is way ahead of communism in this respect.

Here we confront several different issues. First, can we eliminate boring jobs? So far, no society, socialist or capitalist, has solved this problem, and the solution does not seem to depend on who owns the means of production. It depends on technical developments—specifically, on the future of automation.

Secondly, can we drastically reduce the number of hours per week that anyone has to spend on a boring job? Here the United States and other capitalistic countries have done rather well, and further improvements are in sight.

Thirdly, can we shift people around so that they do not have to do the same boring job all the time? If one had to fish eight hours every day one might well find that very trying, and most men would reach the limit of endurance before long. What makes fishing so attractive to so many Americans is that it is so different from almost everything else they do, and that nobody is breathing down their necks. Could uninteresting jobs be rotated in such a manner that variety would drastically reduce boredom? Clearly, much more could be done along this line, but the resistance to any such change would come mainly from those who would benefit from it. Those who hate routine and have few habits are a very tiny minority. Most men desire amazingly little variety. Witness what they do with their spare time.

Any notion that most men, if given the time, would use it to reread the tragedies of Aeschylus every year, as Karl Marx did, is wildly romantic. And for the charge that only capitalism keeps them from doing this, there is no evidence at all. Not only is Marx's assumption that man has an essence open to question, but his conception of man's true nature was without any broad empirical foundation. He seems to have realized this, at least up to a point, by 1848, but many self-styled socialist humanists still seize uncritically upon his immature early manuscripts.

6. "Things have never been worse"

An idea that is not at all specifically Marxist looms large in the literature on alienation: that things have never been worse. Unless one comes to grips with this notion, one misses much of the import of the current vogue of alienation.

The immense popularity of Martin Buber's *Ich und Du* (1923) during the sixties was due largely to the fact that the second of its three parts deals at length with alienation and suggests that ours is a sick age. Less and less do men see one another—or a work of art, or a tree—as another You; more and more they relate to their fellow men, to works of art, and to nature as so many objects of experience and use. Young men and women who have read the book more than forty years after it was written consider it prophetic because it seems to describe so perfectly the world in which they live. It does not occur to most of them that the world in which it was written was like that, too—any more than it struck Buber himself that he tended to glorify a past that had not been as different as he occasionally implied it was. He recognized emphatically that men cannot live entirely in I–You relationships, but he did write at times as if the past had known perfect communities not tainted by "sickness"; and like others who speak in this vein, he failed to substantiate or even investigate this assumption.

Of course, things haven't always been as they are now. But have they been better? That remains to be shown, and the demonstration requires both empirical research and value standards. But even if in some clearly specified respects there has been a manifest decline, this could have been accompanied by progress in other important respects.

What we are witnessing is an understandable reaction against the blithe faith in progress that was fashionable in the nineteenth century. But the new anti-faith in the unique alienation of modern man is as unsound and unsophisticated as the old faith in progress. The notion that things were never so good and are constantly getting better, and the notion that things were never so bad and are steadily getting worse, are entirely worthy of each other.

It is ironical that both notions should have been associated so often with Hegel or Marx, for what is wrong with such naïve conceits is that they are so utterly undialectical. People place their faith or anti-faith in a simple proposition without even inquiring why such an assertion may be countered reasonably with a diametrically opposite claim. "Dialectic" is almost as fashionable a word as "alienation," but few who use it have a clear idea of the meaning of Hegel's dialectic. One knows, of course, that it has something to do with opposites, but it is usually assumed that it involves a denial of the laws of thought or logic.

In fact, Hegel opposed the dogmatism of those who believe in such simple propositions as, Things were never so good (or so bad). Not only is it the philosopher's task to examine the meaning of "good" and "bad" and the implicit standards; it is also important to inquire how that which has become better is related to that which has become worse. And if we consider that something is very bad, it is simple-minded in the extreme to say that we must obviously get rid of it no matter what the cost. And it shows an appalling lack of imagination, learning, and responsibility to claim that anything at all is bound to be better than whatever it is that we do not like. We have to ask what changes would be for the better—and what price we probably would have to pay for each.

Most of the discussion of alienation is historically blind in *three* ways: One fails to inquire how things actually were in the past, and one remains oblivious of the fact that changes usually have side effects that, in the long run, prove much more important than the effects that were intended. Finally, one fails to see the current vogue of "alienation" in historical perspective.

Estrangement from nature, society, one's fellow men, and oneself is part of growing up. One has to detach oneself from the womb of one's environment in order to become a person, an individual, an independent being. Self-consciousness involves such detachment. One has to come to look upon oneself and others and the world as strange and perplexing.

It does not seem to follow from this that it should become extremely difficult for us to relate to other men. Or *does* it follow, after all? Isn't it part of the price one pays for excellence—for being exceptionally sensitive, thoughtful, and honest? There's the rub: What used to be the condition of those who were outstanding has become the condition of millions who are not blessed with any special talent. Goethe's Tasso says:

> And when man in his agony grows mute,
> a god gave me to utter what I suffer.

Now there are masses of men, almost as alienated as Goethe's Tasso, but unable to sing of what they suffer: They merely gripe.

More and more people get more and more education, are exposed to literature and art and music, develop some sensitivity along with the desire to become artists, writers, or creators of some sort—and find that the careers actually awaiting them are disappointingly dull.

Alienation is to be found in all ages, but it does not always take the same form. And many of the phenomena currently lumped together under this label are due in the main to two causes: mass *education* and the *population explosion*.

Long before the days of television, Nietzsche inveighed against the *Verdummung*, or moronization, of his people, and today moronization is widely associated with our mass media. But regardless of the kind of society men live in, moronization commences for most of them in their early twenties, if not before. It may seem fairer to say that it begins as soon as children are sent to school. But while most schools extinguish the sparks of curiosity that have survived that long, students usually also learn something—not nearly as much as they might, but still, something. Once out of school, most people cease to learn much and become progressively less curious. More precisely, their curiosity is perverted: The passion to inquire turns into inquisitiveness, and the magical power to read is used to pry into the private lives of movie stars.

For all that, more people read Plato and Shakespeare than ever before, and any notion that the masses used to be brighter and more knowledgeable than today, or more humane and more appreciative of poets, painters, and philosophers, is wildly out of touch with fact. In the United States more people go to college than ever before, and a higher percentage of the total population gets a higher education than in any other large country. The education most of them receive is scandalously bad, but incomparably better than what any similar percentage of a large population ever got before. Mass education depresses quality in the sense that the education is not as good as the best that used to be available for a very small number; but the best education now available at our best colleges and graduate schools is easily comparable, if not superior, to the best education offered in former times. If it is less good in some fields, it is vastly superior in others. Many things that were learned thoroughly by our parents or grandparents are now neglected, but there are far more things learned by students today that were not, and could not have been, dreamed of fifty years ago. With so much recent history, literature, and science to teach, most teachers—and the fault here clearly lies with the older generation—simply are not up to also giving their pupils a good grounding in the classics, in the Bible, and in foreign languages, not to speak of their own language. It is imperative that we should try to improve education, but there is no reason to believe that things used to be better.

Even the best education must increase alienation. At every turn it shows us how what is familiar is not comprehended, and how what seemed clear is really quite strange. Comfortable prejudices crumble as we discover how little we know. If alienation is more widespread now than it used to be, it is because more people receive more education today than formerly.

Moreover, our educational system not only exposes pupils to great art and poetry and fiction; it also encourages them to believe that they can paint and write as well as anyone. It not only acquaints them after a fashion with some of the most original scientists; it also leads them to think that there is no reason why they should not make comparable discoveries. One does not only study the Presidents of the past; one is also taught that every American boy—and, perhaps, every American girl—can become President. But such wild expectations are doomed to be disappointed in most cases. And there are two reasons.

First, the creative life is full of depressions, and very few have talent enough to find an over-all sense of satisfaction in it. Instead of emphasizing fundamental skills and basic knowledge, training people for the jobs that actually await them, our educators too often talk blithely of projects and of research, promise and originality, discovery and creativity. But disciplined originality is very rare, and few pupils indeed go on to make scientific discoveries or to write, paint, sculpt, or compose anything of lasting interest.

Secondly, the total number of people in most societies is increasing at an alarming rate. Thus, every American boy today has only a fraction of the chance to become President of his country that every American boy had a hundred years ago. This hardly seems to be a serious matter. But the student who chooses to become a scientist or writer, painter or philosopher, is apt to feel that the competition has become so keen that it defies comparison with previous ages. During the long period of his training he has no assurance that he will be able to make a living in his chosen field, and there is much less reason to expect that he will ever make his mark by doing something really worthwhile. And this is one of the most crucial experiences associated with alienation. But while the numbers of those who feel insecure and frustrated are clearly greater than ever, the situation has not become worse in terms of percentages. On the contrary, upward mobility has rarely been greater. But if one of those rare times was only a few years back, a sudden drop may create the erroneous impression that things are worse than ever.

Some of the experiences for which the word "alienation" is often used are an inevitable consequence of education; others are due to particular methods of education, and specifically to the way our system raises high expectations that are bound to remain unfulfilled in most cases. A great many forms of alienation could be avoided by providing much less education—a cure that would be incomparably worse than the disease. But some forms of alienation could be prevented by changing our educational system; by not stimulating utterly unrealistic hopes; by preparing students for the jobs that actually await them—and for the ever increasing leisure time that most men still use so disgracefully.

7. Against Marx's Heritage

As it becomes more and more impossible to keep up with developments in different fields, most people feel a growing need for bargain words that cost little or no study and can be used in a great variety of contexts with an air of expertise.

The point is not necessarily to deceive others; the greatest benefit to the user of such terms is that they reassure *him*. Instead of feeling ignorant and helpless, he feels that he is in on what is going on.

It is one of the major fringe benefits of such terms that they generate questions that can be discussed endlessly, not only at parties and in classes (what would some hostesses and teachers do without them?) but also in print. One large class of such words ends in -ism. Wonders can be worked with "realism" and "idealism" and, of course, with "existentialism": Was X a *y*-ist? Or: *z*-ism in the American drama. But not all bargain words end in -ism; witness "dialectic," "the absurd," and "alienation."

As a first therapeutic step I have suggested that we ask who is supposed to be alienated from whom or from what. It seems reasonable to suggest that if one or both terms of the relationship cannot be specified, "alienation" is the wrong word.

Another suggestion is bound to be more controversial. Some of the ways in which Marx used "alienation" are extremely far-fetched and should be given up—except, of course, in discussions of the thought of Marx and his followers. He was heavily influenced by Hegel and by Ludwig Feuerbach when he wrote his early manuscripts in 1844, and historically it is not difficult to understand why he used the term as he did; but now that it has acquired so many other meanings closer to the literal sense of the word, it would clarify matters considerably if we could draw the line somewhere.

Here is a passage from Marx's manuscript "Alienated Labor," in which he sums up what he means by alienation: "The alienation of the worker in his object finds expression as follows according to the principles of political economy: The more the worker produces, the less there is for him to consume; the more values he creates, the more he loses value and dignity; the more his product is shaped, the more misshapen the worker; the more civilized his object, the more barbarous the worker; the more powerful the work is, the more powerless becomes the worker; the more spirit there is in the work, the more devoid of spirit and a slave of nature the worker."

It is worth noting that the final clause is ungrammatical in the original[8] and that the whole paragraph is placed in parentheses, for it is all too often forgotten that these early manuscripts represent rough and unrevised drafts. Yet these ideas richly merit critical attention. In the first place, they are expressed again and again in the same fragment and in the other early manuscripts. Secondly, this is the birthplace of the fateful Marxian idea that the condition of the workers is bound to become more and more inhuman and intolerable until there is a violent revolution in which, according to *Das Kapital*, "the expropriators are expropriated."[9] Finally, these ideas have been immensely influential not only on Marxism but also on the literature on alienation.

The passage quoted is a fine sample of Marx's style, which wallows in antitheses. But it is not altogether irrelevant that Marx was wrong. What Marx describes as an inevitable development is not what actually happened in England, in the United States, and in the other industrial nations of the West. It is easy to agree with Marx that the developments he pictures are, without exception, terrible: impoverishment, degradation, dehumanization, barbarization, enfeeblement, and moronization. It shouldn't happen to a dog. But why call all this "alienation"? And what led him to think it was inevitable?

The answers to both questions are to be found in Hegel and Feuerbach, whose names are encountered constantly in the manuscripts of 1844. Hegel had used the word "necessary" again and again as a synonym of "natural" and as an antonym of "arbitrary" or "utterly capricious." Among later German writers this confusion is common, and Marx's thought suffers severely from it.

Feuerbach had shown how man projects his best qualities into the deity until God becomes the image of perfection

---

[8] *Je geistreicher die Arbeit, um so mehr geistloser* [sic] *und Naturknecht der Arbeiter* . . . MS, p. XXIII. See, e.g., Karl Marx, *Texte zu Methode und Praxis,* II: *Pariser Manuskripte 1844,* ed. Günther Hillmann, Rowohlt paperback 1966, p. 54.

[9] Vol. I, near the end of Chapter 24. The whole paragraph, which could be said to represent the climax of volume I (volumes II and III were not published by Marx himself), invites comparison with the paragraph from "Alienated Labor."

and man a hopelessly imperfect sinner. Man strips himself of all that is good and strong to clothe God in goodness and strength, and the greater he makes his God, the smaller he makes himself. Now Marx sought to transpose this idea into laws of political economy; and his bold antitheses seem to charm those in search of Marxist humanism. If he had been right that the worker is divested of all the qualities that appear in his product—that its beauty, subtlety, and power leave him ugly, coarse, and weak—it could be argued that this is alienation. Using the German terms, one might even say that in that case we should have not only *Entäusserung* (divestment) but also *Entfremdung* (estrangement). But since it is not at all inevitable that the workers become poorer the more they produce, it makes little sense to call impoverishment "alienation." And if we speak of moronization as "alienation" instead of keeping it clearly in focus as a phenomenon in its own right, we stand much less chance of coming to grips with it and preventing it.

The point here is not directed at Marx and his admirers only. Other writers also often use "alienation" as an antonym of self-realization. Depending on their conception of man's true self, they use "alienation" to designate brutalization, moronization, loss of spontaneity, mindless conformity, lack of "authenticity," or anything at all that one might call dehumanization. But we have words for these phenomena, and it is more discriminating and helps to clarify difficult questions if we take some trouble to find the right term. Serious critics are not satisfied to label what they like "swell" or "groovy" or "divine"; neither should serious writers be content to call what they deplore "alienation."

Let us therefore restrict the term to cases in which someone feels estranged from something or from others. We need not stipulate that previously A was close to B. Estrangement can take the form of A's suddenly feeling or realizing how a gulf separates him from B.

It is imperative to realize that alienation need not be destructive. One cannot participate in all the groups to which one might belong: One has to make choices. Not only are time and energy limited, but some groups define themselves in opposition to other groups. Alienation from B may be the price one pays for belonging to C; and it need not even be felt to be a price.

Moreover, some kinds of alienation are fruitful. Witness, for example, the discourse of Nietzsche's Zarathustra "On the Way of the Creator." We have seen one writer equating alienation with "what in theistic language would be called 'sin'"; and suggestions abound that we ought to prevent alienation. But that would really dehumanize man.

It does not follow that we should be casual or callous about destructive alienation. The evils the young Marx attacked in the passage we have quoted should be fought; but as Marx himself discovered within less than four years, to fight them effectively it is best not to lump them together under the catch-all label of "alienation."

8. A Pluralistic View

We have given reasons for not restricting the term "alienation" to self-destructive conditions. Should we then use it exclusively for fruitful estrangement—for the conditions we have illustrated from the lives of various philosophers and poets? The trouble is that one does not know in advance when estrangement will prove to be fruitful. Moreover, self-destruction and creativity are not mutually exclusive. This last point is central in the Prologue to Nietzsche's *Zarathustra*; but those put off by its flamboyant tone may ponder Nietzsche's own case or that of Franz Kafka. Kafka was one of the most creative and original writers of our century; but he left instructions to burn the manuscripts of *The Trial* and *The Castle* because he felt so sure that he had failed. It would be perverse and unhelpful to say either that he thought he was alienated but, being a great writer, actually was not —or that he was alienated without knowing it. It is much less misleading to say that he was and felt deeply alienated without realizing how fruitful his condition was, how prophetic it made his voice, how within a mere thirty years millions of readers in many different countries would feel: *Mea res agitur*.

Insofar as alienation involves a painful sense of isolation, self-doubt, and frustration, it may seem as if there were two kinds of men: the few who, being creative, can cope with it; and the many, who not being creative, cannot. Nietzsche often wrote as if this were a palpable fact. He also assumed that those who have the gift to utter what they suffer, suffer much more deeply than the mute masses; and his concern was pre-eminently with those whose agony seemed greatest to him. As for the multitude, he occasionally suggested that it might be best to keep them contented with their mediocrity and not raise their hopes by giving them too much education.

Those more concerned with the uncreative masses may take an even dimmer view of life than Nietzsche did. While accepting his tragic account of the creative life, they are prone to feel that the wretchedness of those who lack even the comfort of occasional achievement makes this world a vast hell.

Any such bifurcation of humanity, however, must be rejected. Not only are a man's contemporaries poor judges of his rank, as Nietzsche well knew from firsthand experience, but many, like Kafka, are quite unsure of their own status. Nor do these two crucial objections go far enough: They still leave the dualistic model untouched and show only how difficult it is to decide, at least in some cases, to which camp a person belongs. But any such dualism is ill-founded and pernicious.

Nobody is creative all the time, and nobody is creative none of the time. Unfortunately, many people approximate the latter extreme, especially as they grow older. But this is due in part to two great errors. Their education gives them far too romantic an idea of creativity, and then persuades them that they are creative in this wholly exceptional sense. Most men discover soon enough that they are not, and then give up. In effect, they swallow the false notion that there are two kinds of men, and their resignation is often poisoned by resentment against those who do not give up.

The feeling of estrangement could be minimized by drastically reducing popular education, by brainwashing, by drugs —and even by frontal lobotomies. But if most men are mere caricatures of what they might be, it is quite possible that in order to become more humane they must first become more estranged. This notion finds support not only in Hegel but also in some of the world's great religions.

Judaism and Christianity agree in their original challenge to men to alienate themselves from nature, society, and themselves. The individual is not supposed to feel altogether at home in nature; Judaism lifted man out of nature and stressed the discontinuity between man and nature, the cardinal differences between man and animal. Moreover, it is one of the leitmotifs of the Hebrew Bible that the people are not supposed to be "like all the nations" but a people apart. Theoretically, this could have meant that their sense of community compensated them entirely for their alienation from all other nations. And reading the second part of Buber's *Ich und Du*, one may get the feeling that this was what happened. But in the Hebrew Bible we find no trace of such perfect community. Rather we find a succession of imposing figures who not only tell their people that they should be different but who are themselves thoroughly alienated from their own society. Moses, Elijah, Amos, Hosea, and Jeremiah are among the outstanding examples. They not only remind their people that they were strangers in the land of Egypt; they themselves are strangers among their own people.

Sigmund Freud spoke out of this tradition and gave a clear picture of fruitful alienation when he said at the outset of his *Selbstdarstellung* (1925): "The university, which I entered in 1873, brought me, to begin with, several palpable disappointments. Above all I was struck by the presumption that I should feel inferior and not a member of the *Volk* because I was a Jew. The former notion I rejected quite decisively. I have never comprehended why I should be ashamed of my descent or, as one was then beginning to say, my race. The membership in the *Volk* that was denied me I renounced without much regret. I thought that for an eager fellow worker a small place must be found within the framework of humanity even without such acceptance. But these first impressions of the university had one consequence that remained important later on: early in life I became familiar with the lot of standing among the opposition and being placed under a ban by the 'compact majority.' This laid the foundation for a certain independence of judgment."[10]

In other religions the sense of alienation went much deeper and became more problematic. In primitive Christianity the feeling was widespread that this world belonged to the devil and was altogether hopeless. Nature was the enemy, sex was evil; the body was a prison, as among the Orphics; and society was Caesar's. Messianic hopes were deferred to another world. One despaired of social justice here and now. And Paul offered a classical formulation for self-alienation: "I do not understand my own actions. For I do not do what I want, but I do the very thing I hate" (Romans 7.15).

Nor were Hinduism and Buddhism less alienated. The sages of the Upanishads sought to estrange their disciples from nature, from society, from their own bodies, and from whatever they might consider their own selves: All this was ultimately unreal and unworthy the attention of the true sage. One must detach oneself altogether from this whole world and recognize the sole ultimate reality of Atman, that inmost core of being which transcends all individuality and is identical with Brahma. Salvation was to be found far from society in complete withdrawal.

The Buddha, too, sought to detach men from society, from all desire—from all attachment. He founded a monastic order without teaching any sense of community. His last words were said to have been: "Work out your own salvation with diligence."

To use a phrase dear to Marxists, it is no accident that modern alienated youth so often turns to the wisdom of India. Here is balm for alienated souls and a promise of salvation. One does not have to choose this path to recognize the truth in the great religions that the development of the spirit requires a full measure of estrangement. This insight does not entail otherworldliness or any form of escape at all. In the words of Nietzsche's Zarathustra, we can "remain faithful to the earth."

[10] *Gesammelte Werke*, vol. XIV (1948), p. 34 f. The phrase in single quotes is from Ibsen's *Enemy of the People* (*Volksfeind* in German).

Sartre's Orestes says to Zeus: "Man's life begins on the other side of despair." And Goethe's Prometheus defied Zeus well over a century and a half earlier:

> Did you fancy perchance
> that I should hate life
> and fly into the desert
> because not all
> blossom dreams ripened?

Neither Sartre's Orestes nor Goethe's Prometheus withdrew into solitary defiance. Both chose to suffer for others.

Karl Marx, rereading his Aeschylus every year, saw himself as another Prometheus. He, too, wanted to bring into being a race of free men. He lived to say that he was no Marxist; and the twentieth-century literature on alienation would scarcely have led him to recant his declaration that the "philosophical nonsense" about alienation did not help. Much of it would certainly have struck the hard-boiled old polemicist as sentimental mush.

It is tempting to be as polemical as Marx was and to say that the fundamental alternative is that between Marx and Hegel—and that Hegel was right and Marx wrong. Hegel saw estrangement as the very heartbeat of the life of the spirit, while Marx wanted to get rid of alienation.

It seems odd and historically blind to me that so many writers today want to go back to the young Marx, although I have pleaded extenuating circumstances on their behalf. But we cannot turn back the clock and return to Hegel. He had much wisdom, and we can learn from him; but one would have to be "alienated" in the obsolete psychiatric sense to wish to return to him.

Hegel, of course, was not the only one to realize that as freedom, education, and self-consciousness increase, alienation grows too. Plato warned us long ago that there is no pre-established harmony between liberty and happiness, and Dostoevski's Grand Inquisitor makes the same point more briefly. Both believed that it was possible, and indeed crucial, to make a sharp division among men and to reserve liberty and higher education for the very few. Others have sought different panaceas. Marx placed his faith in a new economic structure, and nowadays the search for new forms of community is sometimes held to be our best hope for salvation. But the forms of alienation are manifold, and no single prescription will fit all, unless we drastically decrease men's potential.

Even the profound and painful sense of isolation that sometimes accompanies the feeling of estrangement is met in a variety of ways by one and the same person. Kierkegaard, for example, was an exceptionally creative individual who, nevertheless, did not rely solely on his creative work; he also sought help from a faith that might ease his otherwise scarcely endurable sense of alienation. Others, though creative, join various groups, cliques, or schools; and sex, friendship, and love are compatible with creativity.

All this is so obvious that one should not have to mention it, but the fashionable talk of alienation generally conjures up either a monochromatic picture or a dualistic one. Against such views one must insist that alienation is a central feature of human existence. Creativity is one response to it, commitment another; and both entail further alienation. There are many forms of detachment and involvement, and creativity can be indifferent to social problems, while work in social causes can be, but certainly need not be, relatively uncreative. There are many paths, but all involve estrangement.

Whoever would try to protect the young from alienation has despaired of man. It would be more in keeping with the spirit of the Hebrew prophets, Confucius, and Socrates to say instead: Life without estrangement is scarcely worth living; what matters is to increase men's capacity to cope with alienation.[11]

[11] I am indebted to my friends Siegwart Lindenberg, Michael Sukale, and Melvin Tumin, who very kindly read a draft and discussed it with me. Their comments have been most helpful.

ALIENATION

Das Bekannte überhaupt ist darum,
weil es bekannt ist, nicht erkannt.

HEGEL
Phänomenologie des Geistes

Sag nicht: "Es *muss* ihnen etwas
gemeinsam sein, sonst hiessen sie
nicht 'Spiele' "—sondern *schau,*
ob ihnen allen etwas gemeinsam ist.

WITTGENSTEIN
Philosophische Untersuchungen

INTRODUCTION

1970

It is becoming increasingly common to hear life in the present age characterized in terms of "alienation." When reviewers of books, films, and theater state—as they often do—that a work deals with "alienation," they usually mean to convey to their readers that it deals with some aspect of "the plight of modern man," or that of some significant segment of the population in modern society. Social commentators contend with growing frequency that "alienation" is one of the greatest problems confronting us today. It is seen in the generation gap, in the hippie phenomenon, in the antiwar movement, in the credibility gap, in the challenge to the "old politics" beginning with the McCarthy candidacy, in the emergence of the S.D.S., and in the Black Culture and Black Power movements. We hear of "alienation" in critiques of the nature of work in modern industry and bureaucratic organizations, the quality of life in middle-class bourgeois society, the relation of government to the governed, and the neglect and despoilment of our environment. Reference is constantly made to it in connection with the growth of superficiality and impersonality in interpersonal relations, the compartmentalization of our lives, the stunting of personal development, the widespread existence of inhuman or neurotic personality traits, the absence of a sense of the meaningfulness of life, and the "death of God." There is almost no aspect of contemporary life which has not been discussed in terms of "alienation." Whether or not it is the salient feature of this age, it would certainly seem to be its watchword.

In spite of the term's great popularity, however, few people have a very clear idea of precisely what it means to say of someone that he is "alienated." The vague ideas people do have often differ significantly. For example, the term is generally used as though it were to be understood to refer to some particular condition; yet different people often have very different conditions in mind when they use the term. There are many such problems; and they concern the usage not only of college students and amateur social critics, but also of many writers of greater stature. There is a tendency among the latter both to assume that the term is antecedently understood (and hence requires no careful explanation), and to feel free to use it as idiosyncratically as may be convenient. Where clear definitions are given, they frequently differ; and it is often unclear precisely how they relate to each other. Hegel observes that the familiar is not necessarily clearly understood simply because it is familiar; and no better case in point is to be found than that of "alienation."

It is not at all difficult to see why the term enjoys the popularity it does today. It occupies a position of importance in the writings of many of those whose ideas have a great deal of influence—Marx, Erich Fromm, Jean-Paul Sartre, and Paul Tillich, to mention only a few. And it has been employed by these and other writers in connection with a wide range of major problems and issues. When it is suggested that man has an essential nature which many men fall short of realizing, or that the relation of most men to nature or to other men is not what it ought to be, or that the work most men do fails to contribute to their own self-realization, people are very likely to listen; for these are matters which affect them directly and importantly. And the problems raised by the rejection of traditional cultural values and established sociopolitical institutions by growing numbers of people are so pressing that discussions of the matter receive a great deal of attention. Many of the writers who discuss these issues speak of "alienation" in doing so; and in this way the term has come to have a powerful grip upon the popular imagination.

If understanding is to supplant mere familiarity, however, a careful analysis of the uses of the term is required. This is true where any term is concerned. Yet "alienation" is something of a special case, in that it is a term which—because its most interesting uses are only now making their way into ordinary speech—cannot be investigated simply through an analysis of its employment by average educated speakers of English (or French or German). The average person depends almost entirely for his understanding of the term upon his direct or indirect acquaintance with the writings of certain philosophers, psychologists, and social scientists. It is the latter, therefore, whose uses of the term are most significant. It would make no sense to say, "Never mind what Hegel, Marx, Fromm and others say *they* mean by 'alienation'; I want to know what the term *itself* means." For it is largely through the influence of these and other recent writers that it has come to have whatever meaning it has today. To analyze what it means to say of someone that he is "alienated" *is* primarily to observe how those who have introduced the term into contemporary discussion have used it.

Of course, since the term has a number of traditional standard uses, it is desirable to take notice of them. There is often little connection, however, between these traditional uses and more recent special uses. An examination of traditional standard uses, therefore, can at most serve simply to prepare the way for an analysis of the special uses. Wittgenstein writes: "When philosophers use a word . . . one must always ask oneself: Is the word ever actually used this way in the language game which is its original home?" (6, §116)[1] But this directive is not really applicable in cases like that of "alienation," if the question posed is understood to mean: Is a given use of the term among its traditional standard uses? For (to use Wittgenstein's metaphors) the term is being given new homes in new language games; and it is thus upon them that attention must be focused.

It was Hegel who first elevated the term to a position of philosophical importance. Marx's more popular discussion of alienation (in his early writings) can best be understood in the light of Hegel's. Their discussions are of considerable interest in themselves; and they also constitute the back-

---

[1] References are identified by an italicized number, which corresponds to the number of the work cited on the list of such works for each chapter, to be found at the back of this volume.

ground of a good deal of the more recent literature on alienation. It is with the critical analysis of these classical and recent discussions that I shall be concerned. I shall not attempt
to resolve the many existential problems in connection with
which the term is employed—to determine, for example, what
the individual must do in order to realize his essential nature
fully, and to be properly related to his work, other men, nature, and the society in which he lives. Many of the discussions to be considered, however, bear directly upon such issues; and the following analysis of them should facilitate both
the understanding and the evaluation of the positions taken
in them on these issues.

While this study might be viewed as a contribution to
Wortgeschichte (the history of words) or intellectual history,
my primary concern is with neither. The writers to be considered must be taken up in some order; and since the earlier
ones often influenced the later, it makes most sense to consider the earlier ones first. But the point of considering their
uses of the term is to discover what is to be understood by
it, and whether it is as important and useful as it is commonly
thought to be. These are questions with important implications for anyone who would talk about alienation today.

It has been said that the idea of alienation is a very old
one, which can be traced back to the beginnings of recorded
thought; and that it figures just as importantly in the thinking
of contemporaries of Hegel and Marx—such as Goethe and
Kierkegaard—as it does in that of Hegel and Marx themselves, even though they did not actually use the term. This
claim may be sound; but it is not justifiable—or even meaningful—until the meaning of the term itself has been analyzed
and clarified. And since this analysis must take the form of
an examination of the actual uses of the term, discussions in
which it is not employed are not relevant to the analysis of
the way (or ways) in which it is to be understood. Of course,
once this analysis has been carried out, parallels and simi-
larities can be observed at leisure, and perhaps with great
profit. Indeed, it may turn out that the conditions in connection with which the term has been used are portrayed more
vividly and discussed more penetratingly in works in which

the word "alienation" is not used, than in those in which it is.

The kind of investigation undertaken in this study may not be very satisfying to those whose idea of a philosophical discussion of alienation is that of a phenomenological description of "the thing itself." But the very idea of a program of the latter sort presupposes some understanding of what "the thing itself" is; and its nature is precisely that which is here taken to be problematical. Indeed, it is problematical whether it is even possible to speak of "*the* thing itself" at all. For this implies that the term "alienation" refers to some *one* thing; and that cannot be assumed at the outset. Here another of Wittgenstein's directives is highly relevant: "Don't say: 'There *must* be something in common, or they would not be called "games" '—but *look and see* whether there is anything common to all." (6, §66) One must likewise "look and see" how the term "alienation" functions in the literature in which it occurs.

A number of writers have attempted to generalize about the way it functions. It has seemed to them that, however different the contexts in which it is employed may be, its various uses still display a number of common features. Arnold Kaufman, for example, offers the following general analysis: "To claim that a person is alienated is to claim that his relation to something else has certain features which result in avoidable discontent or loss of satisfaction." (4, 143) Lewis Feuer suggests that "the word 'alienation' [is] used to describe the subjective tone of self-destructive experience," and states: " 'Alienation' is used to convey the emotional tone which accompanies any behavior in which the person is compelled to act self-destructively." (1, 132) And Kenneth Keniston contends that "Most usages of 'alienation' share the assumption that some relationship or connection that once existed, that is 'natural,' desirable, or good, has been lost." (5, 452) While each of these general analyses may seem plausible, they are by no means identical. It remains to be seen whether any of them is adequate, and indeed whether any such general analysis is even possible. These are questions which can be answered only through a more careful and systematic examination of the literature in which "alienation" is discussed than any of these writers has undertaken.

The term "alienation" today occurs primarily in the writings of men who are not themselves philosophers. But this by no means places it outside the pale of legitimate philosophical concern. The business of philosophy is not confined to such areas of inquiry as logic, epistemology, ethics, and linguistics. It extends further, as Jerrold Katz observes:

> Philosophy takes the conceptual systems developed by scientists, mathematicians, art critics, moralists, theologians, et. al., as its subject matter and seeks to explain and clarify what has to be explained and clarified about such systems in order to render them fully comprehensible. (3, 2)

The present study is a case in point; only, instead of taking as its subject an entire conceptual system developed in a single one of these areas, its subject is a term which has come to figure importantly in the writings of social scientists, psychologists, theologians, social critics, and certain philosophers as well. Irving Horowitz suggests the need for precisely such a philosophical analysis, with particular reference to the use of the term by social scientists:

> Once the various meanings and levels at which the term alienation is employed can be properly understood, then social scientists will be better able to employ alienation as a central variable in discussing other features of social structure and process. The task of philosophy in this area might be a clarifying one, to show how various usages of alienation are either synonymous, overlapping, or entirely different from one another. (2, 237)

It remains to be seen, however, just how helpful the term actually is, how "comprehensible" it may be rendered, and whether the role envisaged for it by Horowitz is consistent with its current employment.

Finally, a procedural note. With a few exceptions, quotations from other works are identified by two numbers, e.g.,

(*12*, 235). The latter number indicates the page number,[2] and the former (italicized) corresponds to the number of the work on the list of works referred to in the chapter in question. (The lists for all chapters are to be found at the back of this volume.) The exceptions consist of a small number of works (by Hegel, Marx, Fromm, and Horney) which are cited extensively; these are more directly identified by letters specified in each case (e.g., Fromm's *The Sane Society*=SS), though they are also included on the numbered lists of works referred to for the chapters in question. In a very few cases —namely, those of Hegel's *Phenomenology of Spirit* and Marx's *Early Writings*—two page numbers are given: The first is the page number in the German edition used, and the second is that in the English translation.

[2] Except where it is customary to use paragraph numbers instead: e.g., in citations from Hegel's *Philosophy of Right*. Where a paragraph number is intended, the symbol "§" will be used.

1 The Linguistic
and Intellectual Background

TRADITIONAL USES OF "Alienation"
AND *Entfremdung*

The English term "alienation," as well as its French and German equivalents, *aliénation* and *Entfremdung*, have traditionally had a number of uses. These uses were well established long before Hegel and Marx. The term *Entfremdung* occurs in Middle High German literature, and "alienation" goes back through Middle English and Old French to classical Latin. The terms still retain some of their original uses; in fact, all of their standard uses mentioned in recent dictionaries derive from them.

I. The Term "Alienation"

The Latin origin of "alienation"[1] is *alienatio*. This noun derives its meaning from the verb *alienare* (to make something another's, to take away, remove). *Alienare*, in turn, derives from *alienus* (belonging or pertaining to another). And *alienus* derives ultimately from *alius* (meaning "other" as an adjective, or "another" as a noun). (17)

[1] The standard uses of the terms *aliéner* and *aliénation* in French are essentially the same as the standard uses of "alienate" and "alienation" in English. See Robert's *Dictionnaire alphabetique et analogique de la Langue Française*. (3)

Alienation as Transfer of Ownership

One of the principal Latin uses of *alienare* (and *alienatio*) is in connection with property. In this context *alienare* means, "to transfer the ownership of something to another person." To do so is to cause something quite literally to come to "belong to another"; hence the appropriateness of derivatives of *alienus*. Similarly, in Middle English, one could "alien away" something one owned, such as lands or a house. Thus in the fifteenth century a man could be ordered to "make no alienation of no parcel of land."[2]

The terms "alienate" and "alienation" still have this meaning today, as recent dictionaries attest. Some form of compensation for the transfer may or may not be involved; the term covers the transaction in either case. It only applies, however, if the transfer is effected "by the act of the owner." And it is appropriate only in those cases in which possession of that which is transferred is institutionally acknowledged (e.g., in the form of a title or deed). As in Middle English, this use of the term occurs primarily in legal contexts. When it does occur elsewhere, it is usually in discussions of economics.

Alienation as Mental Disorder

A second traditional use of "alienation" also goes back to Middle English, and also has its roots in Latin usage. In Latin one can speak of *alienatio mentis*, or simply *alienatio*, in connection with the state of unconsciousness, and the paralysis or loss of one's mental powers or senses—as, for instance, in an epileptic seizure, or as the result of a severe shock. In Middle English "alienation" was used in the same general connection. In the fifteenth century it could be said of someone that he was "aliened of mind or understanding," or "aliened and turned from reason." (20) The editors of the *Middle English Dictionary* suggest that this use of the term was from the beginning a technical "medical" one. Like the "legal" one, it too continues to be a standard—if infrequently encountered

[2] In this and other examples taken from the *Middle English Dictionary* (20) I have modernized spellings for the sake of clarity.

—use in current English; although now this use is designated as special to "psychiatry," rather than simply to "medicine."[3]

Alienation as Interpersonal Estrangement

A third standard use of "alienate" and "alienation"—which is the only one that can in any sense be called "ordinary"—also derives from Latin usage. The verb *alienare* can mean, "to cause a warm relationship with another to cool; to cause a separation to occur; to make oneself disliked." And *alienatio* can refer either to this process or to the resulting condition. (17) These Latin terms are applicable in ordinary interpersonal contexts. In Middle English, however, the derivative use of "alien" and "alienation" was confined primarily to theological contexts. In fact, it is specifically identified by the editors of the *Middle English Dictionary* as "chiefly theological." Illustrations contain references to being "aliened from God," and to "alienation and parting between God and man." (20)

In subsequent centuries the terms ceased to have a peculiarly or even characteristically theological employment. The first volume of the *Oxford English Dictionary* (21), published in 1888, gives the verbs "alien" and "alienate" the following, quite general definition: "To convert into an alien or stranger. . . . To turn away in feelings or affection, to make averse or hostile, or unwelcome." One indicated employment of the terms in this sense is in an ordinary interpersonal context: A person could "alien" or "alienate" another who initially felt close to him. The terms could also be employed in the last century in other than interpersonal contexts. Among the illustrations given in the O.E.D., one finds references to "subjects aliened from their duty," and to the increasing "alienation from the act of worship." In these cases

---

[3] This is the only use of the term mentioned in Baldwin's *Dictionary of Philosophy and Psychology*. (4) Baldwin (in 1911) therefore considered the term to have no special philosophical meaning. The following is the entire entry (excluding etymological material and foreign-language analogies): "*Alienist, Alienism, Alienation.* . . . A medical specialist in the study and treatment of mental diseases. Alienism is the name for such a study, while Alienation is a generic name for the various forms of insanity or mental derangement."

there is a "turning away of feelings"; only it is something nonpersonal to which one ceases to feel attached or becomes ill-disposed.

In the first half of the present century the terms apparently ceased to be employed in such nonpersonal contexts, and came to be associated primarily with the cooling of personal relationships. In recent dictionaries "alienation" in this general sense is defined simply in terms of "making indifferent or unfriendly" or the "estrangement of the affections"; and these are terms which have their primary if not sole employment in connection with such relationships. Of course, one continues to hear the term used in connection with the less than truly "personal" relationships between people and their leaders and political parties. (It is often said, for example, that the Purges of the Thirties "alienated" many Western Communists from the Party.) But these may more accurately be considered attenuated forms of interpersonal relationships than fundamentally different phenomena. One who governs may be remote, but he is still a person. And parties are made up of people, and are capable of sustaining quasi-personal relationships in a way in which "duty" and "the act of worship" are not.

It should be observed that this type of alienation comprehends two distinguishable degrees of coolness in such relationships. A person may be said to have "alienated" another, or to have "alienated himself from" another, if he has done something to inspire feelings of antagonism or hostility in someone who formerly felt a positive attachment to him. This is perhaps the more common and obvious case. But he may also be said to have done so if he has simply caused the other's formerly positive feelings toward him to give way to indifference. The other may never be roused to hostility, but may one day simply realize that the person no longer means anything to him. It is equally appropriate to speak of "alienation" in this case.

A different sort of loss of intimacy can occur quite independently of untoward behavior of any sort, simply as a result of one of the former intimates undergoing a change of some sort. Long separation, for example, can transform people who once were close into strangers who feel they no longer know each other. They need not feel any antagonism toward each other; the bonds which once united them simply cease to exist. Indeed, they may regret the transformation bitterly, all the more so because they find themselves unable to regain their lost intimacy. The term "alienation" finds one of its most common contemporary applications in this context.

II. The Term *Entfremdung*

As in the case of the term "alienation" in English, the German term *Entfremdung* has been in use since the late Middle Ages. In the Grimms' *Wörterbuch* (8)[4] the meaning of *ent-fremden* is given as: "*fremd machen, berauben, nehmen, entledigen*"; that is: "to make alien, to rob, to take, to strip of." The German *fremd* is much like the Latin *alienus* and the English "alien," meaning: "belonging or pertaining to another." *Fremd* originally was used to refer to things literally foreign; but it very early came to be applied in connection with virtually any kind of strangeness or otherness. The literal meanings of the German *Entfremdung* and the English "alienation"—"to make *fremd*" and "to make alien"—are therefore very similar.

Like "alienation" in Middle English, *Entfremdung* also has an application in connection with property in Middle High German. However, the application is a quite different one. The "making alien" involved is not to be conceived in terms of the lawful transfer of ownership, but rather in terms of the activities subsequently listed by the Grimms: robbing, taking, stripping of. In Middle High German, that which one "alienates" (*entfremdet*) is generally something belonging to *someone else*; and the "alienation" consists in taking or stealing it from him. Among the Grimms' illustrations is the statement that we "should not alienate or take away our neighbor's goods."

In later German usage, however, the term ceased to be used in this connection. And *Entfremdung* never has had a standard use in connection with the deliberate and institutionalized transfer of one's property to another, as "aliena-

[4] The relevant volume appeared in 1862. Citations from it in English are my translations.

tion" traditionally has had and continues to have in English. A different German term customarily has been used in this connection: *Veräusserung*. This is the term used by Hegel, for example, in his discussion of such tranfer in his *Philosophy of Right*.

The term *Entfremdung* also had a Middle High German use somewhat similar to the English use of "alienation" in connection with mental disorder. The examples of it which the Grimms cite, however, suggest that it was used primarily in connection with unconsciousness and the temporary paralysis of the senses: e.g., "Their senses were *empfrendet* [*sic*], and they lay as if dead." Again, *Betäubung*—a daze, stupor, or coma—is characterized as a state "in which our soul is *entfremdet* from itself." One interesting survival of this use of the term *Entfremdung* in Hegel's time will be discussed below.[5] Generally speaking, however, this use too seems to have disappeared by the nineteenth century.

Entfremdung could be used at least as early as the sixteenth century in connection with interpersonal estrangement; for it is so used by Luther in his translation of the New Testament.[6] But it apparently was only in the nineteenth century that this use of the term began to have any noticeable currency. At any rate, Heyne, writing in 1890, remarks that this use has been "quite common since the beginning of the century"—thereby implying that it was not particularly common earlier. (14)

While this use of the term may have acquired some currency in the early nineteenth century, it cannot have been very great. For by the end of the century *Entfremdung* disappears altogether from German dictionaries. When it does reappear once again in very recent ones, however, its primary use is indicated once again to be in connection with interpersonal estrangement. And in this context, it functions in essentially the same way as does the English term "alienation."

This is the general linguistic background against which the special uses of "alienation" and *Entfremdung*, to be discussed

[5] See p. 43.
[6] See p. 15.

in subsequent chapters, are to be viewed. Seeing them against this background helps one to understand how some of them have arisen; but it also makes clear how greatly many of them differ from traditional and standard uses.

HEGEL'S PREDECESSORS AND CONTEMPORARIES

An examination of the uses of "alienation" and *Entfremdung* in philosophy and theology prior to Hegel's use of the latter in his *Phenomenology of Spirit* will show that he was the first to use the term systematically in anything like the special ways in which it is used today. But it will also show that he did not write in a vacuum; and by indicating the various themes and strands of usage he brought together in his discussion, we can more clearly understand what Hegel meant by the term.

I. Alienation in Earlier Theology

Lewis Feuer asserts that Hegel "imbibed the concept of alienation from pessimist Protestant theology." (6, 117) This view is questionable. The sense of the term most characteristically associated with earlier theology—basically, that of interpersonal estrangement—is not unique to theology. The only difference in its theological use is in its application: Instead of being used in connection with the estrangement of one person from another, it is usually used in connection with the estrangement of a person from God.

The term occurs in the Bible, in Ephesians 4:18. Paul, speaking of the Gentiles, says (reading with the Revised Standard Version): "They are darkened in their understanding, alienated from the life of God because of the ignorance that is in them, due to their hardness of heart."[7] The sense of "alienated from" in this passage is quite clearly that of being separated or cut off from the life of God.

Luther does not appear to use the term *entfremden* in

[7] In the Vulgate, the Latin phrase is *"alienatae a vita Dei."*

this way at all in his own writings, although he does use it to translate *alienatae* in the above passage in his translation of the New Testament. When he does use the term, it is in the ordinary senses mentioned in the previous section.[8]

The case of Calvin is only slightly more interesting. There is one passage in his commentary on Ephesians in which he himself uses the term *alienatio* in explicating a line of Scripture. Paul says (Ephesians 2:1–2) that Jesus "made you alive, when you were dead through the trespasses and sins in which you walked, following the course of this world." Calvin begins his commentary with the words: "As spiritual death is nothing else than the alienation of the soul from God. . . ."[9] (1, 219) "Alienation" here has essentially the same meaning as in Ephesians 4:18.

As in the case of Luther, however, the term does not occur with any frequency—or in any nonstandard way—in Calvin's writings. It is apparent, then, that while it was used by Reformation theologians in connection with separation from God, it was only used casually and infrequently. While Hegel no doubt was aware of this usage, it is hardly likely in itself to have exerted a very great influence upon him.

II. Alienation in Social Contract Theory

Grotius, Hobbes, Locke

The main philosophical context in which the term "alienation" was employed prior to Hegel was that of political theory —in particular, that of social contract theory. Hugo Grotius seems to have been the first to use it in this context, in his *De Jure Belli ac Pacis*. (9) Grotius conceives "sovereign authority" over oneself, or the right of determining one's actions, as analogous to property rights. This enables him to use the Latin *alienatio* in connection with the transfer of "sovereign authority" over oneself to another person. "As other things

---

[8] See Dietz's *Wörterbuch zu Dr. Martin Luthers Deutschen Schriften.* (5)

[9] "*Nam cum spiritualis mors nihil aliud fit, quam alienatio animae a Deo. . . .*" (2, 122) I am endebted to Feuer (6, 117) for pointing out this passage.

may be alienated, so may sovereign authority." (9, Vol. I, 342)

Grotius further suggests that such alienation provides the basis and justification of all political authority. In his view, political authority is constituted when a group of men relinquish the unrestricted right of each to determine his own course of action, and transfer sovereign authority over themselves to some one man. Grotius does not work this out in as much detail as do the contract theorists who followed him. This approach to the problem of political authority, however, greatly influenced subsequent discussion.

Thomas Hobbes and John Locke do not use the term "alienation," as did Grotius before them and Rousseau later. Their approach to this problem is similar, however, and their terminology is closely related. In his *Leviathan* Hobbes writes: "To lay downe a man's Right to any thing, is to devest himselfe of the Liberty of hindring another of the benefit of his own Right to the same. . . . Right is layd aside, either by simply Renouncing it; or by Transferring it to another." (15, 108)

Hobbes holds that a man can enter into the social contract only if he renounces or divests himself of "the Right of doing anything he liketh," and transfers to the sovereign his "right of Nature" to "use his own power, as he will himselfe, for the preservation . . . of his own life." (15, 108, 106) This alone, according to Hobbes, makes possible the emergence of civil society and the commonwealth.

It is Hobbes's contention that the individual gains a great deal more than he loses through this renunciation and transfer of rights. Life in the commonwealth is held to be infinitely preferable to life in the state of nature. Hobbes expects the individual to come to recognize that this is so, and to make the necessary sacrifice willingly. "It is a voluntary act: and of the voluntary acts of every man, the object is some *Good to himselfe*." (15, 109) In this case the "Good" is a life which is much less "nasty, brutish and short" than life is said to be in the state of nature.

Locke takes a similar position in his *Second Treatise on Civil Government*. (18) The right he would have men relinquish and transfer to society, however, is a much less comprehensive one—that of judging and punishing offenders against one's "life, liberty, and estate." "There, and only there, is political society, where every one of the members hath quitted this natural power, resigned it up into the hands of the community. . . ." (18, 71)

Locke speaks of "resigning up" and "quitting" (i.e., giving up), rather than "alienating," "transferring," or "relinquishing." But his terms have precisely the same force as the latter. And in using them Locke—like Hobbes—has in mind the voluntary sacrifice of a right and of complete freedom of action, for the sake of the existence of political society. Because of the great importance he attaches to the existence of political society, he too considers this sacrifice to be highly desirable.

Rousseau

In *The Social Contract* (23) Jean-Jacques Rousseau uses the French equivalents of both Grotius' term *alienare* and Hobbes's term "renounce": *aliéner* and *renoncer*. The two terms seem to be closely related in his mind; at any rate, he moves freely from one to the other. He speaks interchangeably, for example, of "alienating one's liberty" and "renouncing one's liberty." But he also uses the term "alienate" (*aliéner*) in the sense of "transfer"—as Grotius had done, and as Hobbes had used "divest." In fact, when he proposes to analyze the meaning of the term, he takes as his point of departure its standard use in precisely this sense: "To alienate means to give or to sell." (23, 246)

Rousseau agrees with Hobbes that alienation is a "voluntary act," and that voluntary acts have as their object the good of the agent. From this he infers that the act of "alienation" has no validity when it does not serve the good of the agent. He then proceeds to attack the view that it is even possible for people to transfer sovereign authority over themselves to another individual. Grotius is the proponent of this view on whom Rousseau's attack centers. Rousseau's argument is that nothing comparable to what would be given up can be gained by doing so; and that therefore no such transfer of sovereignty is in fact valid, the opinion of the contracting parties notwithstanding. (23, Ch. IV)

In an earlier, briefer discussion of the same question in his

Discourse on the Origin and Foundations of Inequality (22), Rousseau criticizes Pufendorf in a similar manner. Against Pufendorf, he contends that it is "doubtful that one has the right" to "alienate his freedom" or "divest himself of his freedom in favor of someone else," regardless of the compensation he is offered in return, since "no temporal goods can compensate for [it]." (22, 167–68)

Pufendorf, like Grotius, had held that there is an analogy between property ownership and sovereign authority over one-self. It was on the strength of this analogy that he had argued that, since the former may quite properly be "alienated" to another person, the latter may be as well. Rousseau rejects this argument on the ground that, in point of fact, sovereignty is *not* analogous to property—above all, in one crucial respect: One can relinquish any piece of property he owns without suffering degradation; but if one transfers sovereignty over oneself to another person, "one degrades his being." (22, 168) The former does not involve the loss of anything essential to one's standing as a human being, while the latter would. The analogy does not hold, because it rests on the mistake of regarding freedom from subjection to others as no more essential to one than things one happens to possess.

But Rousseau is not arguing that there are *no* circumstances under which sovereign authority over oneself may properly be alienated. On the contrary, he considers such alienation to be "vain and meaningless" *unless* this authority is transferred to a *community* (rather than an individual), in which all are on an equal footing. And he maintains not only that such alienation *is* possible in this case, but also that it is a condition of the very existence of a community. In fact, he takes the position that it is to be unconditional: "Each gives himself to all," and gives himself "without reservation." (23, 256) "It must be clearly understood that the clauses [of the social contract] can be reduced, in the last analysis, to one only, to wit, the complete alienation by each associate member to the community of *all his rights*." (*Ibid.*)

Rousseau is not completely clear about what is involved in this alienation, and precisely what it is that is to be alienated. For example, the meaning of "alienated to the community" is not entirely clear. In some cases it may be construed in the sense of "transferred to the community"; while in others it must be understood in the sense of "renounced before the community." For certain rights (e.g., that of punishing wrong-doers) may be transferred to the community; but "natural liberty" can only be renounced before it. Rousseau has both things in mind, on different occasions.

But he has more in mind as well. In his discussion of aliena-tion he is moving beyond the meaning associated with this and similar terms in earlier social contract theory, toward a notion of alienation in which not merely certain natural *rights* are renounced or transferred, but moreover the *person him-self* is surrendered to the community. At times he thinks he is saying no more than the former: for example, "What a man loses as a result of the Social Contract is his natural liberty and his unqualified right to lay hands on all that tempts him, provided only that he can compass its possession." (23, 263)

At other times, however, he goes much further, as in the passage in which he states what is "essential" to the social contract: "Each of us contributes to the group his person and the powers which he wields as a person under the supreme direction of the general will, and we receive into the body politic each individual as forming an indivisible part of the whole." (23, 257)

This "contribution" clearly involves a good deal more than the relinquishment of the "natural liberty" and "unqualified right" mentioned in the previous passage. The latter does not constitute a complete surrender of self; but nothing is held back if one "contributes to the group his person and the powers which he wields as a person." Rousseau is thus ex-tending the application of the term "alienation" from the individual's surrender of certain rights to the surrender of his entire particular self, to the extent that this is necessary in order for him to become "an indivisible part of the whole." This surrender is very great; but Rousseau—like his predeces-sors in contract theory—considers the gain greatly to outweigh the loss, and therefore views this alienation in a very positive light.

One of Hegel's two main senses of "alienation" would ap-pear to derive from Rousseau's discussion. Hegel was familiar with this chapter of *The Social Contract*; he even says of it (in his *Lectures on the History of Philosophy*) that it contains much that, while "abstractly stated, we must allow to be correct." (11, Vol. III, 401) The phrase "surrender of the particular self," which fairly characterizes what alienation involves for Rousseau, occurs frequently in Hegel's discussion of alienation in the *Phenomenology*. Much the same thing is involved in one type of alienation as Hegel conceives it; the end to be achieved is similar in both cases; and Hegel's attitude toward this alienation is similar to Rousseau's. In short, Hegel's debt to Rousseau here would seem to be considerable.

III. Hegel's Contemporaries: Fichte and Schiller

Fichte and *Entäusserung*

Hegel's German philosophical predecessors and contemporaries did not make special use of the term *Entfremdung*, at least until after the appearance of his *Phenomenology*.[10] However, J. G. Fichte did use the term *Entäusserung* (meaning "surrender" or "divestiture"), which is closely related to "alienation" and *Entfremdung* in social contract theory and the *Phenomenology*. Because of this fact, and because Fichte exerted a considerable influence upon Hegel, his use of this term is relevant here.[11]

Fichte's basic program is that of bridging the Kantian gap between the phenomenal world on the one hand and the spiritual world revealed by reflection on moral experience on the other. He seeks to work out an interpretation of freedom which is meaningful not solely from the standpoint of man's moral consciousness and practical activity, but also from that of his relation to the phenomenal world. Fichte

[10] Schelling uses the term in speaking of nature as something to be "brought back out of self-alienation, once again into man, into his being." (Cit. Gehlen, 7, 341) But he uses it only in passing, and in a lecture delivered twenty years after the *Phenomenology* was published.

[11] See his *The Science of Knowledge*, ed. & tr. by Peter Heath and John Lachs (New York: Appleton-Century-Crofts, 1969); and his *The Vocation of Man*, ed. Roderick M. Chisholm (New York: Bobbs-Merrill, 1956).

finds it possible to do so, by virtue of his radical idealism.
Man may appear to be bound by the chains of necessity, because his bodily existence places him in the law-governed
phenomenal world; but Fichte views the phenomenal world
as a product of spiritual creativity. Insofar as man is spirit,
therefore, he is not merely a part of this world, but rather
the ground of its existence. And by virtue of his consciousness
and reason, it is within his power to reassert his primacy over
it, by coming to recognize where the true dependence lies.
It is in these terms that Fichte conceives man's fundamental
freedom.

The term *Entäusserung* is introduced at a crucial point
in this scheme: in connection with the process through which
the phenomenal world is brought into being. As Georg Lukács
observes, Fichte uses the term in his *The Science of Knowledge* "in the sense of the object being a divestiture on the
part of the subject." (19, 658)[12] The phenomenal world
(the "object") is produced by spirit (the "subject"). It is
brought forth by spirit out of itself, and is set out by spirit
over against itself, as something that is now in a sense external to it. Fichte characterizes this process as an *Entäusserung* on the part of spirit—an externalization and detachment of something of its own. The term is quite appropriate,
for the literal meaning of its verb form is "to make outer or
external (*ausser*)."

In this sketch of Fichte's general scheme, one can see the
basic elements of much of Hegel's thought, insofar as his
conceptions of both the development of spirit and the nature
of freedom are concerned. With regard to the categories in
terms of which he works them out in the *Phenomenology*,
however, it is doubtful whether Fichte should be given credit
for anything more than suggesting to him that the term *Entäusserung* might fruitfully be employed in this connection.
For while Fichte does make this use of it, he does so only
occasionally. Lukács plausibly argues that it is merely a "ter-
minological experiment" which is "but an episode" in his writings, and concludes: "We can regard the conceptual system
of the *Phenomenology* as a completely original accomplish-

---

[12] Citations in English from Lukács are my translations.

ment of Hegel himself, in spite of these anticipations." (19, 658–59)

Whatever the truth of the matter may be with regard to the term *Entäusserung*, Lukács' conclusion is undeniably valid with regard to *Entfremdung;* for Fichte does not make any use of the latter in his metaphysical writings. Both of Hegel's principal uses of the term are closely bound up with some form of self-divestiture. But this by no means should be taken to imply that in his writings the term is interchangeable with *Entäusserung*, as either Fichte or even he himself uses it.

Schiller

It remains to consider one other writer who strongly influenced Hegel, and Marx as well: Friedrich Schiller. In 1795 Schiller published a work entitled *On the Aesthetic Education of Man, in a Series of Letters.* (24) Walter Kaufmann has pointed out Hegel's acknowledged admiration of the *Letters*, and his "far-reaching agreement" with Schiller, particularly in the *Phenomenology.* (16, 46, 49) It is therefore of interest that, as Kaufmann observes (16, 48 ff.), Schiller is concerned with something similar to Hegel's "alienation" in the *Letters.*[13]

He does not use the term *Entfremdung* itself, in any of its forms. However, he does speak of men experiencing the state as "alien" (*fremd*) under certain conditions. (24, 41) And he says of the "speculative spirit" which "strove after imperishable possessions in the realm of ideas," that it had "become an alien in the material world." (24, 42) These remarks may have suggested to Hegel the employment of the term *Entfremdung* in connection with ceasing to feel at one with the state and with the world.

In the *Letters* Schiller maintains that there presently exists a disparity between man's actual condition ("in time") and his true, essential nature ("in idea"). He proposes that it is the "great task of [every man's] existence" to "harmonize" the two. (24, 31–32) When they are harmonized, "the inner

---

[13] The *Letters* of greatest relevance are the Fourth, Sixth, and Twenty-fifth.

man is at one with himself." As long as they are not, he is "at odds with himself." (24, 33–34)

Schiller further holds that for the inner man to be at one with himself, the two basic elements of man's nature—"Reason" and "Nature"—must occupy their proper positions of equal importance. Only then does his existence "in time" correspond to his existence "in idea." It does not do so when one or the other of these elements oversteps its bounds and predominates. (24, 32–34) One of Hegel's central concerns in his discussion of alienation is with the establishment of just such a balance between roughly the same basic elements. And one of his major uses of the term is precisely in connection with an imbalance between them.

Schiller does not feel that it is the eternal fate of man to exist at odds with himself and the world. Greek man, he suggests, did not display the "fragmentation" and "dismemberment" of contemporary man. But while the former is more admirable than the latter in this respect, Schiller holds that man's spiritual development could be continued beyond the level attained by the Greeks only *through* the disruption of the harmony of Greek spiritual life. "This antagonism of powers is the great instrument of culture." (24, 43) Cultural or spiritual development, he feels, can occur only piecemeal, through concentration on different areas singly. In a sense, therefore, "It was culture itself that inflicted this wound upon modern humanity," through the "division of the sciences" and of labor ("occupations"). (24, 39) That is, this "wound"—this fragmentation—is the unavoidable price of development. Hegel takes up this theme, and Marx after him.[14]

Schiller further makes an observation about man in rela-

[14] Marx's criticisms of modern society, in fact, bear a strong resemblance to some of those expressed in the *Letters*, such as the following:

Enjoyment was separated from labor, means from ends, effort from reward. Eternally chained to only one single little fragment of the whole, Man himself grew to be only a fragment; with the monotonous noise of the wheel he drives everlastingly in his ears, he never develops the harmony of his being, and instead of imprinting humanity upon his nature he becomes merely the imprint of his occupation, of his science. (24, 40) Cf. Chapter Three below.

tion to nature, which Hegel relates to this theme and extends to man's relation to society and culture. He says:

> So long as Man in his first physical condition accepts the world of sense merely passively, merely perceives, he is still completely identified with it, and just because he himself is simply world, there is no world yet for him. Not until he sets it outside himself or *contemplates* it, in his aesthetic status, does his personality become distinct from it, and a world appears to him because he has ceased to identify himself with it. (24, 119)

In the long run, according to Schiller, this loss of immediate unity is not a misfortune, because it is a precondition of the attainment of a new, higher, conscious, and rational unity, which is also a more secure one. "Contemplation thrusts its object into the distance, thereby turning it into its true, never-to-be-lost possession, and thus securing it from passion."[15] This idea is developed at length by Hegel, and is basic to his entire discussion of alienation.

In short, Hegel's use of this term appears to have been influenced significantly by Schiller. Schiller may not have used it himself; but he focused Hegel's attention on many of the most important phenomena in connection with which Hegel employs it.

HEGEL'S EARLY VIEWS

Hegel does not use the term *Entfremdung* in any of his writings prior to the *Phenomenology*. The *Phenomenology*, however, was his first book; and he was thirty-six when he published it. It is not surprising, therefore, that many of the things discussed in it engaged his attention in earlier short pieces—including the phenomena in connection with which he speaks of *Entfremdung*. Indeed, it is often the case that his earlier formulations are clearer than his later ones, so

[15] I have revised Snell's translation of this passage (24, 120) to some extent, to give a more literal rendering of the German (25, 587).

that an awareness of the former often facilitates comprehension of the latter.

I. The "Early Theological Writings"

The Fragment on "Love"

A number of Hegel's earliest essays (which he himself never published) have come to be known as his "Early Theological Writings," thanks to their German editor Herman Nohl.[16] Among them is a fragment on "Love," which would appear to date from late 1797 or early 1798. (12, 302) In it Hegel is concerned with the establishment of true unity between individuals, and also between the individual and the world. Unity between individuals is suggested to be attainable only through love, which he characterizes as a feeling of complete oneness. (12, 304) He places great emphasis upon the completeness of this unity. Love is said to exclude all oppositions and to demand complete surrender. Any unrelinquished independence prevents the achievement of complete unity. "Love is indignant if part of the individual is severed and held back as a private property." (12, 306)

The idea that true union requires the complete transcendence of individuality appears again in Hegel's discussion of alienation in the *Phenomenology*. There, however, the relation in question is that between the individual and the social world. With it reappears a complimentary theme, which also is developed initially in the fragment on "Love": This transcendence of individuality is not tantamount to its simple annihilation. "In love the separate does still remain, but as

16 Nohl published these essays under the title *Theologische Jugendschriften*; and they first appeared in English under the title *Early Theological Writings*, translated by T. M. Knox and Richard Kroner. The appropriateness of so designating them is questionable, since they are not "theological" writings in any usual sense of the term. The title of their latest English issuance has been changed, at the suggestion of Walter Kaufmann, to *On Christianity*, with the original title retained as a subtitle. (12) This title is nearer the mark, in that Hegel does *discuss* Christianity in the two longest essays in the collection, if not also in the shorter pieces included in it. With a few minor exceptions, I follow Knox's and Kroner's translations in my citations.

something united and no longer as something separate." (12, 305) These are companion points throughout Hegel's writings.

The term "spirit," which occupies so important a position in his later discussions, does not occur in this fragment. Instead he speaks of "life." But the three-stage process through which "life" here is said to pass is precisely that through which "spirit" passes in the *Phenomenology:* "The process is: unity, separated opposites, reunion." (12, 308) (The section on "self-alienated spirit" in the *Phenomenology* deals with the stage which here is characterized in terms of "separated opposites.") In this fragment Hegel seems to be suggesting that man's relations to other men and to the world are explicable in terms of this process. And his point is that man's reunion with them is attainable through love. With the emergence of love, "life has run through the circle of development from an immature to a completely mature unity." This reunification is associated with the discovery that others and the world itself share with the individual the same essential nature: life. "Life senses life"; and this discovery "deprives man's opposite of all alien character." (12, 305)

In short, as early as this fragment Hegel is concerned with the problem of the relation of the individual to others and to the world. While he does not yet speak of "alienation," he does already speak of the latter appearing to have an "alien character"; and the latter usage is obviously not far from the former. Here he looks to love and a recognition of a common essential nature to transform the situation; and while he ultimately ceases to assign this role to love, something very like this recognition does continue to perform this function in his discussion in the *Phenomenology.*

The Essay "The Spirit of Christianity"

In "The Spirit of Christianity" (in 12), written in 1799, some of the same themes are taken up again. Schiller's influence is clear in this essay, but so is the extent of Hegel's departure from him. One of Hegel's concerns here is to criticize Kant's acceptance and heightening of the antagonism in man between reason and desire. For Kant these two major elements of man's nature remain at odds with each other. Reason may thwart desire, but the two are never fully harmonized. In a criticism of Kant which reveals his own fundamental concern, Hegel says, "One who wished to restore man's humanity in its entirety could not possibly have taken a course like this, because it simply tacks on to man's distraction of mind an obdurate conceit." (12, 212) Hegel, like Schiller, is anxious precisely to "restore man's humanity in its entirety."

Hegel considers the harmonization of intellect and feeling —or in Schiller's terms, of Reason and Nature—to be a deep human need. In fact, he terms it "the supreme need of the human spirit and the urge to religion." (12, 289) It is his contention in this essay that this harmonization can only be achieved through religion. He does still place considerable emphasis on the importance of love, which here again is connected with the recognition that the other is not "something alien," and on the achievement of unity. In a passage reminiscent of the fragment on "Love" he says: "It is in the fact that even the enemy is felt as life that there lies the possibility of reconciling fate. . . . This sensing of life, a sensing which finds itself again [in the other], is love. . . ." (12, 232)

Hegel now feels, however, that the harmonization of feeling and intellect requires that love be combined with an element of reflection. And when he proposes "religion" as that through which this harmonization is to be achieved, he is conceiving it in terms of just this combination: "What is religious, then, is the *pleroma* [i.e., 'fulfillment'] of love; it is reflection and love united, bound together in thought." (12, 253) It is in this sense that "religious" is to be understood when Hegel says,

> Religious practice is the most holy, the most beautiful of all things; it is our endeavor to unify the discords necessitated by our development, and our attempt to exhibit the unification [of the elements of our nature] in the *ideal* as fully *existent*, as no longer opposed to reality, and thus to express and confirm it in a deed. (12, 206)

Schiller had proposed aesthetic activity as the means of

resolution of these discords. Hegel differs from him on this point, and would substitute "religious practice" instead. But he clearly agrees with Schiller that man is faced with the problem of resolving the discord between the different aspects of his nature. And he further agrees that the emergence of this discord is a necessary, if unpleasant, part of man's spiritual development; and that when this discord is overcome in the lives of existing men, the human ideal will have found realization. All of these themes reappear in the discussion of "self-alienated spirit" in the *Phenomenology*. What is not retained is the idea that this discord can be resolved through religion; for Hegel soon found this solution too to be unsatisfactory.

The "Fragment of a System"

As late as 1800, however, when he wrote the so-called "Fragment of a System," he continued to hold to this solution. At least he continued to speak of "religion" as the key; though his manner of conceiving it had changed to some extent. In this fragment it is characterized in terms of the "self-elevation of man . . . from finite life to infinite life." One who achieves this self-elevation "puts himself . . . outside his restricted self," and "intimately unites himself" with the infinite life which pervades the world. (12, 311–12) In this somewhat mystical union, "as little as possible of the finite and restricted . . . remains." (12, 317) This is reminiscent of Hegel's earlier insistence, in the fragment on "Love," that "true union" requires the transcendence of individuality. When this demand is confronted again in the *Phenomenology*, in connection with the individual's relation to the social world, one should recall its original contexts; for they help to account for the positive coloring it has for Hegel.

This fragment may mark Hegel's transition from speaking in terms of "life" to speaking instead of "spirit." "Spirit" here is identified with "infinite life"; it is that which animates what would otherwise be a dead world consisting of a mere multiplicity of things. By virtue of its presence the world is a living whole, in which "single lives [are] organs." (12, 312) It is therefore something basically universal rather than particular, and infinite rather than restricted. It retains this

character when Hegel makes extensive use of the concept
in the *Phenomenology* and other later writings. And it follows that, since man is essentially "life" or "spirit," he is
not true to his essential nature unless he "puts himself outside his restricted self" and "intimately unites himself" with
the rest of "life" or "spirit," becoming an integrated "organ"
within it. This theme too is central to his later discussion of
"self-alienated spirit."

While his primary concern is with union rather than individuality, Hegel does not mean to deny the importance of
the latter. He contends that man's nature must be conceived
in terms of *both* individuality *and* unity with "infinite life":

> A human being is an *individual* life insofar as he is to be
> distinguished from all the elements and from the infinity
> of individual beings outside himself. But he is only an in-
> dividual *life* insofar as he is at one with all the elements
> and with the infinity of lives outside himself. (*12*, 310;
> emphasis added.)

Still, it is clear that Hegel subordinates considerations of
individuality to considerations of unity in this fragment. And
while he is usually careful in later writings to provide for the
development and exercise of individuality, he always considers it to belong within the limits of a pervasive unity.

II. The Essay on Fichte and Schelling

Hegel's first significant publication, which appeared in
pamphlet form in 1801, bears the main title "Difference of
the Fichtean and Schellingian Systems of Philosophy." (*10*)[1]
The lengthy introductory part contains a section entitled "The
Need for Philosophy." In it he develops the position that
philosophy alone can accomplish that resolution of the discords currently besetting man which he earlier had termed
"the supreme need of the human spirit."

This constitutes an important departure from his previous
position, and represents the first rough statement of his ma

[17] This essay has not yet been translated into English. Citations
from it in English are my own translations.

ture view. In earlier writings he had held these discords to be the source of "the urge to religion," and to be resolvable only through it. Now he suggests them to be "the source of the need for philosophy" as well; and it is now philosophy, rather than religion, to which he looks to restore the "rent harmony." (10, 12) He still sees religion as *one response* to them; but he no longer feels that it can succeed in resolving them among the educated in the present age. Its harmonizing powers, he says, are "only effective up to a certain stage of culture and among the common rabble." (10, 15)

In this essay Hegel uses a special term to refer to these discords: *Entzweiung*, or "bifurcation." While it does not figure importantly in the *Phenomenology*, it is a forerunner of *Entfremdung* in his vocabulary. His most striking use of *Entzweiung* is in connection with one of what he calls the two "presuppositions of philosophy." One "presupposition" is the world as a unified totality, "the absolute itself," which is "the goal that is sought," and yet in a sense is "already there," essentially if not yet actually. The other is "the emergence of consciousness out of totality, the bifurcation [*Entzweiung*] into being and not-being, into concept and being, into finitude and infinity." (10, 16)[18] This bifurcation of consciousness and world is closely related to one type of alienation in the *Phenomenology*.

Nor does the parallel stop here. In this essay, Hegel does not object to this bifurcation, because it is presupposed by the emergence of a higher unity of consciousness and world. "Totality is possible in the highest liveliness only through restoration out of the highest separation." (10, 13–14)[19] This principle is central to Hegel's discussion in the *Phenomenology*. It underlies his view that spirit must go through a stage of alienation in the course of its development. The same idea is at work here as that which he expressed in the fragment on "Love" in terms of the "process" of "unity, separated opposites, reunion."

As a historical phenomenon, this bifurcation is explained by Hegel in a way reminiscent of Schiller, and which also anticipates his account in the *Phenomenology*. He suggests

[18] Kaufmann's translation (16, 75).
[19] Kaufmann's translation (16, 74).

that it is a result of the extension of culture; and this in turn
is understood as life objectifying itself.

> The further culture extends, and the more diverse the
> development of the expressions of life becomes in which
> bifurcation can insert itself, the greater the power of bi-
> furcation becomes, the stronger its aura of sacredness, and
> the more insignificant and alien to the whole of culture
> the attempts of life to restore itself to harmony again.
> (10, 14)

It should be observed that while bifurcation is held to *presuppose* the self-expression, or self-objectification, of life, the
two are not identical. For, obviously, bifurcation can "insert
itself" into life's objectifications only when the latter already
exist; from which it follows that the two must be distinct.
This distinction is important; and it carries over when Hegel
later speaks of "alienation" in place of "bifurcation." The
relation involved is clearly an intimate one for him; but it
is not one of identity.

In the paragraphs following this passage, Hegel criticizes
those who turn to either "superstition or entertaining play"
—to either religion or artistic activity—to escape the effects
of this bifurcation. In referring to the latter he is thinking
in particular of the solution to the problem proposed by
Schiller, whose conception of art as play (24) accounts for
Hegel's use of the term "play" to refer to artistic activity.
His use of "superstition" to refer to religion is a reflection of
his abandonment of his earlier attempt to work out a solution
in terms of a new conception of religion.

His reason for rejecting religion and artistic activity as solutions is that, far from promoting reunification with the
world of cultural institutions, both involve a turning away
from it. In the case of the former there is a retreat to otherworldliness; and in that of the latter, to a world of private
experience. Both, therefore, are "alien to the whole of culture," and consequently are "insignificant" from the standpoint of overcoming the bifurcation in question. This criticism recurs in Hegel's discussion of "self-alienated spirit" in
the *Phenomenology*. Indeed, it is but a short step from characterizing the recourse to religion or art as "alien to the whole

of culture," to speaking of "alienation" in connection with the flight from the world of cultural institutions which it involves.

Having dismissed religion and art as incapable of overcoming the bifurcation of man and world, Hegel turns to philosophy, which he regards as much more promising. But by "philosophy," he is at pains to make clear, he does not mean mere "understanding" (*Verstand*), or analytical reflection; this he considers capable of little more than drawing distinctions, and incapable of grasping underlying unities. Rather, he means "reason" (*Vernunft*), which he conceives in terms of precisely this latter capacity. Its function is to synthesize or unify what has been analyzed or separated through the operation of the understanding. Only reason, he feels, is able to "unite that which was divided and reduce absolute bifurcation to a relative bifurcation which is contingent upon fundamental unity." (*10, 14*)

It has been observed that Hegel suggests that philosophy has two "presuppositions": the totality of things (the world), and the existence of consciousness sundered from it. And, he maintains, "the task of philosophy consists in unifying these presuppositions," i.e., in guiding consciousness to a new, higher unity with this totality. (*10, 16*) Here "philosophy" obviously must be conceived in terms of "reason" rather than mere "understanding"; for the latter is quite inadequate to this task. It was because Hegel had earlier conceived of philosophy along the latter lines that he had rejected it in this connection in his first writings. In this essay of 1801 he develops a new conception of it, which is essentially his mature conception. So conceived, it does not intensify "bifurcation" or "alienation," but rather is instrumental in its overcoming.

III. Early Political Essays

In 1798 Hegel wrote a short essay on the political situation in Württemberg,[20] in which a passion for political reform

[20] *"Über die neuesten inneren Verhältnisse Württembergs."* (*13*) Citations in English are my translations.

is quite evident. In it he is very critical of those who attempt to maintain political institutions "which no longer agree with the customs, the needs, the opinions of mankind, [and] from which the spirit has fled." He argues that "change is necessary," and that the steps necessary to accomplish it must be taken. (13, 151–52) When he wrote this, his inability to feel at home in these institutions led him to demand that they be altered, rather than to try to bring himself to accept them.

Things Are as They "Should Be"

Four years later (in 1802) he wrote a much longer essay, on the German constitution,[21] in which he again finds a good deal to criticize in the existing order. In the Introduction to it, however, his earlier demand for change is unequivocally retracted:

> The thoughts contained in this work can have no purpose or effect . . . other than that of the comprehending of what exists, and thus of the promotion of a more tranquil attitude toward it, together with a moderate toleration of it in word and deed. For it is not what *exists* that makes us vehement and causes us suffering; rather, it is what *is not* as it *should* be. But if we see that it *is* as it *must* be— i.e., that it is not arbitrary or accidental—then we also see that it *should* be as it is. (13, 5)[22]

Here—and for the most part, hereafter—Hegel seeks to reconcile himself with the existing order by reasoning in this manner concerning it. This passage is of special interest because it reveals a number of assumptions and inferences which are basic to, but not explicit in, his discussion of the overcoming of one type of alienation in the *Phenomenology*.

Hegel has an unfortunate tendency to conceive of necessity in two different ways.[23] (The word conveying the concept here is "must.") At times the idea is that of "could not be otherwise"; while at other times it is merely that of "not arbitrary, not accidental." These are two quite different ideas. To establish that it is not purely accidental that something

[21] *"Die Verfassung Deutschlands."* (13)
[22] My translation; emphasis added.
[23] Cf. Kaufmann (16, 85).

is the way it is, is not to show that it could not be otherwise. An example will make this clear. It is not purely accidental or for purely arbitrary reasons that certain crimes are punishable by death in this country; but this does not mean that other punishments could not have been assigned for them, or cannot now be. Two different senses of "necessary" and "must be" need to be distinguished, therefore, corresponding to these two different ideas. The "could not be otherwise" sense may be termed the *strong* sense, and the "not arbitrary" sense the *weak* one.

It obviously invalidates an argument to use a term in two nonequivalent senses, unless their nonequivalence is irrelevant to the argument, or the proper relation of implication holds between them. In the present case the nonequivalence of senses is important, since the needed relation of implication does not obtain. Hegel suggests that if it is not accidental that X is as it is, X *must* be as it is. This is true only if "must be" is construed weakly, rather than strongly. But what Hegel is attempting to establish is that if it is not accidental that X is as it is, X is as it *should* be. And at best, this conclusion follows only if it is true that something which "must be" in the *weak* sense, "must be" in the *strong* sense as well. As the capital-punishment example shows, however, this implication does not hold. The argument therefore fails. This result agrees with our intuitions about the matter; for, e.g., the suggestion would surely be counterintuitive that, death not being a purely arbitrarily selected punishment for certain crimes, it follows that they *should* be punished by death.

The Position Reformulated

It is possible to reformulate Hegel's position in such a way that the logical difficulties encountered in his formulation are avoided. One may believe that existing institutions are far from perfect, but that real, lasting improvement of them can come about only through gradual historical evolution. Indeed, one may believe that agitation for change not only is unlikely to result in the acceleration of this evolution, but moreover is highly likely to have precisely the opposite effect, and to result in a change for the worse. If these assumptions are valid, it would follow that things are as they "should be," in the sense that the world could not be better than it is at this time. Hegel made something like these assumptions, and drew this conclusion from them. The conclusion is sound if the assumptions are valid.

It may be reasonable to fear that attempts to perfect society through radical action will as a rule miscarry. But this should not blind one to the possibility that more moderate attempts to improve social institutions might meet with greater and more enduring success. It is highly implausible to claim that even attempts of this sort will for the most part result in changes which are for the worse. The last century and a half of political and social history provides numerous counterexamples. Thus even this reformulation of the view that things are as they "should be," which is internally more sound, is still not very compelling.

Of course Hegel may have had good reason to be pessimistic concerning the likelihood of anything he said having any effect upon existing institutions. Such pessimism might well lead one to seek the strength to endure a present one cannot change, through the attainment of historical perspective. But it is a quite different thing to take the position that one can aspire to nothing more than "the comprehending of what exists, and thus . . . the promotion of a more tranquil attitude toward it, together with a moderate toleration of it in word and deed."

Resignation and Alienation

Hegel assumes—or hopes—that if one comes to believe things are as they should be, this will remove the source of the "vehemence" and "suffering" occasioned by the recognition of the imperfections of the existing order, and will enable one to become reconciled with it. For he holds that it is not this recognition in itself which causes our vehemence and suffering, but rather the belief that things are not as they *should* be. Eliminate the latter, he suggests, and they will cease.

This is far from convincing. If one grants Hegel the point that things must be as they are, then it is true that one has no right to expect the existing order to be any better than it is. But one may be unable to see how it would be *possible* for it to be improved at the present time, and yet feel irreconcilably at odds with it. One may still find it too repugnant, too "alien" to embrace. One's "vehemence" and "suffering" would in this case be more aesthetic than moral—more a matter of what one finds disagreeable than what one is able to argue should be otherwise. But this would make them no less real; and they would constitute no less substantial an obstacle to reconciliation and unity with the existing order. In such a case, agreement with Hegel's conclusion can perhaps resign one to the existence of this order in its present form. It might well be unable, however, to overcome or even overbalance the feeling of "alienness," and to enable one to feel at home in this order. The resignation to which it can give rise is compatible with intense alienation.

2 Hegel's *Phenomenology of Spirit*

And what is oneness without otherness?
JOHN WISDOM, "Gods"

I. Introduction

On the *Phenomenology*

An adequate understanding of Hegel's use of the term "alienation,"[1] and a proper appreciation of his discussion of "self-alienated spirit," require an awareness of the general character of the book in which they occur: his *Phenomenology of Spirit*. Some idea of its character is obtainable from a literal reading of its title: It is a systematic study of those phenomena collectively describable as manifestations of the human spirit.

This characterization, however, does not adequately describe the astonishing program Hegel sets for himself in this extraordinary book, and gives no indication of his underlying view of these "phenomena of spirit." In brief, he attempts

[1] For the sake of readability and continuity with later chapters, I shall substitute the English equivalent for the German original, and shall for the most part speak of Hegel's use of "alienation," rather than *Entfremdung*.

Since "alienation" is one of the more important special terms used by Hegel in the *Phenomenology*, it is curious that it has received very little attention in the Hegel literature. There is not even an entry for *Entfremdung* in Glockner's *Hegel-Lexikon* (3), which gives copious references for so many other terms Hegel uses.

in the *Phenomenology* to trace the entire development of the human spirit. In the process he tries to take into account all of the great human achievements of the past up to his time, and to present them as aspects of a single continuous development. He is less interested in accurate chronology than in what might be termed the "logical" development implicit in man's history. At the same time, he feels he is describing the various stages through which the individual must pass, in order to attain to the level of spiritual development which the human spirit has reached at this point in history.

This may be illustrated by reference to the section entitled "Spirit," in which his discussion of "self-alienated spirit" occurs. At one level, Hegel is presenting certain developments beginning in classical Greece and running through the late ancient world, the Middle Ages, the Renaissance, the Enlightenment, the French Revolution, and the period immediately subsequent to it. At another level, he is discussing the emergence of the individual out of an unreflective unity with his society and culture, as a distinct and independent personality; and the subsequent establishment of a new and conscious unity, within which there is room for individuality.

The Social Substance

Hegel holds that the world in which man lives is, to a considerable extent, a world he himself has created. Social, political, and cultural institutions constitute what he refers to as "the social substance," or more frequently, simply "the substance." The social substance has come into existence, and has been sustained in existence, through centuries of human activity. As a product of the human spirit, Hegel considers it to be essentially "spiritual." "This world is a spiritual entity, it is essentially the fusion of individuality with being; this its existence is the work of self-consciousness. . . ." (PG, 347/B509)[2]

[2] All references identified with the letters "PG" are references to the *Phenomenology*. The first of the two page numbers gives the location of the passage in question in the German text (5); the second, preceded by a "B," gives that in Baillie's translation (6). In my citations I have followed Baillie, except where a different rendering of the German than his has seemed more accurate or helpful.

This suggests that there is a sense in which a spiritual nature is imparted to everything transformed by human activity, as well as to that which is created through it. In this view, since much of the natural world has been transformed by human activity, it too may be said to have acquired a "spiritual" character. Hegel even goes so far as to suggest that, since to perceive is to transform, the entire phenomenal world is "spiritual" by the same principle. (E.g., *PG*, 550/B790) It is not necessary to go this far, however, to appreciate the point about the social substance. And virtually the whole of his discussion of alienation occurs in a section on "Culture and Its Realm of Actuality," which is precisely the world of social substance.

The social substance is man's creation; but for Hegel, it has a significance which this does not adequately express. He regards it as the objectification of the human spirit, in which spirit finds the objective form that is essential to its actualization. Thus he also speaks of it as "objective spirit." As early as his essay on Fichte and Schelling, he had characterized the various aspects of "culture" as the "outward expressions" (*Äusserungen*) of "life."[3] In the *Phenomenology* he speaks instead of "substance" and "spirit," but he has in mind the same basic point. And he now takes the position that it is only with the emergence of social substance that spirit takes on a form which is not merely particular, subjective, and ephemeral, as is the life of the individual without it. He considers it crucial that spirit should take on such a form; for it is of the very nature of spirit as he conceives it that it should be objective, enduring, and, above all, universal. This view goes back to his introduction of the concept of "spirit" in his early "Fragment of a System," in which "spirit" is identified with "infinite life," as opposed to that which is merely "finite and restricted."[4]

Man's Nature

Hegel recognizes that man is essentially individual. But he insists that individuality is only one aspect of his nature. A

[3] See p. 32.
[4] See p. 29.

more balanced characterization of man's nature, he suggests, can be given in terms of "spirit," which balances the idea of individuality with that of universality.

> Spirit is the nature of human beings generally, and their nature is therefore twofold: at one extreme, explicit individuality of consciousness and will, and at the other, universality which knows and wills what is substantive. (PR, §264)[5]

Hegel takes strong objection to the view that the nature of man consists merely in "particularity of nature and character." He holds that nothing so ephemeral can be endowed with essential significance. Furthermore, he contends that an adequate conception of man's nature must take into account his reason; and reason involves the transcendence of particularity and the movement of thought at a general level. He therefore attaches great importance to "universality" (*Allgemeinheit*). He says of human consciousness that universality is its "essence." "Its universality is its significance and its actuality. . . . Its significance depends . . . on its having made itself . . . conformable to what is universal." (PG, 351/B514) "Universality" is to be understood in terms of conformity to or accordance with the "universal." One example of something "universal," for Hegel, is the "system of reason" he discusses in his *Logic*. Another—and that which he has in mind in this section of the *Phenomenology*—is the social substance.

Of course, the social substance of a particular people is not universal in the sense of extending to all men everywhere. The domain over which its universality extends is limited, covering only the particular people in question. The justification for using the term "universality" in this context is that it contrasts with "particularity"; and the idea Hegel wishes to convey is that the social substance transcends the particularity of individuals. The literal meaning of *allgemein*

---

[5] All references identified with the letters "PR" are references to Hegel's *Philosophy of Right*. In references to this work I shall give paragraph numbers (e.g., "§264"), which are the same in Knox's English translation (7) as in the German (4), rather than page numbers. I have generally followed Knox's translations.

is "common to all"; and the point is that the social substance
is common to the whole of the people in question.[6]

That which is universal in the realm of interpersonal interaction is the social substance; and it follows from this that
if the individual is to achieve universality, he must "make
himself conformable" to it, and live in accordance with it.
This is a theme also developed at length in the *Philosophy
of Right*, in which Hegel says that a "substantive basis" for
universality is to be found only "in social institutions"; they
alone make it possible. (PR, §264) And since man must
attain universality if he is to realize his essential nature as
spirit, Hegel considers unity with the social substance to be
something essential for man. "It is in an ethical [i.e., social]

---

[6] For this reason, Kaufmann contends that "universality" is a
misleading translation of *Allgemeinheit* in this context; and that the
German term is better rendered as "generality," which conveys the
idea of the transcendence of the merely individual, without implying
the notion of something all-encompassing. Thus, according to Kaufmann, the term is to be understood in the same way in which the
term "general" is to be understood when Rousseau speaks of the
"general will"; the "general will" is shared by all members of a particular community, but not by all men whatsoever.

I have retained the term "universality" (which Baillie uses in his
translation of the *Phenomenology*, and Knox, in his translation of
the *Philosophy of Right*) for two reasons. First, when Hegel characterizes the nature of spirit—and therefore of man—in terms of
Allgemeinheit, it is ultimately true universality (in the sense in which
reason is truly universal), rather than mere generality in the above
restricted sense, that he has in mind. Secondly, while he recognizes
that the social substance of one people does differ in various respects
from that of another, he regards the social substance of each people
as a more or less adequate embodiment of the truly universal "system
of reason," and thus itself as truly universal to the same extent. It
therefore is not accidental that he uses the same term (*Allgemeinheit*) to refer both to what is truly universal *and* to conformity to a
particular social substance, although *we* might find it more comfortable to characterize the latter in terms of "generality" only. My retention of the term "universality" is thus motivated by a desire to
remain faithful to Hegel's use of a single term in both connections,
and to what I take to be his ultimate intentions. To avoid misunderstanding Hegel, however, it must be kept in mind that, to the
extent that the social substance of a people does not conform completely to the "system of reason," its "universality" is relative, and
has the character of mere generality; it transcends the merely individual, but is not truly or absolutely universal.

order that individuals are actually in possession of their own essence or their own inner universality." (*PR*, §153)

Hegel's Twofold Use of "Alienation"

One cannot meaningfully speak of "Hegel's concept of alienation," *simpliciter*, because he uses the term in two different ways.[7] At times he uses it to refer to a separation or discordant relation, such as might obtain between the individual and the social substance, or (as "self-alienation") between one's actual condition and essential nature. I shall use the subscript "1" to indicate that the term is to be understood in this sense ("alienation$_1$"). He also uses it to refer

[7] In his translation of the *Phenomenology*, in his introduction to the section of the book in which Hegel's discussion of alienation occurs, J. B. Baillie makes a suggestion which requires comment. He says of Goethe's translation of Diderot's *Rameau's Nephew*:

> It . . . came into Hegel's hands while he was writing the *Phenomenology*. . . . The term "self-estranged spirit" [Baillie's rendering of "*Der sich entfremdete Geist*"] with which he heads this section occurs in Goethe's translation. Rameau is an extreme type of such a spirit. (6, 508)

Baillie is right about Rameau; and it is true that there are a number of references to the work in this section of the *Phenomenology*. But the implied suggestion that Hegel got the expression "*Der sich entfremdete Geist*" from Goethe's translation is mistaken. For this expression does not occur as such either in Goethe's translation of the work itself, or in his appended remarks. The closest thing to it conveys a meaning quite different from anything Hegel ever intends by it. At one point Rameau goes into a fit of musical frenzy; and in the course of the description of him that follows, this passage occurs: "But he noticed nothing, he kept on, in the grip of *einer solchen Entfremdung des Geistes*, an enthusiasm so close to madness that it seemed doubtful whether he would recover." (Barzun's translation [2, 67], except for the German, which is Goethe's rendering [1, 288].)

This occurrence of the term, in the traditional sense of loss of one's senses, is the only one in Goethe's translation. And while Hegel would consider Rameau—as generally portrayed—to provide a good example of what he means by "alienation," it is not this momentary condition which he takes to constitute it. Hegel is indebted to Goethe for making *Rameau's Nephew* available to him (it was not published in French until after the *Phenomenology* was written), but not for the expression "*der sich entfremdete Geist*."

to a surrender or sacrifice of particularity and willfulness, in connection with the overcoming of alienation$_1$ and the reattainment of unity. When it is to be understood in this sense I shall employ the subscript "2" ("alienation$_2$").

The first sense derives relatively directly from the ordinary use of "alien" (*fremd*) in connection with strangeness, foreignness, difference, nonidentity. Alienation$_1$ involves something "becoming alien." This use of the term was not without precedent. It was used in this way by Reformation theologians to refer to the separation of a person from God. And in its standard use in connection with interpersonal estrangement, it conveys the idea of a separation where unity once prevailed. The second sense, on the other hand, derives from the notion—frequently met in social contract theory—of the surrender or transfer of a right to another. It might be said to involve a "making alien."[8]

Alienation$_1$ for Hegel is a condition which occurs when a certain change in a person's self-conception takes place. It is neither something one does nor the intended result of a deliberate action. One *finds* that the condition has come to exist. Alienation$_2$, on the other hand, is—as it was for social contract theorists—something deliberate. It involves a conscious relinquishment or surrender with the intention of securing a desired end: namely, unity with the social substance. Alienation$_1$ is to be overcome completely—in part, precisely through alienation$_2$. The latter, however, is to be permanent, or, more precisely, continuous; for only in this way can alienation$_1$ be kept from recurring.[9]

[8] This use of the English, French, and Latin terms can be traced back from social contract theory to standard traditional usage. *Entfremdung* does not have this use in traditional German usage, however; it would seem to have been an innovation of Hegel's, suggested to him by social contract theorists writing in other languages—above all, Rousseau. (See pp. 16–21.)

[9] Since the claim that Hegel uses the term *Entfremdung* in these two different ways would seem to be rather novel, it would perhaps be well to document the fact that he does by citing instances of each use in the German text. (Since most of the passages in question are cited in English in the discussion which follows, I shall not provide translations of them here.) The term is used in each of the two ways with approximately equal frequency in the section of the *Phenome-*

II. First Sense of "Alienation" (as Separation)

Loss of Unity with the Social Substance

Consciousness of oneself as a distinct individual does not inevitably emerge in the course of life. This sort of self-

---

nology entitled "Der *sich entfremdete* Geist," in which most of its occurrences in the work are concentrated.

In the following passages, the term has the sense of "separation." Speaking of the "unhappy consciousness," Hegel says (in the paragraph immediately preceding the above-mentioned section): ". . . ihre *wirkliche* Wahrheit . . . besteht darin, dass dies *allgemeine Gelten* des Selbstbewusstseins die ihm entfremdete Realität ist." (PG, 346/B506) Speaking of the otherworldly consciousness, he says that "this world," the world of the social substance, "seine ihm entfremdete Wirklichkeit ist." (PG, 348/B510) Also in this connection, he says: "Hier aber ist die Religion teils aus der *Substanz* hervorgegangen . . . ; teils ist dies reine Bewusstsein seinem wirklichen, das *Wesen* seinem *Dasein* entfremdet." (PG, 377/B551) Speaking of that self-consciousness which has ceased to be at one with the social substance, Hegel says that the latter "ist für das Selbstbewusstsein ein unmittelbar Entfremdetes. . . ." (PG, 352/B516) Similarly: "Wenn daher innerhalb der Welt der Bildung selbst das reine Denken als eine Seite der Entfremdung fiel. . . ." (PG, 377/B550) One further example: ". . . Alles [ist] sich selbst entfremdet, das *Fürsichsein* vom *Ansichsein* getrennt." (PG, 375/B546) Cf. also PG, 348/B510, 359/B526, 367/B537, 371/B541, 376/B549, 378/B551, 379/B552.

In the next series of passages, on the other hand, the term *Entfremdung* has the sense of something like "surrender." In one paragraph worth citing at length, because it sums up so much of what Hegel is saying in this section of the *Phenomenology*, Hegel says:

> Wodurch also das Individuum hier Gelten und Wirklichkeit hat, ist die *Bildung*. Seine wahre ursprüngliche Natur und Substanz ist der Geist der *Entfremdung* des natürlichen Seins. Diese Entäusserung ist daher ebenso *Zweck* als *Dasein* desselben; sie ist zugleich das *Mittel* oder der *Übergang* sowohl der *gedachten Substanz* in die *Wirklichkeit*, als umgekehrt der *bestimmten Individualität* in die *Wesentlichkeit*. (PG, 351/B515)

Similarly, Hegel states that the process "wodurch die Substanz wirklich wird, ist die Entfremdung der Persönlichkeit. . . ." (PG, 348/B510) For the individual who is not at one with the social substance "hat die Substanz die Bedeutung eines aus ihm ausgeschlossenen Daseins, mit dem es sich nur durch die Entfremdung seiner conception is a relatively recent historical phenomenon; and it is by no means universal even today. It has been and continues to be quite common for people to conceive of themselves primarily in terms of the roles they occupy and the groups in which they live. Their identification with these roles and groups is not conscious and deliberate; rather, it is immediate and unreflective. Their relation to the social substance is one of complete and immediate unity. Hegel uses the expression "ethical world" (*die sittliche Welt*) to refer to the stage of human development at which this immediate identification with the social substance obtains.

He then observes that conflicts can arise as a result of which one is "driven back into himself out of this actuality," ceases to identify with the substance, and comes instead to limit his self-identification to his own particular person and characteristics. (PG, 346/B506) Hegel considers this to be a desirable development, in that it marks the emergence of a dimension of distinct individuality and independent existence, which is necessary if man's essential nature is to be realized completely. This dimension is "the reality of the self that is not

selbst eins zu setzen . . . hätte." (PG, 347/B509) (These three passages also illustrate the point that Hegel uses the term *Entfremdung* in the sense presently under consideration in connection with the overcoming of that disunity of individual and social substance which is characterized in terms of *Entfremdung* in the first set of passages cited above.) Further: the individual self-consciousness "hat nur *Realität*, insofern es sich selbst entfremdet; hiedurch setzt es sich als allgemeines, und diese seine Allgemeinheit ist sein Gelten und Wirklichkeit." (PG, 351/B514) For this reason Hegel says: ". . . das Fürsichsein [ist] vielmehr der Verlust seiner selbst, und die Entfremdung seiner vielmehr die Selbsterhaltung." (PG, 371/B542) And, speaking of the "noble consciousness" which renders service to the state, he says: "Wessen dieses im Dienste sich entfremdet, ist sein in das Dasein versenkte[s] Bewusstsein; das sich entfremdete *Sein* ist aber das *Ansich*." (PG, 360/B527) Cf. also PG, 348/B510, 353/B517, 360–61/B527–28, 362/B529, 363/B531, 421/B608. In many of these passages, as in the first one cited, Hegel uses the term *Entfremdung* in this way, and then goes on to use the term *Entäusserung* ("relinquishment," "divestiture," "surrender") in its place, in such a manner that it is clear that the former is to be understood along the lines of the latter. In the first set of passages, on the other hand, *Entfremdung* cannot be understood in this way.

found in the ethical world." Because it is not found there, the unity with the substance which characterizes the ethical world "is the universal actuality of the self; but this actuality [maintained at the expense of distinct individuality] is directly the perversion of the self as well, and [is] the loss of its essential being." (*PG*, 346/B506) In order to overcome this deficiency, the complete and immediate unity characteristic of the ethical world must end.

After this original unity is lost, and until a new one is established, the relation of the individual to the social substance is discordant. Absorbed in his new-found distinctness, the individual comes to regard the social substance with which he formerly was at one as something completely "other." A "nonidentity in consciousness between the ego and the substance" emerges. (*PG*, 32/B96) The individual now views the substance as something "external and opposed" to him. (*PG*, 347/B509) It has *become alien* in his eyes; or as Hegel now says, it is "alienated." (*PG*, e.g. 346/B506, 352/B516) This is one of Hegel's uses of the term. The separation in question is the most important instance of alienation₁. —

Other Instances of Alienation₁

Hegel on occasion uses the term in this sense in connection with other kinds of separation as well. On one such occasion he suggests that something analogous to the alienation₁ of the substance occurs in the experience of the phenomenal world generally:

> And experience is the name given to just this movement in which the immediate, the unexperienced, i.e., the abstract, whether sensible being or bare and simple thought, becomes alienated and then returns to itself from this alienation, and is only then presented in its truth and actuality, and becomes the property of consciousness. (*PG*, 32/B96)

There is much more than a passing resemblance between this view and Schiller's view that "contemplation thrusts its object into the distance, thereby turning the object into its true, never-to-be-lost possession," and that "a world appears to man [only when] he has ceased to identify himself with it."[10] In the above passage, Hegel is making basically the same point: Consciousness can only grasp the content of experience "in its truth and actuality" by first ending its initial immediate absorption in this content, and stepping back from it far enough to be able to apprehend it. He reasons in much the same way where the alienation₁ of the social substance is concerned: the immediate original unity of the individual with the substance must end, in order that a higher, conscious, and secure unity may emerge. He thus regards the relation of the individual to the social substance as an instance of a wider pattern in human life. For the most part, however, he confines his use of the term "alienation" to the context of this relation, and does not employ it in connection with experience generally.

There is one other context in which Hegel sometimes speaks of alienation₁. It is that of the loss of independence, which occurs when one becomes dependent upon others for the means through which one wishes to assert one's independence and develop one's individuality. Hegel frames his remarks in terms of the case of dependence upon a benefactor; but they have an obvious application to any such attempt which is made dependent upon wealth or possessions. Wealth and possessions are or can be affected by others at every point from their production to their retention to their use. To the extent that one depends upon them, therefore, one is dependent upon the suffrance of "an alien will." Thus a condition quite other than independence results whenever one attempts to assert and develop one's "independent existence" in a way that involves reliance upon wealth or possessions. In such a situation, Hegel suggests, true independent existence has become "an alien reality" for the person in question.

> That which is alien to self-consciousness here is independent existence itself; it finds its self as such to be alienated—an objective solid reality, which it has to receive from another solid independent being. (PG, 367–68/B537)

[10] See p. 25.

General Characterization of Alienation₁

In all of its occurrences in the *Phenomenology*, "alienation₁" is used in connection with the emergence of an awareness or feeling of the "otherness" of something. Thus Hegel refers to the necessity of taking seriously "otherness, alienation, and the overcoming of this alienation." (*PG*, 20/B81) But he does not use the term to refer to the awareness of "otherness" as such. He uses it only in cases in which the "otherness" in question is of an extreme sort, and in which there is no "oneness" which complements and transcends it.

He does not consider something to be alienated₁ in relation to an individual if it simply *is* viewed as "alien" by him. It must have *become* "alien" to him, subsequent to a period in which he was at one with it, if the term is to be applicable. Thus, for example, Hegel does not speak of independent existence as alienated₁ at the stage of the ethical world, even though he holds it to be lacking at this stage. It is simply absent. One must previously have acquired a sense of independence, and have attempted to assert it, before he considers it appropriate to speak of alienation₁ in connection with the absence of it.

In Hegel's usage, it is generally that which has become *alien to the individual* that is termed "alienated₁." For example, it is the social substance that is said to be alienated₁ (in the eyes of the individual), when the individual ceases to identify with it. Today, on the other hand, it is usually said that it is the individual who is alienated (from something like the social substance), when the same lack of unity exists. The two ways of speaking are equally reasonable; and far from being incompatible, they are complementary. It is simply a historical fact that Hegel tended to speak in the former way.

Self-alienation₁: First Sense

He does, however, speak of the individual as "self-alienated₁" in this situation. He holds that man is essentially spirit; and that universality is essential to anything essentially spiritual. Loss of universality thus has the result that one "thereby alienates himself from his inner nature and reaches the extremity of discord with himself." (PG, 366/ B535) Universality at the interpersonal level is attainable, according to Hegel, only through unity with the social substance. In ceasing to be at one with the social substance, therefore, the individual loses his universality; and when this happens he is no longer "in possession of his essence." (PR, §153) He thus "alienates himself from his inner nature," or in brief, becomes "self-alienated$_1$."[11]

It follows that one who adopts an otherworldly religious orientation, and one who conceives of himself solely in terms of his own particularity, are both self-alienated$_1$. For the relation of both to the social substance is not one of unity. Otherworldliness, Hegel observes, is precisely "the flight from the world of actuality, and is characterized by opposition [to it]." It is thus the rejection of that which makes universality possible. "By its very nature," therefore, the otherworldly consciousness "is self-alienated." In turning away from the world of social substance, it is "alienated from its actualization, its inner nature from its existence." (PG, 377–78/B551)

One who limits his self-conception to his particular self also turns away from the social substance, though in a different direction. He seeks to develop his particular nature and character, and to assert his independence, as completely as possible (in *this* world)—at the expense of unity with the substance. He closes his eyes to his essential universality, and "is proud and well-satisfied in this self-alienation." (9, 91) There is just as great a disparity between his "existence" and his "inner nature" as there is in the case of the otherworldly individual. These are the two instances of self-alienation$_1$ to which Hegel devotes the most attention.

In all such cases the expression "self-alienation" is used to refer to a separation or disparity between actual condition

---

11 Here too, "alienated" has the sense of "separated"; and so I shall continue to employ the subscript "1" when the expression is to be understood in this way. The subscript merely indicates the sense of the term "alienation" in this compound expression, however. Because the term "self" may be understood in different ways, the compound expression can take on different meanings, even though "alienation" has the same sense.

and essential nature, resulting from the loss (rather than the mere absence) of some element of the latter in the life of an individual. The connection between the alienation₁ of the social substance and of independent existence, and the condition to which self-alienation₁ refers, should be obvious.

Hegel's concern with the disparity which may obtain between man's actual condition and essential nature goes back to the period of his early writings. It is to be seen, for example, in the essay "The Spirit of Christianity," in which he suggests that man's greatest task is to "exhibit the unification in the ideal [of the elements of his nature] as fully existent."[12] The problem associated with self-alienation₁ is that one or the other of these elements has been lost, and that therefore the proper combination and balance of these elements is not "fully existent" in the life of the individual.

Self-alienation₁: Second Sense

There is another way in which self-alienation₁ must sometimes be understood. For Hegel, the social substance is not merely the creation of spirit, but moreover its objectification. This means that the substance *is* spirit, in objectified form. From this it follows that when the substance is alienated₁ from the individual, it is objectified spirit that is alienated₁ from him.

It is not difficult to follow Hegel this far. But he goes further. He envisages a fundamental identity between the spirit which animates the individual and the spirit which has objectified itself in the social substance. The latter, for him, is the individual's *true* "self." This leads him to the remarkable conclusion that when the social substance is alienated₁ from the individual, it is the individual's *own true self*-objectified—that is alienated₁ from him. This is a second sense in which Hegel considers one who stands in this relation to the social substance to be self-alienated₁. In such a case the individual consciousness fails to recognize that "what seems to happen outside it, as an activity directed against it, is its own doing." (*PG*, 32/B97–98) In other words, one fails to see that the social substance which seems

12 See pp. 27–28.

alien to one is not really so, but rather is one's own creation
and objectification.

Hegel had long been persuaded of the essential identity
of the individual and spirit generally which this view presupposes. In his early essays, he had suggested that life is
essentially "infinite," rather than "finite and restricted," and
had spoken of "single lives" as "organs" of the living whole of
the world.[13] He continued to think along these lines; though
he tended subsequently to speak only of the identity of the
individual with the spirit of his people, when discussing something like the social substance.

References to this identity are common, for example, in
his *Lectures on the History of Philosophy*. There he speaks
of individuals as "parts of the state, like members of an organic body." He suggests that "the spiritual content" of the
state "constitutes the essence of the individual as well as that
of the people," and likens "the particularities, the whims of
individuality" to "the dust playing over a city or a field, which
does not essentially transform it." For him, "the spiritual
individual" is "the people, insofar as it is organized in itself,
an organic whole," rather than the individual person. (8, 51–
52) He says of the state that "it is this temporal totality
which is one being." "To it the individual belongs. . . . This
spiritual being is his—he is one of its representatives—it is
that from which he arises and wherein he stands." (8, 66)

It is within the framework of assumptions of this sort that
one must understand Hegel's assertion that "what seems to
happen outside" the individual "is his own doing." It makes
sense to take this position only if one holds that "the people"
is the irreducible "spiritual individual," rather than the individual man; and that the ultimate identity of a person is
that of a "representative" or "organ" of such an "organic
whole," rather than that of an irreducibly individual being.
And it is only on this view that the idea is coherent that,
when the social substance is alienated$_1$ from the individual,
it is his own self (objectified) that is alienated$_1$ from him.

This would be a second respect in which such an individual could be described as self-alienated$_1$, in addition to the

13 See pp. 27 ff.

respect of having lost the universality required by his essential nature. And if one can bring such an individual to accept this view of his relation to his people, one has at hand a relatively easy way of reuniting him with the social substance. For then it remains only to show him that this substance is the objectification of the "spiritual individual, the people" of which he is a part. This in fact is Hegel's preferred solution to the problem of the alienation$_1$ of the substance.

If one cannot accept the view in question, however, then while one may grant that such an individual is self-alienated$_1$ in the respect discussed previously, one will reject the idea that he is also self-alienated$_1$ in this second respect. In fact, one will very likely reject the very notion of self-alienation$_1$ of this sort, unless—as Marx did—one finds a different application for it, in connection with something which may more plausibly be viewed as the objectification of the individual's "self."[14] And one will also have to find another solution to the problem of the alienation$_1$ of the substance (if it is considered desirable to find one).[15]

Self-alienation$_1$ and "Self-alienated Spirit"

The entire section of the *Phenomenology* under consideration is entitled "Self-alienated Spirit." In the light of the foregoing discussion, it is not difficult to perceive Hegel's meaning in referring to spirit generally as "self-alienated," when a discordant relation obtains between the individual and the social substance. Concrete existence on the one hand, and universality and objectivity on the other, are the two basic aspects of spirit as he conceives it. Spirit requires both in order to be fully "actual."

Hegel recognizes that only existing individuals can enable spirit to exist concretely; and he contends that it can attain a concrete universality and objectivity only in the form of

[14] See pp. 108–09.
[15] There is another solution at least implicit in Hegel. In brief: If there is a desire in man to actualize his essential nature, then if one can persuade the individual that unity with the social substance is necessary to this end, he will have been given a motive to seek unity with it. See pp. 66 ff.

the social substance. Their unity is essential to the realization of the desired "twofold actuality" of spirit—individuals who have achieved universality as well as concreteness, and universal and objective forms (i.e., the social substance) which are at the same time concretely embodied. (*PG*, 352–53/ B516–17, 360/B527) When the social substance is alienated₁ from the individual, spirit is bifurcated within itself; and it is between its bifurcated aspects that this relation of alienation₁ holds. The unity between these aspects which is essential to spirit has been lost. In short, spirit is self-alienated₁; and this section of the *Phenomenology* is a study of spirit in this condition.

III. Second Sense of "Alienation" (as Surrender)

Hegel uses the term "alienation" to refer not only to various separations, but also to a kind of surrender or sacrifice, which is necessary if certain of these separations are to be overcome. The latter is the sense of the term which has been designated as "alienation₂." While he regards the alienation₁ of the social substance (together with the self-alienation₁ he takes it to imply) as something unfortunate—although necessary—and to be overcome, he regards alienation₂ as something desirable and to be perpetuated.

He distinguishes between that individuality or independence which is consistent with and limited by the requirements of universality, and that which involves a disregard of these requirements and an elevation of particularity (of nature and character, desire and will) to a position of supreme importance. The latter involves "the possession of an individual will which is not yet surrendered *qua* will," and which is indulged at the expense of universality, thereby in effect destroying it. (*PG*, 361/B528) Unity between the individual and the social substance can be restored (and self-alienation₁ overcome) only if willful self-assertion is given up.

Hegel often uses the term "alienation" to refer to this renunciation. Having emerged out of its original immediate unity with the substance, the individual consciousness can again "make itself one with the substance only through the alienation of its self." (PG, 347/B509) The individual for whom the substance is alienated$_1$ can overcome this alienation$_1$ and his self-alienation$_1$—his separation from his *essential* self—only through the alienation$_2$ or surrender of his *particular* self (self-alienation$_2$).

Alienation$_2$ and Social Contract Theory

This second use of the term has close parallels in the writings of the social contract theorists discussed in the previous chapter. Grotius, it will be recalled, speaks of man's ability to "alienate" his "sovereign authority" over himself. Hobbes talks of the individual "renouncing" or "divesting himself" of "the Right of doing anything he liketh"; while Locke speaks of men "quitting" or "resigning up" the "natural power" of judging and punishing offenders. And Rousseau discusses the idea of the individual "alienating," "renouncing," or "divesting himself of" his "natural liberty," and "giving himself to all, without reservation."[16]

It should also be remembered that all of these writers view the surrenders in question very favorably, at least when they are made under the proper circumstances. They are regarded as prerequisites of the establishment and maintenance of something of much greater worth than absolute individual freedom: a social order. These writers suggest that it is only within the framework of a social order that a person can adequately maintain and develop himself; and that there is a place for individuality, but only within the bounds set by the requirements of the existence of society.

While Hegel is not simply echoing their views, it is illuminating to keep them in mind when considering his use of the term "alienation" in the sense presently in question—and, more generally, his entire position on the relation of the individual to the social substance. The term here is virtually synonymous with such terms as "renunciation" and "relinquishment" in contract theory; and it is similarly interchangeable with the German equivalents of these terms (*Entsagung*, *Entäusserung*) in the *Phenomenology*. For Hegel, as for Rousseau, it is the individual's "natural being" (Hobbes and

[16] See pp. 16–21.

Locke: "natural right" and "natural power") that is to be "alienated" or "renounced." And like the contract theorists, Hegel regards this development in a very positive light; for it makes possible the attainment of a similar and equally highly desired end.

Rousseau had gone beyond earlier contract theorists, in suggesting that the surrender the individual is called upon to make is of *himself,* and not merely of certain rights. Hegel uses the term "alienation₂" in connection with a comparably extensive and fundamental "surrender" of "self," which involves the "renunciation of independent existence," and even the "relinquishment of personality." (*PG,* 350–52/B514–15) Like Rousseau, however, he is strongly opposed to such alienation₂ when it results in dependence on or subordination to *another person.*[17] And even in the right circumstances he regards it as necessary only insofar as the attainment of a broad universality requires it. Particularity is to be subordinated to universality, but not eliminated altogether.

Yet while the result Hegel has in mind should not be exaggerated, neither should it be underestimated. He envisages a situation in which "the original *determinate* nature [of the individual] is reduced to an *inessential* difference of quantity." (*PG,* 351/B515) Rousseau had spoken of the individual coming to be "an indivisible part of the whole."[18] This expresses Hegel's idea exactly, and conveys some notion of what is involved in the "alienation" of which both speak in this connection.

Mitigating Considerations

The idea of so considerable a relinquishment of independence and a subordination of particularity to universality is not likely to be as acceptable to most people today as it was to Hegel. It loses some of its initial objectionability, however, when considered in the context of the circumstances of Hegel's introduction of it, and the lack of compulsion associated with it in his mind.

First, Hegel's positive attitude toward alienation₂ is not

[17] Compare, for example, Rousseau's criticisms of Grotius and Pufendorf (pp. 18–21) with Hegel, *PR,* §§66 and 67.
[18] See p. 20.

word
star heel

grounded in any preference for totalitarian political systems.
Rather, it is an outgrowth of his early concern with the establishment of solidarity among men through "love," and of
an "intimate union" of the individual with "spirit" or "infinite
life." In his fragment on "Love" he had observed that love
requires the relinquishment of independence, and is incompatible with "separateness of individuality." And in his so-
called "Fragment of a System" he had suggested that one can
achieve unity "with all the elements and with the infinity of
lives outside himself" only if he "puts himself outside his
restricted self," so that "as little as possible of the finite and
restricted . . . remains."[19] The universality of which he
speaks in the *Phenomenology* retains overtones of these sorts
of unity for Hegel; and the relative reasonableness of the
kinds of sacrifice which they require is correspondingly reflected in his attitude toward the alienation$_2$ required by
this universality. He recognizes that alienation$_2$ involves a
loss; but as in these other cases, he feels that the gain it makes
possible outweighs it by far.

Next, one must consider the cultural situation in which
Hegel was writing—a cultural situation in some ways similar
to our own. There was no danger of a stifling conformity to
social and cultural institutions and traditions, particularly
among the educated members of the younger generation. On
the contrary, the Romantic cult of the individual and of inwardness was flourishing. There was an increasing tendency
to view involvement in the institutions and traditions of the
society with disdain; such involvement was held to entail
something like a surrender of one's authenticity and a sacrifice
of one's personal integrity. Enthusiasts of the "beautiful soul,"
concerned only with the attainment and preservation of a
state of inner purity, viewed participation in the social, political, and economic life of the society as something to be
avoided as much as possible.

Hegel was greatly disturbed by this development.[20] He had
a profound awareness of the importance of these social and

[19] See pp. 26–27 and 29–30.
[20] See, for example, his scathing attack on the "beautiful soul,"
or "self-consciousness withdrawn into the inmost retreats of its being," *PG* 461 ff./B665 ff. and 470/B676.

58 ALIENATION

cultural forms, and felt it crucial that they not lose their power. We tend to take it for granted that all life that can be called genuinely human is structured by these forms. But this has not always seemed so obvious; and one of Hegel's great contributions was to help make it so. He further saw that if life is to be structured by these forms, subjectivity and particularity cannot be given precedence over them and indulged at their expense, as the more extreme Romantics in effect urged. His call for the alienation₂ of the particular self must be viewed in this light, and should be regarded as directed, above all, at these excesses of Romanticism.

Finally, it should be recognized that, at bottom, alienation₂ is the relinquishment of a self-*conception*—the conception of oneself as an essentially particular, absolutely independent, and distinct being. A person comes to view the social substance as something "alien" as a result of coming to conceive of himself in this way. He abandons the one-sided conception of himself as a mere member of the social order, only to adopt another self-conception that is equally (but oppositely) one-sided. And it is only because he entertains this new self-conception, Hegel suggests, that he clings to his particularity and asserts it at the expense of his universality.

But a person can in turn abandon this self-conception in favor of a more balanced one, according to which he is inherently universal as well as particular. If he does, and if he sees that universality is attainable only through the relinquishment of particularity in cases of conflict, then he will cease to regard alienation₂ as inherently objectionable. There is no question of external compulsion. A person with the proper self-conception, according to Hegel, will undertake alienation₂ willingly, in order to realize the conception he has of himself.

Alienation₂ and the Overcoming of Alienation₁

In the first pages of the section on "Culture and Its Realm of Actuality," Hegel both elaborates upon his conception of alienation₂ and describes its role in overcoming the alienation₁ of the social substance (and thus also the corresponding form of self-alienation₁). He directs our attention to the situation in which the substance "is in the eyes of self-consciousness something that is directly and primarily alienated." When self-consciousness comes to the realization that "this is its own substance," through coming to a better understanding of the nature of the substance and of its own nature, it "proceeds to take possession of the substance." The process through which it does this is that of "making itself conformable to this actuality." This is the process of *Bildung*[21], through which the individual assimilates the content of his society and culture, simultaneously making it his own and making himself a part of it. (*PG*, 352–53/B516–17)

In this way the individual eliminates the gulf that had separated him from the social substance. Its alienation$_1$ is overcome, and he attains the requisite universality: "Through *Bildung* he achieves significance and actuality." (*PG*, 351/B514–15) Only then is his unity with the social substance properly grounded. His earlier, immediate unity with it was not—as is shown by its having become alien to him. He may have been brought up in unreflecting conformity to it; but his unity with it is secure only when he has self-consciously made its content his own and shaped himself in accordance with it.

Hegel summarizes this development in the following words:

> For the power of the individual consists in making himself conformable to that substance, i.e., *in relinquishing his self*, and thus establishing himself as the objectively existing substance. (*PG*, 353/B517; emphasis added.)

[21] There is no term in English which adequately conveys the meaning of *Bildung*. Baillie translates it as "culture" (in *PG*), and Knox as "education" (in *PR*); but the term has overtones of both, and neither rendering conveys this fact. Perhaps the best English rendering would be "acculturation"—a term which is used by some social scientists in discussions of alienation. Kenneth Keniston, for example, says that where "alienated subjects" are concerned, "we can speak of a *failure of acculturation*." (11, 197) The primary association of this term with the early periods of life, however, renders it less than satisfactory as a translation of Hegel's term; for he has in mind less one's initial introduction to the social substance than one's deliberate and mature attempt to appropriate the content of the social substance to which one has been exposed in the course of one's upbringing. In the absence of an adequate English equivalent, therefore, I have retained the German term. In the light of these remarks, its meaning should be sufficiently clear.

He can achieve unity with the social substance only by surrendering his particular self—only by sacrificing his particular interests and desires to the extent necessary. This is precisely alienation$_2$.

It may overstate the point to suggest (as Hegel seems to here) that this relinquishment or alienation$_2$ is the *same thing* as the assimilation of the content of the social substance it makes possible. But the two certainly go hand in hand, and constitute the negative and positive aspects of the endeavor through which a mature unity with the social substance is achieved. It should be clear, therefore, how important a role alienation$_2$ plays in overcoming the alienation$_1$ of the social substance and the self-alienation$_1$ it entails.

Alienation$_2$, Service, and the State

So far this development has been viewed from the standpoint of the individual. It can also be viewed from the standpoint of the social substance: The alienation$_2$ of independent existence and particularity enables the social substance to acquire concrete embodiment and thus actual existence. This is Hegel's point when he suggests that alienation$_2$ helps "produce" the social substance. (PG, 347/B509, 360/B527) It helps accomplish the transition of a merely "thought-constituted universality into actuality." (PG, 352/B516)

Social contract theorists had thought along similar lines in their discussions of the origin and basis of civil society. Rousseau, in particular, had traced the existence of the community to a comparable sort of alienation. This part of the social substance, which Hegel designates as the "state-power" or "state," is one he explicitly discusses in this connection. He suggests that the "state-power" is actualized through the performance of *service* by individuals; for through their service it attains embodiment in concrete existence. And he observes that the proper performance of service involves the alienation$_2$ of independence and particularity. In the course of actualizing the "state-power" through such sacrifice and service, the individual also brings his own existence into accord with his essential nature. He thus "produces a twofold actuality."

The individual consciousness shapes itself in accordance with essentiality [i.e., universality] through this surrender. That from which it alienates itself through service is its consciousness immersed in mere existence; but the condition of being thus alienated is its essential nature. (*PG*, 360/B527)

The last remark underscores the distinction between the alienation$_2$ of the particular self and self-alienation$_1$; for the latter involves precisely the *non*realization of one's essential nature.

Alienation$_2$ is not purely a matter of what one *does*; it is a matter of the state of mind underlying what one does. It has not occurred when "deeds of honor" are performed, but with a "secret reserve of private intention and self-will." Hegel uses the term in connection with service only where "the isolated inner spirit, the self as such," has been surrendered, and the will of the individual has been brought into complete harmony with the "universal will" or "state-power." (*PG*, 361–62/B528–29) This affords another contrast of self-alienation$_2$ with self-alienation$_1$; for Hegel speaks of the latter in connection with the very opposite situation, in which there is an *opposition* between the particular will of the individual and the universal will. (*PG*, 422/B610)

Alienation$_2$, *Bildung*, and Culture

If Hegel's remarks concerning the actualization of the social substance through alienation$_2$ had been confined in their application to the state, their originality would have been quite limited; for the basic point here had already been advanced by social contract theorists. Their real originality is to be found in their application to the social and cultural aspects of the social substance. These aspects, like the state, have no actuality independently of their embodiment in the lives of men. They too are a mere "thought-constituted universality" except insofar as they attain it. They do so through the process of *Bildung*, in which men appropriate their content. "Their *Bildung* . . . is the process of making the substance itself actual and concrete." (*PG*, 353/B517) And Hegel observes that this process—no less than the process through which the "state-power" is actualized—involves a very real and considerable "alienation of personality," or "relinquishment of the self."

It should be observed that it is appropriate to speak of *Bildung* and alienation$_2$ only in connection with an existing body of social and cultural institutions. Their function is that of making such a body of institutions "actual and concrete." Both are conceivable only in a situation in which these institutions already exist as a "thought-constituted universality," in accordance with which the individual can shape himself. This situation is similar to that in which a body of subject matter is to be mastered; for a similar kind of sacrifice is required in both cases. If mastery of a body of subject matter is to be achieved, self-discipline and even self-denial are required. Preoccupation with oneself is incompatible with the attainment of this end; one must forget about oneself and concentrate upon the subject matter. Other interests and desires that would interfere with its mastery must be sacrificed. Moreover, practical considerations aside, subjectivity and the indulgence of particularity are simply out of place here. For the attempt to master a body of subject matter is by its very nature an attempt to elevate oneself to the level of something transpersonal.

It is of course possible to place a high value upon particularity and subjective thinking, in the manner of Kierkegaard. Given the desirability of the universality possible only through *Bildung*, however, self-sacrifice or self-alienation$_2$ along these lines is necessary. Since Hegel supposes that the "significance" and "actuality" of the individual are contingent upon his attainment of universality through *Bildung*, the importance he attaches to the sacrifice in question becomes at least comprehensible.

IV. Alienation, Objectification, and Otherness

The relations between the two senses of "alienation" and certain other notions Hegel discusses in connection with them —objectification, objectivity, and otherness—are rarely clearly understood. Perhaps due to the influence of Marx, the distinctions between the two senses of "alienation" and these other concepts are often completely obscured. Marx gives the impression, in his early writings (12), that Hegel overlooks these distinctions; and many of those whose understanding of Hegel is influenced by Marx tend to see Hegel accordingly. This view, however, is mistaken.

The Concept of Objectification

A distinction should be recognized, of which Hegel clearly is aware, and which he would appear to take for granted. The creation of the social substance may reasonably be viewed as an "objectification" of the human spirit—i.e., a process through which it provides itself with a realm of objective spiritual forms. This is something quite different from the development in the individual of the *feeling* that this substance is *alien* to him. At the stage of the "ethical world," the social substance has already been created, but the individual remains completely at one with it. It is only when he ceases to identify with it that it takes on the appearance of something alien. The alienation$_1$ of the substance is thus to be distinguished from "objectification," even though the former presupposes the latter.

With regard to alienation$_2$, Hegel does speak of the "production" of the substance *as an actuality* through the alienation$_2$ of the particular self. But first, even when this sort of "production" is in question, it is not alienation$_2$ *per se* that in fact accomplishes it, but rather *Bildung* and service. Thus the two are not to be identified.

Secondly, and more importantly, "production" here is something quite different from "objectification"; and therefore the alienation$_2$ associated with the former also differs from the latter. This is particularly clear where *Bildung* and the aspects of the substance associated with it are concerned. "Objectification" refers to the initial establishment of a set of objective spiritual forms; whereas the question of *Bildung* (and hence of alienation$_2$) only arises when these forms are already in existence, but are not adequately embodied in the life of the individual. "Production" here is to be understood in the sense of "actualization" rather than "creation." Even to the extent that one can speak of alienation$_2$ accomplishing the "production" of the substance as an actuality, therefore, it is still to be distinguished from "objectification." Thus in neither of Hegel's senses of "alienation" is the term equivalent to "objectification."

Alienation₁, Objectivity, and Otherness

The establishment of a realm of objective forms, or "objectivity," is the outcome of the process of "objectification." The concepts of "objectivity" and "otherness" have a similar relation to the alienation₁ of the substance in the *Phenomenology*, and therefore may be discussed together.

It is a mistake to hold, as Marx does, that for Hegel "consciousness is offended not by alienated objectivity but by objectivity as such," and by otherness as such. (12, 210) Hegel does not consider it desirable to eliminate all otherness and all objectivity. He shares the low estimation of "oneness without otherness" suggested by John Wisdom in the line cited at the outset of this chapter. It would be pointless for spirit to establish a realm of objectivity only to annihilate it. Hegel states quite explicitly that even at the level of absolute knowledge, otherness remains as a "moment." Spirit at this highest level is said to be "at home in its otherness as such." (*PG*, 549/B789-90) There is a great difference between eliminating otherness and coming to feel at home in it. In the latter case otherness endures; only it is no longer felt to be complete and absolute. It is its absoluteness—otherness experienced as alienness—that is eliminated. The same holds true of objectivity. The situation Hegel ultimately envisages is one in which the social substance appears

> . . . as an objective world, that has lost, however, all sense of alienness for the self, just as the self has lost all sense of having an . . . independent existence by itself, cut off and separated from that world. (*PG*, 314/B458)

Hegel considers the emergence of objectivity and otherness to be an essential development in the evolution of spirit. Even after it ceases to be appropriate to speak of alienation₁, it continues to be appropriate to speak of them; for they constitute an enduring "moment" in the life of spirit. Alienation₁ is thus to be distinguished from both. (The same obviously holds true of alienation₂.)

V. The Overcoming of Alienation₁

Hegel's views concerning the ways in which the alienation₁ of the social substance and that of independent existence are to be overcome are sufficiently interesting to merit consideration in more detail. The overcoming of self-alienation₁ need not be discussed separately; for since self-alienation₁ occurs precisely by virtue of the occurrence of these sorts of alienation₁, it is overcome when they are.

Alienation₁ of Independent Existence

Hegel devotes a good deal of attention to the way in which the alienation₁ of independent existence can be overcome, in his discussion of the type of person exemplified by Diderot's Rameau. The basic point may be stated quite briefly. Where such alienation₁ exists, it may be overcome through the recognition that one has been conceiving and asserting one's independence in a way that renders one dependent upon others; and through the rejection of this way of conceiving and asserting it, in favor of a more genuinely independent one. "Only as self-consciousness roused to revolt does it know its own shattered condition, and in knowing this it has *ipso facto* risen above that condition." (PG, 367/B548)[22]

Dependence upon others can rarely be eliminated completely. But it is possible to conceive and assert one's individuality and independence in ways which minimize such

[22] Rameau (the namesake nephew of the "Rameau" in the title of Diderot's work, *Rameau's Nephew*), is a good example of an individual from whom the social substance is alienated₁. However, Hegel seizes upon the character in a different capacity. Rameau had been living quite comfortably by making himself agreeable to a wealthy family. He had come to recognize, after doing so for a time, that the kind of independence he gained by being supported by a benefactor was being purchased at the expense of his independence in a much more fundamental sense. In effect, he had come to recognize that his independent existence was alienated₁. This had "roused him to revolt," in Hegel's phrase, and he had deliberately put himself out of favor with his benefactor—thus losing his support, but regaining his independence. (2, 39–41) He was no closer to unity with the social substance for having done so, but that is beside the point.

dependence. Hegel has in mind much the same sort of inner freedom and independence of spirit—as opposed to an existence centered around possessions and wealth—which is the aim of those who today are rejecting what they perceive to be the materialism of modern society. Many things are impossible if wealth and possessions are lacking; but one is not independent insofar as one takes them for one's object.

Alienation$_1$ of the Social Substance

Hegel's views concerning the overcoming of the alienation$_1$ of the social substance are less simply stated, and more questionable. Two proposed solutions to the problem may be discerned in his discussion, which reflect two different interpretations of what it means to say that men are essentially "spirit." The point may be that man's nature is to be conceived in terms of certain "spiritual" characteristics; or it may be that the individual's essential identity is that of an individuation of a transpersonal "spiritual" entity. It means both of these things for Hegel. One solution presupposes only the former view; while the other presupposes the latter as well.

The latter view, and the solution suggested in connection with it, have already been discussed.[23] The problem with this solution is that the view of man on which it rests is hard to accept. The other solution is more interesting, because the view of man it presupposes is more plausible. Here one need grant only that universality is something essential to man. If one is persuaded of this, and desires to realize his essential nature, and if he can be convinced that universality is attainable only through unity with the social substance, he will have a motive to seek unity with it. The general program through which this unity may be pursued is that of *Bildung*, in conjunction with the necessary alienation$_2$ of willfulness and particularity. Hegel does not regard the feeling of the alienness of the substance (alienation$_1$) as an insurmountable obstacle to the attainment of this unity, once its desirability is adequately recognized.

The major shortcoming of this solution concerns this last point. Even if a person is willing to grant that realization

[23] See pp. 51–53.

of his essential nature requires unity with the social substance, he will seek unity with it only if his desire to realize his essential nature is stronger than any countervailing feelings he might have. This difficulty may not pose serious problems where the cultural aspect of the substance is concerned; but it assumes considerable proportions in relation to social and political institutions. Hegel holds that, properly understood, "they are not something alien to the subject. On the contrary, his spirit bears witness to them as to its own essence." (PR, §147) As soon as I achieve a proper grasp of my own nature and that of the social substance, he suggests, "this very other is immediately not an other in my eyes, and in being conscious of this fact, I am free." (PR, §268) And, he might have added, the alienation₁ of the substance is in principle overcome.

This sounds plausible enough, as long as social and political institutions are considered abstractly, with regard to their essential function. But when a person is confronted with particular existing institutions, his view of the matter may be quite different. (One may think of a Russian worker in 1910, a German intellectual in 1940—or a considerable number of Americans in 1970.) It may be true that one must conform to these existing institutions if he is to conform to any, since they are the only ones at hand. But it may also happen that he may find them objectionable in various respects. And if he objects to them strongly enough, his negative feelings toward them may override his motivation to conform to them springing from his desire to realize his essential nature. Under such circumstances, these institutions would remain "alien" in his eyes, and he would make no effort to attain universality through unity with them.

This reaction is not invariably to be condemned. There are conditions—such as those which existed in Nazi Germany —under which opposition to existing institutions would be preferable to unity with them, and alienation₁ to universality, even if the realization of one's essential nature were (as Hegel claims) at stake. Hegel seems to acknowledge this where conditions are such that *no* allowance is made for the development and expression of personality. He does not take account of the possibility of less extreme cases, however, in which opposition to existing institutions may still be justified, in spite of the cost.

This difficulty may be mitigated to a considerable degree if one restricts the kind of situations in which the alienation$_1$ of the substance is conceived to be a *problem*—something to be overcome—in the light of these considerations. That is, one might distinguish between those cases in which it results from the emergence of the individual's awareness of his own distinctness (type A), and those in which it is grounded in principled opposition to certain features of the social or political order (type B). It is the possibility of cases of type B which casts most doubt upon the effectiveness of Hegel's suggested way of overcoming the alienation$_1$ of the substance— and upon the desirability of overcoming it. One might therefore regard Hegel's remarks as applicable only to cases of type A.

Most probably, however, Hegel would not have been satisfied with this restriction. His actual discussion is devoted largely to cases of type A. But his underlying concern is with the realization of the individual's essential nature and the concretion of the social substance, both of which require the attainment of universality by the individual. He places too high a value on these ends to view with equanimity the situation that would result from the perpetuation of cases of type B. He presumably would have held, therefore, that even in these cases (except under the extreme conditions mentioned above), the alienation$_1$ of the substance *should* be overcome. If it is true that his proposed way of overcoming it is in fact inadequate in these cases, he would have regarded this as a serious problem.

VI. Evaluation

Hegel's Twofold Use of "Alienation"

In attempting to evaluate the fruitfulness of Hegel's use of the term "alienation," one is immediately confronted with the question of his reason for using it in two very distinct senses, with quite opposed applications. While the German term *Entfremdung* has a traditional use in one of these senses (that of "separation"), only its foreign-language equivalents deriving from the Latin *alienatio* had previously been used in the other sense (that of "surrender" or "relinquishment"). Hegel must have had something in mind, therefore, when he used it in the latter sense as well as in the former, and employed it in connection with opposed but related phenomena.

His reason for doing so, however, probably lies no deeper than his fascination with categories which can formally comprehend opposed conditions.[24] It is in fact intriguing to be able to say of a person who is at one with the social substance *and* of a person who is not, that each has "alienated his self" —only in radically different senses. And the idea of self-alienation₁ being overcome (in part) by self-alienation₂ has a certain appeal—particularly since this is a way of saying something important without being purely arbitrary in the use of language. Hegel was greatly drawn to such twists; one finds them throughout the *Phenomenology*.

The delights of such twists and wordplays notwithstanding, however, the use of the term in the two senses together would not appear to add to the fruitfulness of its use in each sense taken by itself. In fact, Hegel's twofold employment of it detracts from its usefulness by creating confusion about how it is to be understood in its particular occurrences. This confusion can be avoided only by specifying in each case how it is to be understood; and this complicates discussion. The use of the term in both senses will be warranted in spite of this difficulty if there are good reasons for using it in each sense considered individually—but only if there are.

Generally speaking, the use of a term is helpful only if it enables one to talk about something more easily than one otherwise could, or to characterize something in a more penetrating way than other terms enable one to do. The same holds true with regard to the use of a term in a new or extended sense. If other terms are or become available which

[24] Cf. Hegel's remark in his *Logic:* "But it should strike us that a language should have come to use one and the same word for two opposed definitions. For speculative thinking it is a joy to find in the language words which are characterized by a speculative significance." (Cit. Kaufmann, 10, 192.)

better perform these functions, the term in question is dispensable without loss—and indeed with advantage. It is with reference to such considerations that Hegel's twofold use of "alienation" must be evaluated.

Second Sense of "Alienation"

In its second sense, "alienation" is one of a number of terms used interchangeably by Hegel to refer to the same general phenomenon. The importance of the phenomenon is not in question. What *is* in question is the helpfulness of characterizing it as the "alienation" of willfulness and particularity, in addition to characterizing it as their "surrender," "relinquishment," "renunciation," or "sacrifice."

The traditional use of "alienation" which places it in the company of these other terms is currently very uncommon; and the German term never has had this sense at all in standard usage. Any complete characterization in which it is employed must contain the terms required to explicate *its* meaning as well, in order to be comprehensible. The characterization is equally complete, therefore, and its expression *more* economical, if these other terms alone are employed.

The most one can get out of the term "alienate" itself is that it involves somehow "making something alien" ("*alienating*" something). But this casts no light on the phenomenon, even when the "something" is understood to be the willful, particular self. It is helpful to explain that the process in question involves self-denial and self-sacrifice, the renunciation of certain interests, and the surrender of absolute independence. But to add that this involves making something *alien* clouds rather than clarifies the issue. In short, it is important in reading Hegel to recognize that he speaks of "alienation" in this connection; but this would not appear to be a use of the term which is particularly fruitful. The same holds true of "self-alienation$_2$."

First Sense of "Alienation"

The situation is quite different with respect to Hegel's first sense of the term. Used in this sense, it enables him to characterize and relate an important range of phenomena more accurately and precisely than does any other term available to him. The use of the term in this general sense was not new; for it had previously been used to convey the idea of a discordant relation or separation between individuals, and between men and God. Hegel's departure from conventional usage here consists in his employment of the term in connection with a discordant relation between the individual and the nonpersonal social substance. This innovation in application was fruitful. The term "alienation" conveys an idea of the quality and origin of this relation, as it does in its traditional applications; and this renders it superior to other terms available—such as "separation" or "discord" or Hegel's own, earlier "bifurcation"—in its ability to characterize the phenomenon. Unlike "alienation$_2$," therefore, it would not be dispensable without loss.[25]

Self-alienation$_1$

The entire plausibility of using the expression "self-alienation$_1$," as Hegel does is contingent upon the plausibility of speaking of an essential nature of man which may or may not be actualized.[26] For it refers to a disparity between a person's actual condition and his essential nature; and the concept of such a disparity obviously presupposes that he has such an essential nature (or "self"). In this respect, self-alienation$_1$ differs from alienation$_1$; for the latter refers simply to a discordant relation between the individual and the social substance, which is conceivable quite independently of any such presupposition.

It has become rather unfashionable, both on the European Continent and in the English-speaking world, to suggest that man has an "essential nature." There are, however, few who do not in fact consider man to have something like an essential nature of some description. For example, Marx is often

[25] The term "estrangement," of course, would do equally well. There would be no advantage in using it instead of "alienation," however, since it is no more ordinary or suggestive a term. The issue does not even arise in German, since both are translated by the single term Entfremdung, and are alternate renderings of it.

[26] I shall restrict my comments to the "first sense" of this expression discussed in Section II.

represented as being highly anti-essentialistic; yet he regards the development of several basic qualities as essential to man's humanity.[27] Even among modern analytical philosophers, it is often allowed that certain conditions must be fulfilled to render appropriate the use of terms like "human" and "person." Hegel's suggestion, therefore, that there are certain characteristics which are essential to man, should not in itself be regarded as unworthy of serious consideration. And the employment of the expression "self-alienation" in this general connection should not be dismissed out of hand.

It may be that Hegel's conception of man's essential nature is not completely satisfactory. But there is much to be said for his basic point: that the most important thing about man is his capacity for spiritual life; and that spiritual life in its completeness involves both distinct individuality and participation in a social, cultural, and political community. Support for this suggestion is to be found in the fact that most people would not consider life to be truly *human* if either of these elements were completely lacking. Hegel does make further claims which are much less plausible; but this much at least is quite reasonable. One can thus appreciate his specific application of the expression "self-alienation₁," which rests on this conception of man's nature, as well as the general use of it in any such context.

[27] See Chapter Three, Section II.

3 Marx's Early Writings

Alienation is apparent . . . in the fact that everything is something different from itself, that my activity is something other than mine, and that . . . an inhuman power rules over everything.

MARX, "Economic and
Philosophical Manuscripts"

I. Introduction

In the century following Hegel's death, his analysis of "self-alienated spirit" in the *Phenomenology* attracted little attention, and the term "alienation" gained little if any currency. Interest in both was aroused only with the publication of Marx's "Economic and Philosophical Manuscripts" in 1932. Marx's name had commanded widespread attention for some time; but the publication of these "Manuscripts" of 1844 revealed a side of him which previously was largely unknown: that of the passionate "humanist," concerned above all with the issue of man's self-realization.

Many people were intrigued by this revelation of a "humanistic" Marx, with the result that the "Manuscripts" were (and continue to be) widely read. This in turn resulted in the popularization of the term "alienation,"[1] used extensively in the "Manuscripts" in Marx's criticism of contemporary

[1] As in the last chapter, I shall for the most part employ the English "alienation" in place of the German *Entfremdung*.

society and his characterization of contemporary man. Many
recent writers who use the term do so under their direct influence. The "Manuscripts" thus occupy a position of great
importance in relation to current discussion of alienation.

In addition to popularizing the term "alienation," the
"Manuscripts" also drew attention to Hegel's discussion of
alienation in the *Phenomenology*, through Marx's extensive
analysis of it, and through the importance he attributes to
the *Phenomenology* in virtue of it. Indeed, he contends that,

> . . . in so far as it grasps the *alienation* of man . . . ,
> *all* the elements of criticism are contained in it, and are
> often presented and worked out in a manner which goes
> far beyond Hegel's own point of view. (*FS*, 644/B202)[2]

"Early" and "Late" Marx

Marx's interpreters are far from unanimous about whether
the concept of "alienation" has a place in his mature thought.
Sidney Hook takes the position that, "Aside from the specific
sociological doctrine of 'the fetishism of commodities' . . .
the central notion of 'self-alienation' is foreign to the historical, naturalistic humanism of Marx." (*8, 5*) Robert Tucker,
on the other hand, suggests that "Alienation remains his central theme, but it has gone underground in his image of society." (*13, 176*)

Even the proponents of the latter view must admit, however, that the "Manuscripts" are the last writings in which
the *term* "alienation" figures at all centrally. By the time of
The German Ideology (1846), Marx's only explicit references
to alienation are derisive ones. (*12, e.g., 24, 68*) And in *The
Communist Manifesto* (1848), in a pointed piece of self-
criticism, he scornfully says,

---

[2] All references identified with the letters "*FS*" are references to
Marx's early writings. The first of the two page numbers gives the
location of the passage in the collection entitled *Frühe Schriften*,
edited by Lieber and Furth. (*10*) The second, preceded by a "B,"
gives its location in the English collection edited and translated by
Bottomore. (*9*) Both collections contain other writings in addition
to the "Economic and Philosophical Manuscripts." I have followed
Bottomore's translation in my citations, except where a different
rendering has seemed preferable.

The German literati . . . wrote their philosophical nonsense beneath the French original. For instance, beneath
the French criticism of the economic functions of money,
they wrote 'alienation of humanity.' . . . (11, 37)

It may be, as Tucker claims, that "alienation remains his
central theme," and that "wage labor" has the same force
in his later writings as does "alienated labor" in the "Manuscripts." (13, 176) But such questions can be settled only
after an analysis of his use of the expressions "alienation"
and "alienated labor" in the "Manuscripts" has been carried
out, and a comparable analysis of his "image of society" and
his concept of "wage labor" in his later writings has been
undertaken.

Before turning to Marx's discussion of alienation and alienated labor, it is necessary to consider the relation in which
he stands to Hegel and to Ludwig Feuerbach. The content
of his discussion reflects a strong Hegelian influence, but
Marx's approach to Hegel owes a great deal to Feuerbach.

Marx and Feuerbach's Program of Reduction

In his early writings, Marx holds Feuerbach in high esteem.
His works, according to Marx, "are the only writings since
Hegel's *Phenomenology* and *Logic* which contain a real theoretical revolution." (FS, 508/B64) Feuerbach's "revolution-
ary" idea is that the abstract systems of thought developed
in previous philosophy and theology describe the actual structure of things, but are not applied properly. The right configurations of predicates are attributed to entities which are
mere abstract images of the actual concrete ones. It follows,
according to Feuerbach, that a program of reduction is necessary, revealing the objects of metaphysics and theology to be
"nothing other than" these concrete ones, and thereby re-
directing attention to the real world. "*Nichts anderes als*"
is his byword.

His best-known implementation of this program is in connection with religion. In his *The Essence of Christianity* (1)
and his *Lectures on the Essence of Religion* (2), he subjects
the body of views associated with Christianity to "anthro-
pological" reduction. He is particularly concerned to establish

that the conception of the nature of God is "nothing other than" a conception of the essential nature of man, which has been mistakenly applied.

> My doctrine in brief is as follows: Theology is anthropology. I.e., that which reveals itself in the object of religion—in Greek, called *Theos*, in German, *Gott*—is nothing other than the essence of man. In other words, the God of man is nothing other than the divinized essence of man. (2, 21)[3]

For Feuerbach, man has created God in his own essential image. The two seem dissimilar because there is a disparity between man's actual nature and his essential, or ideal, nature; and it is the latter, rather than the former, which is reflected in the idea of God. The nature of the disparity has been misinterpreted, and has come to be conceived as a difference between actual man and a being distinct from him: God. Moreover, this difference has taken on the aspect of something to be respected, with the result that man has not dared to aspire to the qualities which he attributes to this other being. In renouncing these qualities, however, he in fact is denying his own essential nature. The situation may be summed up in Fichtean language: Man has "posited an object" with his own essential qualities in opposition to himself, and in doing so has "relinquished" what is essential to him.

Marx does not concern himself with the reduction of religion to "anthropology." To his mind, little more needed to be said along these lines than Feuerbach already had said. That which *he* feels requires reduction is Hegel's philosophy of "spirit," and in particular his discussion of "objective spirit" and the social substance. And the reduction that is called for, he suggests, is the reduction of this to "political economy."

This is a form of reduction which is quite foreign to Feuerbach. He too undertakes a reduction of speculative philosophy, but only to religion (and thereby, indirectly, to "an-

[3] My translation. See also Chapter Three of *The Essence of Christianity*.

thropology"). For present purposes, his reduction is of no special interest. Marx says that he is to be credited with a "great achievement" for having "shown that philosophy is nothing other than religion brought into thought and developed by thought." (*FS*, 639/B197)[4] But Marx is far from satisfied with this reduction, and feels that the proper one has yet to be carried out: "The task has not yet been accomplished." (*FS*, 508/B64) It is his intention to accomplish it. For him, Feuerbach's "achievement" really lies in the general suggestion that philosophy *is to be reduced* to something other than philosophy, because it in fact is "nothing other than" *something else* which has been "brought into thought." But Feuerbach had failed to see that this "something else" is "political economy," rather than "religion" or "anthropology." The reduction he had attempted thus had not been the proper one.

In short, Marx both differs from Feuerbach and follows him, in his treatment of Hegel's philosophy. He considers it necessary to carry out a reduction of it different from Feuerbach's; but he is indebted to Feuerbach for the basic idea of subjecting it to reduction.[5]

[4] "Philosophy," for both Marx and Feuerbach, is, above all, Hegelian philosophy. Its characterization as "religion brought into thought and developed by thought" thus hardly represents a penetrating new insight into its nature. Hegel himself had regarded religion as an anticipation of philosophy, and philosophy as the comprehension in concepts of truths the most important of which are anticipated by religion. Feuerbach's originality (if it can be called that) consists merely in proclaiming such philosophy to be "nothing other than" religion conceptualized, and thus in suggesting that the former constitutes no real advance over the latter. Hegel seeks to increase our respect for religion by relating it to his philosophy; while Feuerbach seeks to decrease our respect for Hegel's philosophy by relating it to religion. In both cases, however, a connection between them is recognized.

[5] It is sometimes suggested that Marx is also indebted to Feuerbach for the idea of "self-alienation," which is supposed to have come to him from Hegel via Feuerbach. But while Feuerbach may have drawn Marx's attention to Hegel's discussion of "self-alienated spirit," through his own discussion of man's relinquishment of what is essential to him, it is only in Hegel's discussion that the term *Entfremdung* has a role of any significance. In the whole of *The Essence of Christianity* the term occurs only a few times, and with

Marx's Criticism of Hegel

Marx criticizes Hegel on the ground that "Hegel has merely discovered an *abstract, logical,* and *speculative* expression of the historical process, which is not yet the *real* history of man." (*FS*, 640/B198) In the *Phenomenology*, he says, "man appears only as spirit" or "self-consciousness." (*FS*, 644/B202, 647/B204) He feels that to characterize man in this abstract fashion is to misrepresent "real, corporeal man, with his feet planted on the solid ground, inhaling and exhaling all the powers of nature." (*FS*, 649/B206)

He levels the same charge of overabstraction at Hegel's conception of alienation. "The distinctive forms of alienation which are presented are but different forms of consciousness and self-consciousness." (*FS*, 645/B202) They are "merely the thought of alienation, its abstract and hence vacuous and unreal expression." (*FS*, 659/B215) This is also what he feels to be wrong with Hegel's idea of the way in which this alienation is to be overcome: The procedure he proposes can accomplish "merely an abstract and vacuous supersession" of it. (*FS*, 659/B215)

The fairness of this criticism is questionable. Marx is correct in suggesting that the instances of alienation of which Hegel speaks are "different forms of consciousness and self-consciousness." But it does not necessarily follow that they are therefore unduly abstract. In particular, it need not follow from this that they are "merely the thought of alienation," *as opposed to something else* which is alienation itself.

Consider, for example, the situation which Hegel describes in terms of the alienation of the social substance from the individual. In this situation the individual *regards* the social substance as something alien to him. When he regards it in this manner, it *is* alienated from him. The "thought" *is* the reality of this alienation. The individual regards the social substance as something alien as a result of *conceiving* of himself in a certain way. He ceases to do so when he comes to *see* himself and the substance in a different light. All of this

---

no special fanfare. Its centrality in the "Manuscripts" thus quite clearly derives from Hegel rather than from Feuerbach.

takes place at the level of "consciousness and self-consciousness," and would be inconceivable in any other terms. It thus is no objection to Hegel's discussion that it is cast in these terms, even if there should prove to be phenomena of a more "concrete" nature which are also characterizable as instances of alienation.

Marx's Task and "Alienation"

Marx views Hegel's account of "the historical process" as an abstraction, but one in which the outlines of "the *real* history of man" can be discerned. Accordingly, he undertakes to bring it down to earth, to cut away the accretions due to its development in abstract form, and to set forth "the *real* history of man" in the concrete terms appropriate to it— those of "political economy." He finds justification for this endeavor in Hegel himself; for he persuades himself that "Hegel's standpoint is that of modern political economy." (*FS*, 646/B203)

Given this as his conception of his task, one can easily see the reason for his fascination with the term "alienation." Here was a term which both figured importantly in Hegel's account of the development of spirit, and occupied a significant position in the language of political economy itself! Moreover, Hegel had used the term *Entäusserung* in connection with property transfer and the labor contract in the *Philosophy of Right*; and he had at times used *Entfremdung* interchangeably with this term, in the *Phenomenology*. Here, then, was an excellent place to begin the reduction of Hegel's philosophy to the concrete; for its transformation into political economy is suggested by Hegel's own usage! One had simply to interpret his remarks about the "relinquishment" and "alienation" of self-consciousness in the *Phenomenology*, in the light of his discussion of the "contracting" and "relinquishment" of labor and property in the *Philosophy of Right*.

Hegel and the Alienation of Labor

Hegel does not speak of the *Entfremdung* of labor in either of these works. (Neither, for that matter, does Feuerbach.)

In fact, Hegel does not use the term at all in the *Philosophy of Right*. He does, however, speak of the *Veräusserung*, or "contracting," of labor, i.e., the agreement to perform labor for another, usually in return for wages. This *Veräusserung* may be either of part of my time or of "the whole of my time, as crystallized in my work, and everything I produce." In the latter case, Hegel suggests, I "make into another's property the substance of my being . . . , my personality." (PR, §67) He uses the term *Entäusserung* to characterize this result, referring to it as "the *Entäusserung* [i.e., relinquishment] of personality and its substantive basis." (PR, §66) Thus in the *Philosophy of Right*, *Entäusserung* stands to complete *Veräusserung*—loss of personality to contracting away one's entire labor potential—as general effect to concrete cause.

In his essay "On the Jewish Question," Marx states: "*Veräusserung* is the activity of *Entäusserung*." (FS, 487/B39) This essay was written at the very time he was studying the *Philosophy of Right* intensively;[6] and this assertion clearly derives directly from his reflection upon it. Turning to the *Phenomenology*, Marx found Hegel speaking of the *Entfremdung* as well as the *Entäusserung* of personality. This quite naturally suggested to him that *Entfremdung* is bound up with the same concrete practice of *Veräusserung*. The close connection between the three terms, and between the concepts of "labor" and "personality," further suggested to him that the submission of one's labor to the direction of another could itself be characterized as its *Entäusserung* and *Entfremdung*.[7] For to contract it to another is, after all, to "sur-

[6] 1843. In the same year, he began to write a critique of the *Philosophy of Right*, to which he therefore obviously was then devoting a good deal of attention.

[7] It is unfortunate that Bottomore, in his edition and translation of Marx's early writings, uses the term "alienation" to render both of these German terms. He attempts to justify doing so on the ground that Marx "does not make a systematic distinction between them." (9, xix) The terms are closely related in Marx's mind—so closely that in certain contexts he uses them interchangeably. There are other contexts, however, in which he does not. He is not uttering a mere tautology, for example, when he says that "*Entfremdung* . . . constitutes the real interest of this *Entäusserung*." (FS, 643/

render" it to another, and thereby to "make it alien" to one-self. Wishing to stress this point, Marx relies exclusively upon these formulations in the "Manuscripts." This, it would appear, is how he came to speak of the *Entfremdung*, or "alienation," of labor.[8]

II. Man and Labor

Marx's discussion in the "Manuscripts" centers on the concepts of "(self-)alienated man" and "alienated labor." These concepts can best be understood in relation to his underlying concepts of "man" and "labor."

Man's Nature and Man's "Life-activities"

Marx approaches the question of man's essential nature—and for the most part refers to it—in terms of the kinds of "activity" or "life" which correspond to it, on the ground that "the whole character of a species, its species-character" is manifested "in its type of life-activity." (*FS*, 567/B127)[9] Pre-

---

B200-01) Since Marx employs the one term on some occasions and the other on others, since there are numerous passages in which they are not interchangeable, and since the normal rendering of *Entäusserung* is "relinquishment" or "surrender," it would seem obvious that the two terms should be distinguished both in translation and discussion.

[8] Tucker observes that it is commonly assumed that "the work of Hegel's from which Marx took his departure in the creation of his own system was the *Philosophy of Right*." But he suggests that the "Manuscripts" serve to "make it unmistakably plain that the assumption is erroneous, and that Hegel's *Phenomenology* is the work with which Marxism is immediately affiliated." (13, 125–26) Tucker is right in stressing the importance of the *Phenomenology* in the formation of Marx's views; but his depreciation of the influence of the *Philosophy of Right* upon Marx is unwarranted, as the example of the central Marxian concept of the alienation of labor shows. For while the term "alienation" occurs only in the *Phenomenology*, Marx's concept of the alienation *of labor* clearly has its origin in the *Philosophy of Right* as well. And his extremely important view that the alienation of labor and of the self involves the direction of labor by *another man* is comprehensible only in the light of the latter work. Thus "early Marxism is immediately affiliated" with it as well as with the *Phenomenology*.

[9] Under the influence of Feuerbach, Marx tends to use a group of terms which have a more scientific sound than "essential nature"

cisely because of this relation between the two, however, it is not difficult to identify what he takes to be man's nature from what he indicates to be the types of "life-activity" characteristic of genuinely "human" life. The one on which he places greatest emphasis is production: "Labor, productive life . . . is man's species-life." (FS, 567/B127) In addition, he designates as essential two other general kinds of life: "social life," or existence in fellowship with other men, and "sensuous life," or cultivation and enjoyment of the senses.

His specification of the latter two kinds of "life" indicates that he regards man as an essentially social and sensuous being. It may be less immediately obvious what "species-characteristic" is associated with "production"; but for Marx, as for Hegel, productive activity corresponds to the dimension of individuality or personality, and is that through which the individual personality expresses and thereby realizes itself.

Thus for Marx, man's essential characteristics are those of individuality, sociality, and sensuousness. For Hegel, they are those of individuality and universality. By including sensuousness, Marx feels that he is correcting a serious omission on the part of Hegel, whom he considers not to have given man's sensuous nature its due. With regard to his other two characteristics, however, there is a striking similarity between his conception of man and Hegel's. Both conceptions make reference to individuality; and while sociality and universality are not the same thing, the former is clearly the Marxian counterpart of the latter. The two conceptions do differ; but even where differences exist, it is helpful to keep in mind the Hegelian conception of man which Marx had before him as he developed his own. It was his point of departure; and his reaction to it was not to reject it completely, but rather to modify it and add to it.

Production and Self-realization: Hegel

The importance Marx attaches to production derives from the connection he conceives to exist between it and the self-

does: species, species-character, species-existence, and species-life (*Gattung, Gattungscharakter, -existenz, -leben*). They have much the same force, however, as is shown by his occasional use of the term *Wesen* ("essence" or "nature") interchangeably with them.

realization of the individual person. He does not argue for this connection, apparently taking it for granted. Hegel, however, discusses it at length in the *Philosophy of Right* and the *Phenomenology*; and it presumably was this discussion which persuaded Marx of the idea.

One section of the first part of the *Philosophy of Right* is devoted to a discussion of "Property." The underlying issue in this section is that of the nature of the institutions associated with the development of "personality." *Qua* "person," according to Hegel, one is characterized by one's particular characteristics and by the freedom to express them. (*PR*, §35) Production is related to personality in that it is the primary activity through which "property" comes to exist; and "property is the *embodiment* of personality," through which alone personality achieves objective reality. (*PR*, §51)

"Property," Hegel contends, "is the first embodiment of freedom." (*PR*, §45) That is, through the possession of property, an objective domain comes into existence for the individual in which he can act freely and independently. Hegel suggests that while my will is *essentially* free, "I as free will . . . for the first time am an actual will," i.e., am *actually* free, only when such a domain exists for me. (*PR*, §45) Personality is something actual only when freedom is something actual. It becomes an actuality, therefore, only when one "translates his freedom into an external sphere," by acquiring property. (*PR*, §41)

Having made this point, Hegel then observes that we acquire property by "taking possession" of "things." He distinguishes three different ways of doing so. "We take possession of a thing (a) by directly grasping it physically, (b) by forming it, and (c) by merely marking it as ours." (*PR*, §54) The first of these three ways, he says, is "only subjective, temporary, and seriously restricted in scope." (*PR*, §55) And the third is a "very indeterminate" mode of taking possession, which in reality "is not actual but is only representative." (*PR*, §58) It is thus the second—that of "forming" the thing —which is of the greatest significance. "When I impose a form on something, the thing's determinate character as mine acquires an independent externality. . . ." (*PR*, §56) The thing's relation to me is neither fleeting nor superficial, for

it is essentially transformed through my productive or
"forming" activity in such a way that it bears my imprint.
I have "put my will into it"; I have made it reflect my will,
my personality. (PR, §44)

Moreover, in doing so, I have *objectified* my will and personality. In the "formed" thing they attain objective embodiment in the actual world. (PR, §46) Through the "forming"
activity of production, therefore, I both secure for myself an
objective domain of property in which my freedom can be
exercised, and give objective expression to my personality.
Thus there is for Hegel an essential connection between production and the actualization of personality.

Turning to the *Phenomenology*, one finds the same point
being made in the section entitled "Lordship and Servitude."
Hegel here suggests that until consciousness gives itself concrete embodiment through "formative activity," it is merely
"ephemeral" and "evanescent." It is only through engaging
in production that "self-existence . . . becomes truly realized." The "lord" or "master," who lives off of the production
of his servants and does not himself engage in productive
activity, thereby deprives himself of the means of realization
of his "self." In this respect, Hegel suggests, the situation of
the servant ironically is the more advantageous one; for the
necessity of producing with which he is confronted places
him in a position to achieve this end. "In the work one
does, self-existence is externalized and passes into the condition of permanence." Through productive activity, one becomes "factually and self-consciously self-existent." In the absence of it, one does not. (PG, 148–49/B238–39) Here again,
the realization of the particular self or personality is presented as occurring through production.

Production and Self-realization: Marx

Marx follows Hegel closely here, even in the language he
uses to state his position. The individual is said to find himself confronted with "the sensuous external world," which is
"the material . . . out of which and through which he produces things." (FS, 562/B123) The "thing produced" is the
"product of labor"; and "this product is an *objectification* of

labor," in which "his labor becomes an object, assumes an external existence." (FS, 561–62/B122) Production, for Marx, is "the direct activity of individuality." (FS, 595/B157) Through the production of objects the individual "reproduces himself . . . actively and in a real sense, and he sees his own reflection in a world which he has constructed." (FS, 568/B128) This "reproduction of himself" constitutes an actualization of his otherwise merely implicit "self" or personality in the realm of objectivity. Marx refers to this process as one of "externalization." (FS, 586/B148) Through it, man becomes "an objective fact for himself"; and this accomplishes "his self-realization." (FS, 598/B159) The things he produces are "the objectification of himself," which "confirm and realize his individuality." (FS, 600/B161)

Marx even retains the Hegelian emphasis upon the importance of property in this connection. He is commonly thought to have advocated the complete abolition of private property. This is a profoundly mistaken interpretation of his position as it is set forth in the "Manuscripts." He terms the communism which proposes this a "crude communism" and rejects it, arguing that this would "negate the *personality* of man in every sphere." And he accepts Hegel's contention that property is essential to the realization of personality, and urges instead its "genuine appropriation." (FS, 591/B153) Anyone who views it as inherently objectionable, he says, "has not yet grasped the positive nature of private property." (FS, 593/B155) To be sure, the institution of private property *as it presently exists* is something he finds strongly objectionable. But "the meaning of private property—released from its alienation—is the existence of essential objects for man, as objects of enjoyment and activity." (FS, 631/B189)[10]

10 One reason why Marx is commonly misunderstood on this point is that in later writings his focus is not upon the inherently positive nature of private property, but rather upon its presently existing form. Another reason, pertaining even to his early writings, is that he employs a term in this connection which can be understood in two quite different ways: *Aufhebung*. This term—which Hegel uses extensively—can mean simply "abolition." But it can also convey the idea of elevation to a higher form (the literal meaning of *aufheben* is "to lift up") and preservation in that form. In the

Marx was well acquainted both with Hegel's discussion of property and personality in the *Philosophy of Right*, and with the section on "Lordship and Servitude" in the *Phenomenology*. And his position concerning the relations between production, property, and personal self-realization is clearly similar to Hegel's. He differs from Hegel only in holding current conditions to be such that production and property do not in fact contribute to self-realization. Hegel had properly stated their essential connection; but he had not, in Marx's view, seen that in capitalistic society production and property are perverted, and that they prevent the worker from objectifying his personality and realizing his individuality through them.

Characteristics of Production

Human production, as Marx conceives of it, contrasts with that of animals in several respects. He recognizes that animals also "produce"; but he contends that only man produces "in accordance with the laws of beauty." He also holds that human production alone is essentially "free" production. While animals produce "only under the compulsion of direct physical needs, man produces when he is free from physical need and only truly produces in freedom from such need." (*FS*, 568/B128) In other words, the kind of production considered by Marx to be man's "life-activity" is motivated by nothing more than the need to create, to express oneself, to give oneself external embodiment.

Marx further suggests that man alone is capable of consciousness of the fact that this is his "life-activity." He criticizes Hegel for representing man as "self-consciousness"; but he nonetheless conceives man as a self-conscious being, who not merely produces freely, but also can perceive that it is his

---

latter sense, that which is *aufgehoben* is abolished, but only *in its existing form.*

Marx's call for the *Aufhebung* of private property is frequently understood in the former, narrower sense, as a call for its simple abolition. In fact, however, it is a call for the transformation of the institution of private property, to bring it into accordance with its essential function. This is clear from the passages cited above, and from his use of the adjective *positive*: What he desires is "the *positive Aufhebung* of private property." (*FS*, 593/B155)

nature to do so. "*Conscious* life-activity distinguishes man from the life-activity of animals. Only for this reason is he a species-being." (*FS*, 567/B127) From Marx's use of the Feuerbachian term "species-being," it is clear that he means more than that man alone is conscious of what he is *doing* while he is producing. For Feuerbach uses the term specifically to indicate that a being so designated is conscious of itself as belonging to a certain species, and thus as having a certain essential nature.[11] Of course, neither Feuerbach nor Marx mean to suggest that all men in fact *are* conscious of their essential nature. Their point is that man alone is *capable* of such self-consciousness.

Finally, Marx considers the fundamental form of production to be material production. However, he also recognizes that "religion, the family, the state, law, morality, science, art, etc." are also human "products." He attempts to subsume such "particular forms of production" under the "general law" of material production; but he at least is not blind to the wide range of man's productive activity. (*FS*, 594/B156)

The Nature of Labor

The concept of "labor" (*Arbeit*) is central to Marx's early (and later) writings, and to be understood properly, it must be viewed in relation to his concept of production and its function. Essentially considered, there is no difference between "labor" and "production" for Marx. He does not employ the terms "labor" and "alienated labor" interchangeably, at least in the first of the three "Manuscripts," in which his main discussion of the nature of labor occurs. For here he is concerned with the conditions under which labor—which is not alienated as such—*becomes* alienated. When he *means* "alienated labor," he either uses the adjective "alienated," or else specifies that he is speaking of labor as it exists for "political economy." Otherwise "labor" refers to (un-"alienated") production or "practical human activity."

To be sure, Marx has a negative attitude toward "labor . . . in the form of acquisitive activity." (*FS*, 518/B77) And he speaks critically of it "insofar as its purpose is merely the

[11] See the first chapter of his *The Essence of Christianity*.

increase of wealth." (*FS*, 517/B76) But it is a perversion of labor that he is considering in these passages. Viewed from the standpoint of its essential nature, it is "an end in itself," which has "human significance and worth." (*FS*, 572–73/B132) Its essential identity with production in his mind is indicated by his equation of "labor, life-activity, productive life." (*FS*, 567/B127)

Marx suggests that labor should be an activity through which man "fulfills himself," and "develops freely his spiritual and physical energies." It should be itself "the satisfaction of a need," rather than a mere means through which other needs can be satisfied. Above all, it should be "voluntary" and "free," a man's "own work," "his own spontaneous activity." (*FS*, 564–65/B125) The paradigm of such activity would seem to be artistic creation, or at least some form of activity in which craftsmanship can be exercised. (Recall Marx's characterization of human production as production "in accordance with the laws of beauty.")

In the second and third "Manuscripts," and in later writings, Marx does tend to use the term "labor" to refer to the perverted forms of labor actually prevailing in contemporary capitalistic society. In the second "Manuscript," for example, he speaks of "labor, that is . . . , activity which is alien to itself, to man and to nature, and thus to . . . the expression of life." (*FS*, 578/B139) But the fact that he refers to it as "alien *to itself*" is a reminder that, essentially, labor is something very different from the current reality. Essentially, its nature and function are identical with those of production.

Man as a Social Being

For Marx, man is essentially *social* as well as individual. Life is genuinely "human," he maintains, only if it is characterized not simply by productive activity, but also by fellowship with other men. Human life is essentially "communal life." Marx contrasts the individual who views other men "antagonistically" with "man as a *social*, i.e., really human, being." (*FS*, 593–94/B155) And in discussing the currently prevailing relations between men, he speaks of the possible "return of man . . . to his *human*, i.e., social, life." (*FS*, 595/B156) An individual does not fully conform to his essential "species-character" when his "species-bonds" with other men are severed, as they are in civil society. (*FS*, 486/B38) The concepts of community, solidarity, harmony and fellowship—as opposed to those of disunity, antagonism and exploitation—would seem to convey what Marx has in mind when he speaks of "social" life.

His justification of his contention that man has an essential "social" nature is a poor one; for it involves introducing the expression "species-being" in one sense, and then making use of it in another. Marx establishes that man is a "species-being" on the ground that man is a being capable of consciousness of his essential nature. Here he follows Feuerbach's usage. Considered by itself, however, the expression suggests the idea of a being whose nature it is to exist together with —and thus in harmony with—other beings of its kind. Marx takes advantage of this fact to imply that, because man is a "species-being," he is a social being. But possession of a social nature is by no means entailed by the capacity for self-consciousness. To establish that man is an essentially social being, more is required than the establishment of the fact that he is a "species-being" in the Feuerbachian sense.

Marx's line of reasoning adds nothing to the intuitive plausibility of the idea that man is essentially a social being. Indeed, by making the point seem dependent upon so unsatisfactory an argument, he makes the case for it appear to be much weaker than it in fact is. He himself undoubtedly did not become convinced of it on the strength of this argument; rather, it would seem simply to have been one of his most profound convictions, the basis of which he could not adequately express.

Hegel, in his early writings, exhibits a concern with unity among men which is similar in intensity to Marx's.[12] This concern is part of the background of his later insistence upon the importance of "universality," and his acceptance of the sacrifices involved in its attainment. Still, it is universality as such, rather than the solidarity among men resulting from their common attainment of it, which he ultimately concludes to be essential to man; and thus Marx's concept of

[12] See pp. 26 ff.

"sociality" is to be distinguished from it. The issue for Hegel
is that of one's relation to impersonal institutions; for Marx,
it is that of one's interpersonal relationships.

One must even distinguish between Marxian sociality and
the interpersonal solidarity associated with Hegelian universality. For in the case of Hegelian solidarity, the individual's
unity with others is mediated by social institutions; whereas
in the case of Marxian sociality, it is direct and personal. In
the one case he may be related to others simply as one member of a society to other members of it; in the other case he
is related to them as one individual to other individuals.
Common membership in a society insures no more than a
general and diffuse solidarity, which is compatible with the
absence of genuine fellowship. It is just such fellowship,
however, that Marx has in mind. Hegel may have hoped for
the eventual emergence of this more intimate kind of interpersonal unity; but it is not implied by his concept of
universality.

Man as a Sensuous Being

Marx considers it essential not only that men realize their
personalities through productive activity and live in fellowship with each other, but also that their "subjective *human*
sensibility" be "cultivated or created." In fact, he goes so far
as to say, "The cultivation of the five senses is the work of all
previous history." His basic point is that a man cannot be
considered fully "human" until his "senses have become
human," i.e., refined. (*FS*, 600–01/B160–61) This follows
from the contention that this side of man's life is a "truly
ontological affirmation of his essence." (*FS*, 631/B189)

Marx insists upon the distinction between "humanized
sense" and "sense which is subservient to crude need." The
latter regards things merely from the standpoint of the use
to which they may be put. The former, on the other hand,
"relates itself to the thing for the sake of the thing." The
terms "human" and "humanized" serve to distinguish not
only the sensibility of man from that of animals, but also
the refined sensibility from the crude and brutish, and the
aesthetic from the materialistic. (*FS*, 599–601/B160–62)

It is clear that Marx has in mind, above all, the cultivation of the capacity for aesthetic appreciation. His examples of "subjective *human* sensibility" are: "a musical ear, an eye which is sensitive to the beauty of form." (*FS*, 601/B161) However, he does not restrict himself to works of art. The "*human* sensibility" will be sensitive to the "beauty" and "particular characteristics" of "minerals." He also conceives it to encompass the lower senses; for he contrasts the "human form of food" with the "feeding-activity" of animals and starving men, thus suggesting that it involves a cultivated palate. (*FS*, 601/B162)

Possession of a cultivated sensibility, according to Marx, is connected with "social" existence and "self-objectification" through production. (*FS*, 600–01/B161) There is an obvious difference, however, between living in fellowship with others and being able to appreciate things aesthetically. There is also a difference between the latter and giving oneself expression through productive activity, as may be seen in the different relation to "things" in the two cases. The former involves an appreciation of things in virtue of their *having* a certain form, either naturally or through the efforts of someone else; whereas the latter consists of *giving* them a new form which reflects one's own personality. Whatever their factual interconnectedness, therefore, these three dimensions of life are conceptually distinct, and reflect three distinct essential characteristics of man's nature as Marx conceives it.

Marx's Use of the Term "Alienation"

In Marx, Hegel's two senses of "alienation" come together, and a single general sense emerges, which may be characterized as "separation through surrender." This is not to say that he deliberately synthesizes Hegel's two senses; on the contrary, he fails to distinguish them in his discussion of Hegel. His own use of the term is the result of a (perhaps fruitful) confusion of them, through which the ideas of both "separation" and "surrender" come to be suggested. He gives the term many different applications. In each case, however, it is used to suggest the existence of a separation of some sort. And in each case, the separation to which the term "alienation" refers is related in some way to a certain surrender: namely, the surrender of one's control over one's

product and labor. This affords a contrast with Hegel's two
senses of "alienation." In Marx, the separation is the *result
of* the surrender; whereas in Hegel's discussion of the relation of the individual to the social substance the separation
(alienation$_1$) is *overcome through* the surrender (aliena-
tion$_2$).

Because Marx gives the term many applications, and the
things he terms "alienated" differ so considerably, the exact
way in which the term is to be understood depends very
much upon the context in which it occurs. Its basic sense is
the same; but the point it conveys differs according to the
nature of that to which it is applied.

III. The Alienation of One's Product

The human product which Marx terms "alienated" from
the individual under certain conditions is not the "social substance," as it had been for Hegel. The closest thing to the
social substance from which he ever terms the individual
alienated is "community" (*Gemeinwesen*), which he conceives in terms of "communal life" and "social existence,"
rather than cultural, social, and political institutions. Of
course, he was far from being at one with the society in which
he lived. And he notoriously undertook to bring the individual worker to the point of open hostility to the socioeconomic order which oppresses him. But he does not characterize the discordant relation between individual and society
in terms of "alienation," as Hegel had done.

The human product which Marx *does* speak of in these
terms, in place of the social substance, is the product of the
individual's labor. In working this change upon Hegel, Marx
feels he is taking the first, crucial step in reducing Hegel's
overly abstract account of alienation to its proper concrete
form. In effect, he is adapting Hegel's concept of the alienation of the social substance in terms of the objectification of
personality in the product of the individual's labor.

The "Alien and Hostile Object"

It is important to recognize that, like Hegel, Marx neither considers production to constitute alienation, nor holds production as such to result in the product's alienation. He does not term the product alienated from its producer merely by virtue of the fact that in it "his labor becomes an object, assumes an *external* existence." For if no more profound separation than this exists between them, Marx (like Hegel) regards the product as the objective embodiment of its producer's "self," and thus as far from alien to him. He explicitly states that it is alienated from its producer only when, in addition, "it exists independently, outside himself, i.e., outside of his control, and alien to him, and . . . stands opposed to him as an autonomous power." (*FS*, 561–62/B122–23) Thus Marx clearly distinguishes between externalization or objectification and the alienation of the product.

In terming the product alienated (from the worker) when "the worker is related to the product of his labor as to an alien object," (*FS*, 561/B122) Marx follows Hegel's usage. (Hegel had referred to the social substance as alienated when the individual is related to it as to an "alien reality.") For both, the term becomes applicable when the object in question is related to the individual as something remote and foreign, which he no longer experiences as his own.

More specifically, in the situation Marx has in mind (i.e., under the capitalistic system of production), the product ceases to be the objective embodiment of the individual's own personality and the distinctive expression of his creative powers and interests. On the contrary, it is not at all distinctive, and has no relation to his personality and interests. He does not choose to make it, but rather is directed to do so. He does not even choose *how* to make it; he is compelled to suppress all individuality in the course of its production. And when its production is finished, it is not his to do with as he pleases. In reality, it never is *his* product at all; he is merely the instrument of its production. In a word, it is *alien* to him.

It is not simply alien to him in a passive way, however; it is also said to exert an actively detrimental influence in relation to him. It is "a power independent of the producer,"

which "sets itself against him as an alien and hostile force."
(FS, 561–62/B122–23) But though Marx thus attributes
"hostility" to the alienated product itself, the actual source
of its hostility lies beyond it, in the powers which govern it.
There are two such "hostile powers" for Marx, which render
it "alien and hostile" to its producer. One is the "other man"
for whom it is produced. The other is the set of economic
laws which govern the behavior of capital and thereby the
system of production under capitalism. The first is a human
power; the second, Marx characterizes as an altogether "inhuman power."

The Alienated Product and the Other Man

Marx contends that the product becomes an "alien, hostile, powerful and independent object" in relation to its producer when "another alien, hostile, powerful and independent
man is lord of this object." (FS, 570/B130) This view profoundly affects his later program of political action as well as
the further development of his theoretical position. He holds
that if my product is related to me as an alien and hostile
object, this must be because it belongs to someone alien and
hostile to me. Its alienation from me must be grounded in
my surrender of it to another person. To understand why he
takes this position, it is necessary to refer to the Hegelian
background of his discussion of the subject.

There is a familiar kind of transaction in which one ex-
changes one's products for payment. Hegel deals with this
kind of transaction in the *Philosophy of Right*. He refers to
the consignment of one's products to someone else as their
Veräusserung. In asserting that something can be *veräussert*
only if it is "capable of passing into the possession of someone
else" (PR, §66), Hegel is simply observing that the consignment of something involves its consignment *by* someone *to*
someone else. It is just as with the word "sell": One cannot
sell something without selling it *to* someone.

Where Hegel would speak of the *Veräusserung* of the product, Marx speaks of its *Entäusserung* and *Entfremdung*.[13]
Hegel considers the process objectionable only when one con-

13 See pp. 77–80.

signs *everything* one produces to someone else. (*PR*, §67) Marx, however, finds it objectionable under any circumstances. When he refers to the *Entfremdung*, or "alienation," of the product, he is thinking of its *Veräusserung*; only he is attempting to characterize it in a way that brings out the alienness to the producer of things which are produced to be *veräussert*.

When something is *veräussert*, someone else comes into possession of it. Marx's concept of the alienation of the product is based on the notion of its *Veräusserung*, and retains this feature of it. And it is only in this light that one can see why the alienation of the product for Marx involves the fact that "another . . . man is lord of this object."

He suggests that the product such another man requires of me will serve his interests, at my expense. In return for the means of mere subsistence, I produce the product he desires, at the cost of my own self-realization, and often even at the cost of my physical well-being. Once it is finished, it is his to do with as he pleases, regardless of how that might affect me. It becomes an instrument of his will, and he becomes all the more powerful in relation to me by possessing it. My product thus contributes to my own oppression. In these circumstances, Marx suggests, my product is a force "hostile" to me as well as unrelated to my personality.

The Alienated Product and the "Inhuman Power"

In a market economy, Marx contends, the worker's product is controlled not only by "another man," but also by other, impersonal forces. "Alienation is apparent not only in the fact that *my* means of life belong to *someone else* . . . , but also that . . . an *inhuman power* rules over everything." (*FS*, 619/B177–78) This "inhuman power" is the set of laws governing capital and the market. These laws operate upon the products of the workers' labor, and thus ironically are brought into operation by the workers themselves. Where they prevail, however, the worker's product is governed by them, rather than by his own will.

Under this economic system he produces large quantities of the same item, which he himself cannot use. "The more objects the worker produces, the fewer he can possess." (*FS*,

561/B122) He is both required to do so to secure the necessities of life, and encouraged to do so in order to enrich himself. This renders him "dependent upon all the fluctuations in market price and in the movement of capital." These fluctuations are controlled by economic laws, which are "powers" quite alien to him. They are not subject to his control, and have no regard for his welfare. In fact, according to Marx, the "inevitable result" of their operation for at least "a part of the workers" is "beggary or starvation." (FS, 514/B72-73) Thus to speak of them rather anthropomorphically, their alienness is tinged with "hostility."

As in the case of the "other man," Marx considers the product to take on the characteristics of "alienness" and "hostility" which are attributable to the "inhuman power" that controls it. The product here is "alien" to its producer in that it reflects the profile of the market rather than of his own personality. And it is "hostile" to him in that it strengthens the "inhuman power" which operates to his detriment, and satisfies the demands of the market only at the cost of the sacrifice of his physical well-being and personal self-realization.

In short, Marx terms the product "alienated" from its producer when it comes under the sway of an "alien, hostile power," human or inhuman. He speaks of "the alienation, the *loss* of the object, his product," when it is submitted to the control of these powers, and thereby becomes alien and hostile to its producer. (FS, 562/B123) Here Hegel's two senses of "alienation" have come together. The alienated product is *separated* from its producer (alienation₁); but it is separated from him precisely because he has *surrendered* it (alienation₂) to another man, and more generally, to the market. Its "alienation" consists in its "separation through surrender."

IV. The Alienation of Labor

Marx applies the term not only to the product of labor, but also to labor itself. The prominence of this application is reflected in the fact that the major part of his discussion of alienation in the first "Manuscript" now bears the heading: "Alienated Labor" (*"Die entfremdete Arbeit"*). For Marx, the alienation of labor is related to that of the product not merely as a parallel form, but rather as its basis. "The alienation of the object of labor merely summarizes the alienation, the surrender, in the work activity itself." (*FS*, 564/B124)

Alienated Labor and the Other Man

Marx terms labor "alienated" when it ceases to reflect one's own personality and interests, and instead comes under the direction of an "alien will," i.e., another man. As in the case of the product, he holds that it is the surrender of one's labor power to another man which severs the connection between one's labor and one's personality and interests. "As he alienates his own activity, so man bestows upon an alien person [*dem Fremden*] an activity which is not the latter's own." (*FS*, 571/B131) The alienation of labor and its "surrender" (*Entäusserung*) are so intimately related for Marx that he often employs the two formulations interchangeably.[14]

This is understandable, since he conceives the alienation of labor to involve its surrender, and its surrender to involve its separation from the worker's personality. Labor is alienated, according to Marx, when one is related to "his own activity as something alien and not belonging to him." (*FS*, 565/B126) He then considers it not only legitimate but crucial to ask: "If my own activity does not belong to me but is an alien, forced activity, to whom does it belong?" It is his view that if it "does not belong to me," it must "belong" to someone else. He thus answers his own question:

If the worker is related to his own activity as to unfree activity, then he is related to it as activity in the service, and under the domination, coercion and yoke, of another man. (*FS*, 569/B130)

To see why he takes this position, one must refer again to the *Philosophy of Right*. In it, Hegel discusses the various types of "contract" into which men may enter. Among them is the "contract for wages." In this commonplace type of contract, Hegel observes, "I can give someone else the use of my abilities" in return for whatever compensation the other is willing to give me. (*PR*, §67) He may then direct my activity

14 But see footnote 7, p. 80.

as he sees fit. My labor thus reflects his interests, rather than my own.

Hegel refers to the "giving" of "the use of my abilities" as the "*Veräusserung* of my productive capacity or my services." This *Veräusserung* clearly is inconceivable in the absence of another man who assumes the direction of "my productive capacity." As in the case of the product, Marx's concept of the alienation of labor derives from that of its *Veräusserung*, and incorporates a number of the fundamental features of the latter. Among them is that of the essential involvement of the "other man."

The sense of "alienation" in this context is thus similar to Hegel's second sense of the term, in that the alienation of labor involves its surrender. Even in this context, however, Marx's application of the term differs from Hegel's in several important respects. In Marx's discussion, another man is the recipient of that which is alienated or surrendered; whereas in Hegel's, that which is alienated$_2$ (viz., willfulness and particularity) is simply given up. Moreover, in Marx's discussion it is something essential, rather than something inessential, that is alienated. And as a consequence, he regards the process very negatively, rather than with approval. Furthermore, his fundamental concern here is with the *separation* of labor from the worker and from its true nature under the conditions he describes. This is presumably why he prefers to speak of the *Entfremdung* of labor, rather than of its *Veräusserung*, as Hegel had done. His use of the term in this connection thus is related to Hegel's first sense at least as closely as it is to his second. As in the case of the product, the alienation of labor consists of its "separation through surrender."

Alienated Labor and the Worker

One whose labor is alienated from him views his labor as an "alien activity." By this Marx means that the individual does not "feel at home" in the work he does. He is said to "avoid it like the plague" whenever circumstances allow. "It is not part of his nature"; that is, it has no connection with his own interests, and is no expression of his personality. In fact, it is detrimental to him:

   . . . he does not fulfill himself in his work but denies himself, has a feeling of misery rather than well-being, does not develop freely his spiritual and physical powers but is physically exhausted and spiritually debased. (FS, 564–65/B125)

A man's labor is truly "his own labor," for Marx, only when it is "spontaneous," "free and self-directed activity." (FS, 564/B125, 567/B127) It is his own only if it reflects his own interests, manifests his own personality, and is prompted by his own need to build or create or do something of his own choosing. It must, in short, be precisely what he wants to do.[15]

If he works for another man, his labor is not of this sort. In the "contract for wages," he agrees to do the work stipulated by his employer. In this situation, "The activity of the worker is not his own spontaneous activity. It is another's activity and the loss of his own." His labor here is "imposed, forced labor." It is no longer "free and self-directed," but rather is an "external," "alien" activity. (FS, 564–65/B125) It is this relation of the worker to his labor that Marx characterizes in terms of "alienation." It is a relation of "separation through surrender."

It should be clear that for Marx, this alienation is a relation involving not merely two terms—the worker and his labor—but also a third: another man to whom the worker surrenders direction of his labor. His occasional reference to "alienated labor" as "slave labor" (e.g., FS, 513/B71) corroborates this point; for slavery is a relation in which another man is involved in addition to the slave and his labor. Marx's basic concern is with the disassociation of labor from the worker's interests and personality; but because his thinking is dominated by the model of the Veräusserung of labor, he tends to regard the submission of labor to the direction of another man as the necessary and sufficient condition of its alienation from the worker.

[15] Cf. the famous passage in The German Ideology in which Marx suggests that in "communist society" it will be "possible for me to do one thing today and another tomorrow, to hunt in the morning, fish in the afternoon, rear cattle in the evening, criticize after dinner, *just as I please.* . . ." (12, 22; emphasis added.)

This is unfortunate, given his basic concern. His characterization of labor as alienated from the worker when disassociated from the worker's interests is appropriate and helpful. But the submission of labor to the direction of another man need not entail this disassociation, nor is it invariably presupposed by it. Consider, for example, a camera man in a film studio, or a member of an orchestra. The "labor" of both is not and cannot be "self-directed" and "spontaneous." In each case it is directed by another man—the director or the conductor. Yet this "other-direction" by no means precludes self-fulfillment; on the contrary, it may be that each would find no other activity as personally rewarding. Labor performed under the direction of another man thus need not be "alien activity." To conceive "alienated labor" in these terms, therefore, is to render the concept too inclusive.

Conceived in these terms, it is also not inclusive enough. It is not difficult to think of cases in which one's labor is disassociated from one's interests and personality, even though it is *not* subjected to the direction of another man. One need think only of an independent farmer or shop owner who is able to sustain himself only through a total expenditure of his time and energy, and therefore is never able to do the things he really wants to do. He is oppressed by physical need, and thus on Marx's own criterion does not "truly produce." (*FS*, 568/B128) Yet he has not contracted to work for another man. The connection between one's labor and one's interests and personality thus can be severed without the mediation of an "alien will." If "alienated labor" is conceived in terms of such mediation, the scope of the concept is artificially restricted.

In short, the alienation of labor from the interests and personality of the individual is an interesting and important phenomenon. In conceiving of this alienation in terms of a separation *through surrender to another*, however, Marx obscures its basic character, and encounters problems of both over- and under-inclusiveness. It would seem more fruitful to drop all reference to the mediation of an "alien will" in the explication of the concept of such alienation itself, and to focus solely upon the relation of labor to the individual. It might of course turn out to be the case that this alienation very frequently *does* involve the surrender of labor to the direction of another man; but this would be a factual correlation rather than a matter of definition.

Alienated Labor and Labor's Nature

For Marx, when labor is subjected to the direction of another man, its resulting separation from the interests and personality of the one who performs it also involves its divorce from its essential end and function. This is a second dimension of Marx's concept of the alienation of labor, and a second level at which his expression "alienated labor" is to be understood. At this level his usage is similar to Hegel's, when Hegel employs the expression "self-alienated independence" to convey the idea of independence which is not *true* independence (because it involves dependence upon another man). (PG, 366/B534)

Essentially considered, labor for Marx is productive activity through which the individual objectifies and thus realizes himself, simultaneously expressing and developing himself as an individual personality. It is what it should be only when it has no end other than this. It is therefore a perversion of its essential function, according to Marx, when it is undertaken merely "under the compulsion of direct physical needs" or of that "selfish need" which he terms "greed." Under these circumstances it is *not* what it should be; man "only truly produces in freedom from such need." (FS, 568/B128)

This is suggested to be the condition of labor "in the wage system." When it is regarded as something to be exchanged for pay, "labor appears not as an end in itself but as the servant of wages," and thus loses its "human significance and worth." (FS, 572–73/B132) Here it "is not the satisfaction of a need, but only a *means* for satisfying other needs." (FS, 564/B125) It is unimportant whether these "other needs" are "physical needs" or "selfish needs"; in both cases labor is pressed into the service of needs other than that of self-realization. In return for wages, it is placed under the direction of another man, and thus no longer performs the function of self-objectification.

There is thus a radical disparity between the character and function of labor in the kind of economy Marx describes, and those in terms of which he conceives the essential nature of labor. He characterizes labor of the former sort as "the alienated form of human activity as species-activity." (FS, 623/B181) When he speaks of alienated labor, he has in mind this general disparity between such labor and its essential nature, as well as its separation from the interests and personality of the worker as such. It is not only alien to the worker, but also "alien to itself." (FS, 578/B139)

The sentence-type "X is alienated" is elliptical, implying a "from" clause; and as a rule the object of this clause is distinct from X. Nothing about the expression "alienated labor" indicates, however, that the object of the implicit "from" clause does not refer to something distinct from labor, but rather refers to the nature of labor itself. Of course, it might simply be stipulated that "alienated labor" is to be understood in this sense. But since the expression is not particularly transparent to the intended meaning, little advantage derives from using the term "alienated" rather than some other term, to make the point in question. And other, quite ordinary terms *are* available—and are even used by Marx—which more readily convey the idea of labor that is not as it should be, with regard to both its character (e.g., "unfree") and its function (e.g., "perverted"). This is one Marxian use of the term which is not particularly helpful.

V. Alienation from Other Men

According to Marx, it is "in the relationship between each man and other men" that the "economic fact" of the "alienation of the worker and his production" is "first realized and expressed." In particular, it has the "direct consequence" that "man is alienated from other men." (FS, 569/B129) This passage indicates that "alienation from other men" is an important type of alienation for Marx. However, he employs the term in this connection rather infrequently. To grasp his meaning, therefore, one must rely largely upon passages in which he does not use it, but discusses the same sort of relation of men to each other.

Alienation from Others and Egoism

Marx follows his suggestion that the alienation of men from each other is a consequence of the alienation of production with the statement: "In the relationship of alienated labor every man regards other men according to the standards and relationships in which he finds himself placed as a worker." (*FS*, 569/B129) He further contends that communism, through which "human self-alienation" is overcome, is thereby also "the definitive resolution of the antagonism . . . between man and man." (*FS*, 594/B155) In the first passage Marx seems to have in mind a situation in which men regard others as rivals rather than fellows, and as of no inherent worth. The second suggests a state of constant and general interpersonal strife prior to the advent of communism.

These are among the features which for Marx characterize the relation of men to each other in capitalistic or "civil" society. He speaks of the "member of civil society—that is . . . , man separated from other men." (*FS*, 472/B24) And he refers to civil society as "the sphere of . . . the *bellum omnium contra omnes*"—of the war of all against all. (*FS*, 463/B15) In it, he contends, one "only exists for another person, as the other exists for him, insofar as each becomes a means for the other." (*FS*, 623/B181) Since in these passages he has in mind the same sort of relation between men as he does when he speaks of "alienation from other men," his characterization of their relation to each other in civil society may be taken as a guide to his meaning in employing this expression.

"Civil society," according to Marx, is "the sphere of egoism." (*FS*, 463/B15) It is "a world of atomistic, antagonistic individuals." (*FS*, 486/B39) Man in civil society is "egoistic man," "man regarded as an isolated monad, withdrawn into himself." (*FS*, 472/B24) Marx describes "egoistic man" as:

. . . an individual separated from community, withdrawn into himself, wholly preoccupied with his private interest and acting in accordance with his private caprice. . . . The only bond between egoistic men is natural necessity, need and private interest, the preservation of their property and their egoistic persons. (*FS*, 474/B26)

Egoistic man is motivated solely by self-interest; and "self-interest . . . leads every man to see in other men not the *realization*, but rather the *limitation* of his own liberty." (*FS*, 473/B25) Instead of regarding other men as his fellows, therefore, he regards them as his rivals and adversaries. Accordingly, he is hostile to them. His antagonism toward them is mitigated only to the extent that enlightened self-interest suggests cooperation with them to be desirable, and shows him that they may be of use to him.

Thus the alienation from other men of which Marx speaks is to be understood as involving a complete absence of fellow feeling, an estimation of others as of no more positive significance than that of means to personal ends, and an antagonism based on a feeling of rivalry and the anticipation of attempted counterexploitation. It is grounded in a self-centeredness which attends only to private advantage, and in a self-conception which excludes any idea of sociality.

In the latter respect Marx's "egoistic" man who is alienated from other men is similar to Hegel's "particularistic" individual whose relation to the social substance is one of alienation₁. For in both cases the alienation in question is the consequence of a restriction of self-identification to the particular self. Of course, in Marx's case it is other men who consequently are regarded as alien; whereas, for Hegel it is the social substance. This difference reflects the difference in the elements of man's essential nature which they consider this overly narrow self-conception to neglect—namely, "sociality" for Marx, and "universality" for Hegel.

Marx and Standard Usage

There is an obvious precedent for Marx's use of the term "alienation" in this connection, in the standard use of the term to refer to interpersonal estrangement. But his conception of such alienation differs from the ordinary one in a number of respects. Perhaps most importantly, "egoism" would appear to be the necessary and sufficient condition of its occurrence for Marx. Secondly, when Marx's alienation occurs, it is total; one is "separated from other men" *generally*. In the case of the ordinary conception, on the other hand, it is possible, and even usual, for one to be estranged only from certain individuals, while remaining close to others.

Further, in ordinary usage such alienation in no way implies that one regards the others in question merely as means to one's own ends. On the contrary, it is quite compatible with a high estimation of their intrinsic worth. The ordinary conception also comprehends cases of mere indifference and regretted lost intimacy, as well as cases of antagonism. And even when antagonism is present, it need not have arisen out of the feeling that the other person poses a threat to one, or stands in the way of the exercise of one's freedom.

A final difference between Marx's conception of alienation from other men and the ordinary one concerns the background presupposed by the use of the term. In an ordinary case of interpersonal estrangement, the background situation is one of previous actual unity of some sort, which has given way to a feeling of alienness; someone has "become alien," who formerly was not so. Marx, on the other hand, presupposes no previous actual unity of the "egoistic" individual with other men. The absent unity with them in this case is rather the *ideal* unity of the individual with other men generally, which Marx predicates of him on the ground that man's essential nature requires it. (Nothing of this sort is presupposed by the ordinary conception.)

The differences between Marx's concept and the ordinary one do raise problems. A number of his remarks in this connection cannot even be taken seriously if they are viewed as applying to interpersonal estrangement generally. For example, communism may accomplish the "definitive resolution" of the "antagonism between man and man," and thus of the alienation of men from each other as Marx conceives it, through the elimination of the bases of egoism. (*FS*, 594/B155) But no one could suppose that it would thereby also bridge the generation gap, restore to intimacy erstwhile friends who have drifted apart, or rekindle love grown cold.

Precisely because the term "alienation" has an established use in connection with interpersonal relations, a different use of the term in this connection—such as Marx's—leads to confusion. One cannot help thinking of the ordinary associations of the term when one encounters it in Marx; and because the two uses of the term are related, it is difficult to retain a proper perspective upon his claims. Moreover, if a person uses the term in this connection both as Marx does and as it is ordinarily used, he exposes himself not only to the danger of misleading others, but also to that of reasoning erroneously by slipping from one concept to the other.

The standard use of the term in this connection does render Marx's reasonable, at least in principle. His use of it is bound to give rise to difficulties, however, unless some way can be found of clearly distinguishing the alienation of which he speaks from ordinary interpersonal estrangement generally. (This could be done, for example, by systematically referring to such alienation as "egoistic.")

Relation to Other Forms of Alienation

Marx terms "alienation from other men" a "direct consequence" of the alienation which occurs at the level of "production." Taken at face value, this seems to suggest—rather implausibly—that when one contracts to work for someone else, one thereby cuts himself off from other men. Marx's actual point, however, is a rather different one, for which (given certain assumptions) more can be said.

One must first recall the relation he conceives to exist between "egoism" and "civil society." He holds civil society to be structured in such a way that in it egoism is both encouraged and virtually required for survival. It is "the sphere of egoism," in which man becomes "egoistic man." "Civil society . . . severs all the species-bonds of man, establishes egoism and selfish need in their place, and dissolves the human world into a world of atomistic, antagonistic individuals." (FS, 486/B38–39) While it is true for Marx that "alienation from other men" is a consequence of egoism, therefore, he suggests that egoism itself—and with it this alienation—is the consequence of living in civil society.

To live in civil society is to live under what Marx terms the economic "system of alienation." This economic system is the essence of civil society as he conceives it. The whole society is purportedly organized to facilitate the accumulation

of private property through exploitation. To this end the
"contract for wages" has been developed, into which men are
both encouraged and compelled to enter. Marx characterizes
the system as he does in virtue of the alienation of labor and
the product which results.

He is able both to trace the alienation of men from each
other to existence in civil society, and to say that it is the
consequence of the "alienation of the worker and his production," because in speaking of the latter he is referring to the
economic "system of alienation" which he considers to be the
basic structure of civil society. His position is not that the
act of contracting to work for another man *itself* alienates
the individual from his fellow men. Rather, the point is that
the alienation of the individual from others is related to the
alienation of his labor and product as one result to another
of his existence under the general economic organization
which is the basis of civil society. It is the latter of which
this alienation is the "direct consequence."

The Generality of Alienation from Others

The connection Marx suggests between thoroughgoing
egoism and alienation from other men is plausible. Moreover,
it is a reasonable supposition that in a society that both
places a high premium on egoism and makes the contracting
of labor for wages a necessity, many of those who must thus
alienate their labor will also be egoistic, and consequently
alienated from others. He overstates his case, however, when
he asserts that under these conditions *all* are infected with
egoism, to the point that "*each man* is alienated from others."
(*FS*, 569/B129; emphasis added.)

Marx seems to think that everyone who exists in civil
society necessarily becomes a creature of it—i.e., becomes
egoistic. As Hegel observes, however, it is quite possible for
an individual to cease to identify with the values of his
society, and to adopt an attitude of opposition to them. Marx
himself is a perfect case in point. Moreover, his own belief
in the possibility of solidarity among the members of the
working class within the framework of capitalistic society presupposes the ability of men who continue to live in this
society to overcome their egoism and alienation from each

other. His call to the "workers of the world" to "unite" and overthrow capitalism (at the conclusion of the *Manifesto*) would be pointless if men could only remain egoistic and therefore mutually antagonistic creatures of "civil society" as long as they live in it.

His own beliefs about what is possible, therefore, as well as the apparent truth of the matter, suggest the necessity of a modification of his position concerning the generality of alienation from others in civil society. This alienation should not be considered a "direct consequence" of existence under the "system of alienation." The strongest plausible claim would be that it is a common result of such existence. If Marx's position is modified in this way, a case can be made for it. For existence under the conditions he describes would certainly seem to be *conducive* to exclusive devotion to one's private interests, and thus to alienation from others.

VI. Self-alienation

Like Marx's concept of the alienation of labor, his concept of "self-alienation" involves the idea of a twofold separation. In this case, he has in mind both the separation *from* a person of something which is very much a part of him, and the resulting separation *of* the person from his essential nature. There are thus two senses of "self-alienation" in Marxian usage. In both cases the term "alienation" has the same basic sense of "separation through surrender." In the former, however, the term "self" refers to something which is a part of the person; whereas in the latter, it refers to his essential nature.

Self-alienation: First Sense

In one sense the expression "self-alienation" is used by Marx to characterize more profoundly the alienation of labor, and occasionally, that of the product. The point he wishes to stress in doing so is that a man's labor is his life, and his product is his life in objectified form; and that therefore when they are alienated from him, his own "self" is alienated from him. In "the relationship of the worker to his own activity as something alien and not belonging to him," Marx argues, it is "his personal physical and spiritual energy, his personal life" that is alien to him—"for what is life but activity?" (FS, 565/B126) When his "personal physical and spiritual energy," as manifested in his productive activity or labor, is subjected to the direction of another, his very life is no longer his own. He is, therefore, "self-alienated."

Hegel had considered "giving someone else the use of my abilities" unobjectionable, as long as it is only "for a restricted period." He had not felt that the Veräusserung of my labor, if limited in this way, results in "making into another's property the substance of my being," because "on the strength of this restriction, my abilities acquire an external relation to the totality and universality of my being." (PR, §67) Marx disagrees, and takes the position that the substance of my being, or my "self," is made into another's property to the extent that I give another the use of my labor. A restriction in time merely renders my "self-alienation" less than total; and it does not even do this if I must expend all of my "physical and spiritual energy" in the time during which I work for another. Marx reasons along similar lines with regard to the product of labor.

His position is reasonable, given the sense of "self" in operation here. For if my "self" is conceived in terms of my "physical and spiritual energy," it follows that the more of my labor-potential I surrender to another, the more of the "substance of my being" I surrender to him, and thus render alien to me. Hegel takes a different position—which is also reasonable—because the conception of the self with which he is working here is somewhat different. It is to be conceived in terms of independence; and my independence is intact so long as another does not control all that I do.

Self-alienation: Second Sense

Marx also uses the expression "self-alienation" to refer to one's separation from his truly "human" self, or essential nature. In this sense, it conveys the idea of "a total loss of humanity." (FS, 503/B58) Here, too, the "separation" in question is a "separation through surrender"; for Marx conceives of it as intimately related to the alienation of labor. "Alienated labor," he states, "alienates from men . . . his spiritual life, his human life." (FS, 568–69/B129) It "produces man as a spiritually and physically *dehumanized* being." (*FS*, 577/B138) At this level, "self-alienation" is virtually synonymous with "dehumanization" (*Entmenschung*).

A man is self-alienated for Marx if his true "human" nature is something alien to him—if his life fails to manifest the characteristics of a truly human life. There are three such characteristics for Marx: individuality, sociality, and cultivated sensibility. Self-alienation thus takes the form of dehumanization in the spheres of life which correspond to them: production, social life, and sensuous life. It may best be understood in terms of dehumanization in each of these areas.

Marx considers the worker in contemporary "civil society" to be dehumanized *qua* producer in a number of respects. He is dehumanized in the sense of being reduced to the level of an animal, because he produces merely "under the compulsion of direct physical needs." When he does not "produce in freedom from such need," his production falls to the level of mere animal production, and he thereby loses his "advantage over animals." (*FS*, 567–68/B128) He is also dehumanized in the sense of being reduced to the subhuman condition of a slave, by virtue of his surrender of his labor power to another man; for Marx views labor directed by another man as "slave labor." (*FS*, 513/B71) Finally, "as a result of the division of labor," the worker is dehumanized in the sense of being "reduced . . . to the condition of a machine." (*FS*, 514/B72) The activity required of him is merely "simple mechanical motion." (*FS*, 630/B187–88)

In short, Marx variously describes the worker under the "system of alienation" as reduced to the level of an animal, a slave, and a machine. Common to all of these descriptions is the idea of sinking to a subhuman level, or dehumanization. The alienation of labor is thus associated with the dehumanization of the worker, who is truly human only if his labor is truly human (i.e., manifests and develops his personality). This is one dimension of his self-alienation, one respect in which his actual condition fails to correspond with his essential nature.

A man who is preoccupied with the satisfaction of physical (or selfish) needs, who expends all his physical and spiritual energy in the service of another man, and who is little more than an appendage of a machine, will also be dehumanized (or at any rate, "unhumanized") in another respect. Marx holds that a man is not truly human until his senses and feelings have been "cultivated" or "humanized." One who fits the above description, however, will have had no occasion to develop "the wealth of subjective *human* sensibility (a musical ear, an eye which is sensitive to the beauty of form, [etc.])," and an appreciation of things in virtue of their intrinsic qualities. (*FS*, 601/B161) His sensibility will be subhuman; and therefore he himself will be less than human as well.

A third respect in which a man's actual condition can fail to correspond with his essential nature, for Marx, concerns his relations with other men. Marx holds that life is not truly human unless it is "social" life, life in genuine "community" with other men. If one is alienated from other men, therefore, one's existence is "inhuman" existence. It fails to manifest one's essential sociality; thus one is self-alienated. As has been suggested, Marx traces alienation from others to existence under the conditions which prevail in civil society. In his view, therefore, all three forms of dehumanization, or "self-alienation," have the same origin, and thus tend to occur together.

Marx's concept of self-alienation can also be explicated in terms of the perversion of productive, social, and sensuous life. It has been seen that he uses the expression "alienated labor" in part to convey the idea of labor the actual character and function of which do not correspond to its essential ones. He also speaks of "the alienation of the senses" in characterizing the sensibility which views things as mere "means of life" to be "utilized in some way." (*FS*, 599/B159–60) In like manner, he terms the "exploitation of human communal life" its "alienation." (*FS*, 610/B169) In these contexts the term "alienation" serves to indicate that the forms of life in question are *not as they should be*. In the sense being considered, the expression "self-alienation" functions similarly, and is applicable under precisely these circumstances. For Marx, man's nature is realized only when these forms of life *are* as they should be. In his view, therefore, their perversion entails that the person affected is not as *he* should be. Their alienation is his self-alienation.

Self-alienation in Marx and Hegel

The two senses of self-alienation in the "Manuscripts" are similar to Hegel's two senses of self-alienation$_1$ in the *Phenomenology*.[16] In each, the expression is used to refer both to the separation from the individual of something which is importantly "his," and to a disparity between his actual condition and his essential nature. It does not follow, however, that the corresponding *conceptions* of self-alienation are to be identified. For to speak of the *conceptions* of self-alienation in question is to make reference not only to the *senses* in which Marx and Hegel use the expression, but also to the *applications* they give it.

It is important to distinguish these categories. In one *sense* of self-alienation, for Marx and for Hegel, the expression refers to a disparity between actual condition and essential nature. This characterization is formal and abstract, in that it does not specify what the essential nature or "self" mentioned involves. When the expression is associated with a specific conception of man's essential nature, it is given an *application*; and it is only then that a *conception* of self-alienation emerges. Two people may use the expression in the same sense; but if they conceive man's essential nature differently, their applications of the expression will be different, and their conceptions of self-alienation will differ accordingly.

Marx and Hegel give the expression different applications in each of its two senses. In the sense in which it refers to the separation from the individual of something importantly "his," Marx is concerned with the individual's labor and particular product; Hegel, with the social substance. And in the sense in which the expression refers to a disparity between the individual's actual condition and his essential nature, the unrealized essential nature is conceived by Marx in terms of individuality, sociality, and cultivated sensibility; by Hegel, in terms of individuality and universality. Thus, while they

[16] See pp. 49–54.

employ the expression in the same senses, their conceptions of self-alienation differ.

Marx's use of the expression in the first sense is of considerably greater interest than Hegel's, because of the difference in his application of it. One may question whether the social substance generally may legitimately be considered the individual's objectification, and a part of his "self"; but his own product may quite reasonably be so conceived. The same is true of his productive capacity. Given the notion of the alienation of labor and the product, therefore, the expression "self-alienation" is useful; for it enables one to indicate the deeper significance of this alienation explicitly and economically.

As with Hegel, one's estimate of Marx's use of the expression in the second sense will depend upon one's estimate of his conception of man's essential nature, and of his suggestion that a disparity can exist between it and a person's actual condition. If the latter is considered plausible, it will be useful to be able to refer to the existence of such a disparity conveniently; and the expression "self-alienation" will serve the purpose quite well.

With regard to Marx's conception of man's nature, there is much to be said for his insistence upon the inclusion of reference to man's senses and his interpersonal relationships. But his modification of Hegel's conception of man's nature would not seem to constitute an unqualified advance. Marx is keenly aware of the power of social institutions to shape men; but he shares the Romantics' tendency to view the influence of these institutions as detrimental to human development. In his eyes, they serve primarily to further the interests of the dominant class. He has little to say about them, therefore, in his characterizations of "truly human life" in the ideal, classless society.

Here Hegel may have had the deeper insight, in his insistence upon the importance of the "social substance" in human life. For him the idea of participation in sociocultural institutions is inseparable from the idea of life that is truly human. Marx's depreciation of their importance may have been due to the fact that his obsession with the exploitative character of existing political and economic institutions blinded him to the broader functions of sociocultural institutions generally. While it may be understandable, however, it would not appear to be justifiable. In this respect at least, Hegel's concept of man's nature seems superior to Marx's—and with it, his associated concept of "self-alienation."

VII. The Origin and Overcoming of Alienation

Alienation and "Egoistic Need"

It was observed, in connection with Marx's concept of alienation from other men, that he traces this alienation to egoism. Similarly, he traces the existence of the other forms of alienation to the predominance of "egoistic need." This expression immediately suggests the idea of greed or acquisitiveness. For Marx, however, this is only one type of such need. Another, on which he places equal emphasis in the "Manuscripts," is "physical need," or the kind of need associated with mere survival. He attributes the existence of alienation in its various forms not merely to the former, but also to the latter.

This is clear, for example, in the case of alienation of the senses. Marx conceives of this "alienation" in terms of an orientation toward things as nothing more than material to be "utilized in some way." To illustrate it, he cites "the dealer in minerals," who sees in the minerals with which he deals "only their commercial value, not their beauty or their particular characteristics." The sensibility of such a man may reasonably be characterized as dominated by acquisitiveness or greed. But Marx also cites as examples "the needy man, burdened with cares," who "has no appreciation for the most beautiful spectacle," and the "starving man," for whom "the human form of food does not exist." These are termed examples of "sense which is subservient to crude need." Clearly, the "need" in question here is simple "physical need," rather than greed. (FS, 601/B161–62)

Marx also refers to both factors in his discussion of the alienation of labor and of the product. In explaining why men surrender control of their labor to others, Marx observes that workers may be motivated by "the same desire for enrichment as is the capitalist." (*FS*, 514–15/B73) "The more they want to earn, the more they must sacrifice their time and perform slave labor in which their freedom is totally surrendered in the service of greed." (*FS*, 513/B71) He thus considers greed to be a definite source of this alienation.

Greed is not, however, its only source, according to Marx. Numerous passages are to be found in the "Manuscripts" in which physical need is also assigned a position of great importance: for example, "labor, *life-activity*, *productive life* now appear to man only as a *means* for the satisfaction of a need, the need to maintain his physical existence." (*FS*, 567/B127) Again, Marx contrasts labor as "free and self-directed activity" with labor as a mere "means of physical existence." This contrast is also the background of his statement that man "only truly produces in freedom from [physical] need." (*FS*, 568/B128) In short, he considers physical need as well as greed to be a source of the "alienation" of labor. This "alienation" results, in his view, when *either* form of "egoistic need" predominates.

Alienation and Civil Society

At this point one might be tempted to conclude that this is the final result of Marx's analysis, with regard to the origin of this and the other forms of alienation. To stop here, however, would be to miss one of the most important points of his discussion. He does regard "egoistic need" in its two basic forms as the source of the various forms of alienation—but only as their *immediate* source. He locates the source of egoistic need itself—and thus the *fundamental* source of alienation—in the nature of civil society, and in particular, in the institution of private property around which it is organized.

This has profound implications for the issue of whether and how such need can be eradicated, and the resulting alienation overcome. It is commonly held that human nature and human or natural inadequacy are responsible for the greediness and the neediness of men. In this view, the latter either are ineradicable or can be mitigated only by changes effected at the level of the individual person and in the technological sphere. Marx, on the other hand, takes the position that both the "despotism of physical need" and the greed which prevail in civil society are the results of the nature of civil society itself. He concludes, therefore, that their eradication can *only* be accomplished by changing the socioeconomic system of civil society.

He quite explicitly takes the same position, and draws the same conclusion, with regard to the origin and overcoming of the various forms of alienation. It has already been seen that he locates the source of alienation from other men in civil society. He regards the institution of private property as the heart of civil society. Therefore, with regard to the alienation of the senses, he writes: "Private property has made us so stupid and partial that an object is only [felt to be] *ours* when we have it, when it exists for us as capital or when it is . . . *utilized* in some way." (*FS*, 599/B159) And he contends that the dominance of the institution of private property "is the basis and cause of alienated labor," and thus also of the alienation of the product. (*FS*, 572/B131)[17]

He is equally explicit concerning the overcoming of these forms of alienation through the transformation of civil society generally, and of the institution of private property in particular. "The *positive Aufhebung* of private property"—its positive supersession—would purportedly be "the *definitive* resolution of the antagonism . . . between man and man." (*FS*, 593/B155) It would also accomplish "the complete emancipation of all the human qualities and senses" from subjection to "mere utility." (*FS*, 599/B160) And it would mean the end of the alienation of labor and of the product. In short, "The positive supersession of *private property* . . . is the positive supersession of all alienation." (*FS*, 595/B156)[18]

In this light, one can understand Marx's intense dissatis-

[17] He also says, "Private property is . . . the product, the necessary result, of alienated labor." (*FS*, 572/B131) But here he is thinking of the accumulation of possessions and capital, rather than of the *institution* of private property.

[18] Because of the connection between the forms of alienation mentioned here and self-alienation conceived in both of the ways distinguished in the preceding section, Marx's conclusions concerning the origin and overcoming of the former apply equally to the latter. Self-alienation exists when these other forms of alienation exist, and is overcome when they are overcome.

faction with Hegel's program for the overcoming of alienation. It can hardly be overcome, in his view, by conforming
to the existing social order; for he holds that entrapment in
it is precisely the root of the problem. For both Hegel and
Marx, the problem is to resolve "the conflict between existence and essence." For Marx, however, "the true solution of
the conflict" is possible only through a fundamental socioeconomic reorganization—namely, "the positive supersession
of private property." It is in these terms that he conceives
communism. The solution of this conflict thus requires that
civil society give way to communism. Indeed, Marx states that
communism *is* this solution. (*FS*, 593/B155)

Civil Society, Physical Need, and Greed

Marx views the "despotism of physical need" which prevails in civil society as a function of the exploitation and the
inequality of distribution made possible by the economic system associated with it, rather than of scarcity or low produc-
tivity. It is only because Marx traces it to this source that he
can speak of "the categorical imperative to overthrow all those
conditions in which man is an abased, enslaved, abandoned,
contemptible being." (*FS*, 497/B52) For the suggestion that
a different organization of socioeconomic institutions would
alleviate the plight of the worker presupposes that his plight
is the result of the operation of those which presently exist.

It must be granted, however, that desperate physical need
can result from other causes, such as natural disasters and
human devastation. Moreover, Marx observes that it is only
when industry is very highly developed that "the emancipation of humanity" from the necessity of working simply in
order to live becomes a possibility. (*FS*, 603/B163) Prior to
this stage of development, labor is a mere "means of physical
existence," regardless of the character of the prevailing socioeconomic institutions. It is only under certain circumstances,
therefore, that the "despotism of physical need" can legitimately be attributed to the operation of socioeconomic
institutions, and that its elimination can reasonably be expected through their transformation.

Acquisitiveness, or greed, which Marx claims drives men in
civil society as soon as physical need becomes less pressing,

is also purported to be engendered by the institutions of this society. If he did not hold this view, he could not take the position that egoism can be eliminated by changing these institutions. And that he does take this position is clear: "An organization of society which would abolish the preconditions and thus the very possibility of huckstering, would make the [egoist] impossible." (*FS*, 482/B34)

While this view is attractive, there is a serious weakness in Marx's case for it: He provides no satisfactory explanation of how civil society could come to have the character he attributes to it, if not because men are inherently egoistic. For one who believes that men *are* inherently egoistic, its character is easily explained: It simply reflects man's innate disposition. Marx rejects this explanation, but has no adequate one of his own.

In his only attempt to provide one, he suggests that Christianity is to blame. He contends that it taught men to be spiritually self-centered, and thereby gave rise to a "spiritual egoism" which "in practice becomes a material egoism." The character of civil society thus is suggested to reflect not an innate disposition of man, but one acquired under the influence of Christianity. This, however, leaves the spiritual self-centeredness of Christianity to be accounted for. Marx attempts to do so by tracing it to the "practical need and egoism" of Judaism, which in Christianity is "raised into the ethereal realm." (*FS*, 486–87/B38–39) But this does not solve the problem either, because now the egoistic character he attributes to Judaism must be accounted for. His detour through Christianity and Judaism only postpones the need for an explanation of the emergence of egoism.

Marx proposes this explanation in his early essay "On the Jewish Question." Perhaps because he realized it accomplishes nothing, he does not suggest it in the subsequently written "Manuscripts." In the "Manuscripts" he is either content or compelled to pass over the question of the ultimate origin of the "organization of society" the "basic principle" of which is egoism. The mere fact of physical need does not suffice to account for its character. Marx does say that "the materials necessary for cultural development" and the industrial basis necessary for "the emancipation of humanity" could not have emerged except "through the development of private property." (*FS*, 602–03/B162–63) But while these results of this development are fortunate, they do not explain its occurrence. It may be possible to give such an explanation, but Marx fails to do so; and this renders questionable his entire discussion of the origin and overcoming of alienation.

VIII. Concluding Remarks

Alienation as Separation Through Surrender

Hegel uses the term "alienation" in two distinct senses: in the sense of "separation" and in the sense of "surrender." Marx neither rejects one of these senses, nor introduces a radically new sense of the term, but rather fuses Hegel's two senses, with the result that the term for him has the single sense of "separation through surrender." It is a shortcoming of Hegel's discussion that he uses the term in two distinct senses, in that this is a source of confusion. At first glance, Marx would seem to improve on Hegel, by eliminating this source of confusion.

Actually, however, even more serious confusions result. His retention of the ideas of both separation and surrender allows him to emphasize first the one and then the other, even when speaking of the same kind of alienation, thereby giving rise to ambiguities concerning its necessary and sufficient conditions. In one passage, for example, he characterizes the alienation of labor as "the *relationship* of the worker to his own activity as something alien and not belonging to him." (*FS*, 566/B126; emphasis added.) In another, he refers to it as "the *act* of alienation of practical human activity." (*FS*, 565/B125; emphasis added.) The former suggests that labor is termed "alienated" primarily by virtue of its separation from the worker's interests and personality; while the latter suggests that its surrender by the worker is the definitive factor. Hegel at least avoids ambiguities of this sort.

Further confusion results from the fact that even where the term clearly has the sense of "separation through surrender," the relation of the separation to the surrender must be understood differently where different types of alienation are concerned. In some cases this relation is direct; labor and the product are both separated from the worker *by being* surrendered by him. The schema "X is separated from Y by being surrendered by Y" does not suffice, however, to explicate the notions of the self-alienation of the worker *qua* producer, and of the alienation of labor from its essential nature. The separations involved here *result from* the worker's surrender of his labor; but their relation to this surrender is more complex and less immediate.

In short, Marx's incorporation of the ideas of both separation and surrender into the concept of alienation has undesirable results—above all, because he applies the term to separations which are related differently to the surrender in question. Barring a return to Hegel's use of the term in two different senses, two alternatives remain. One would be to restrict the use of the term to those cases in which separation and surrender are similarly related. The other would be to restrict its sense, for example, to that of "separation," and to retain its breadth of application, indicating the relation of the various separations to the surrender in question by other means. Each alternative has its merits and its drawbacks. The usefulness of the term, however, depends upon a choice being made between them.

Marx's Applications of the Term "Alienation"

In his early writings Marx employs the term "alienation" in connection with a wide variety of things, including labor, the product, the senses, communal life and other men, and man himself. He considers the various kinds of alienation involved to be interrelated, sometimes conceptually and sometimes factually. They constitute what might be termed his "alienation syndrome."

Because this syndrome comprehends very different relations, however, the use of the term "alienation" to designate all of them severely limits its descriptive content. My relation to my product is one thing; my relation to other men is another; and the degree of correspondence of my actual condition to my essential nature is yet another. Since the term "alienation" is employed in connection with all three (and others besides), and since they share little more than a common origin and the idea of separation, it cannot convey anything very specific. Remarks in which the term appears alone are informative only when they apply to the syndrome as a whole; and because of the diversity of the members of the syndrome, the occasions on which this stricture can be satisfied are few—Marx's all-too-frequent use of the term without modification notwithstanding. It may not have been his intent, but in his hands the term becomes little more than a general term whose utility lies primarily in the initial specification of a certain syndrome of separations, rather than in their closer analysis.

Marx's assertion that "alienation is apparent . . . in the fact that everything is something different from itself," (*FS*, 619/B177–78) is implicitly restricted to a range of interrelated phenomena. Yet it and others like it seem to have inspired writers like Erich Fromm to refer to virtually *anything* which is not as it should be as an instance of "alienation," regardless of whether the problems involved are in any way related. Such unrestricted usage renders the term virtually meaningless; yet its occurrence in the works of such writers is, if anything, more common than in Marx's writings.

Marx cannot be held responsible for what later writers have done; but his use of the term set a precedent for theirs. Once its employment in connection with a variety of different phenomena was established, it is quite understandable that it should have continued to be so employed even when his views concerning their interrelation were questioned. And once their interrelation ceased to be regarded as an important consideration, the only obvious barrier to the complete generalization of the employment of the term was removed.

Marx's use of the term manifests a tension between the tendency to allow it to comprehend a variety of different phenomena, and the desire to construe it concretely enough that it has at least some specific descriptive meaning. He is able to have it both ways only by virtue of the interrelation he envisages between the phenomena in question. If their interrelation is denied, or if the term is employed in connection with other phenomena, it is no longer possible to do so. And if one continues to treat the term as though it were a determinate descriptive one, while employing it too broadly for it to function as such, it loses its utility and becomes a source of confusion and misunderstanding. This, unfortunately, is what happens all too frequently in more recent discussions in which it is employed. The following chapter deals with a case in point.

4 Erich Fromm and Karen Horney

Today it is not Baal and Astarte but . . . the all-pervading alienation which threatens the spiritual qualities of man.

FROMM, *The Sane Society*

Erich Fromm has had a great deal to do with the popularization of the term "alienation" in the United States. Having become acquainted with Marx's "Manuscripts" when they were first published in Germany, it was he who made them available to English-speaking readers in his *Marx's Concept of Man* (6).[1] And "the problem of alienation" has been a constant theme in his own very popular writings, beginning with his much earlier *Escape from Freedom* (5).[2] Indeed, it is the central issue in what is perhaps his most important subsequent book, *The Sane Society* (7).[3] There he says: "I have chosen the concept of *alienation* as the central point from which I am going to develop the analysis of the contemporary social character." (*SS*, 103) And "the concept of alienation" is assigned an equally important role in his more recent *Beyond the Chains of Illusion* (4).[4] The influence enjoyed by these books renders desirable a critical examination of his discussion of alienation in them. Then, in the second part of this chapter, I shall consider the conception of

---

[1] 1961. Henceforth identified as "MC."
[2] 1941. Henceforth identified as "EF."
[3] 1955. Henceforth identified as "SS."
[4] 1962. Henceforth identified as "BC."

alienation developed by a writer whom many people associate with Fromm: Karen Horney.

ERICH FROMM

I. Introduction

Fromm's Use of "Alienation"

Fromm often speaks of alienation as though it were a single phenomenon. He employs the term in such a variety of ways, however, that it is difficult to imagine what this phenomenon might be. He uses the term to characterize certain possible relations of a person to himself, other men, nature, his work, and things. He variously refers to alienation as a "relation," a "mode of experience," a "failure" to have a certain kind of "experience," an "act," a "sickness," an "attitude," and a "process." And there are occasions on which he appears to speak interchangeably of alienation and "idolatry," "bureaucratization," "instrumentality" (the treatment of others and oneself as mere instruments), "transcendence," and "automatization" (the transformation of men into "automatons").

Further, it seems that whenever he feels that something is not as it should be, he characterizes it in terms of alienation. He does this in connection with such different things as "love," "thought," "hope," "work," "language," man's relation to "the world," contemporary "culture" or "society," and the processes of "consumption" and "production."

Faced with this profusion of uses of the term, the best procedure would appear to be to focus on those which occur most frequently in Fromm's writings. The relations to which he devotes the most attention in his discussion of "alienation" are those of a man to himself, others, nature, and, in a different way, to society.

"The World" and "Man"

"The world" is not included on this list, despite the fact that Fromm often speaks of it as "alien" to man. On several occasions he rather definitively characterizes alienation in

terms of the alienness of "the world" to man; but his paren-
thetical explanation of what he means shows that he is simply
thinking of a number of the other things mentioned, considered collectively. For example: "The essence of this concept [of alienation] . . . is that the world (nature, things,
others, and he himself) have become alien to man." (BC,
46)

Fromm almost always speaks of "man" in general, rather
than of "a man," "some men," etc. In the passage just cited,
the world is said to have "become alien to *man*." Sometimes
it is "modern man" who is "alienated." On other occasions,
particularly when Fromm is speaking of the "split" between
man and nature and others, he seems to imply that "man"
as such is "alienated."

In passages of the former type (by far the most common),
it is by no means clear about whom Fromm is talking. Sometimes he takes the extreme position that *all* people today are
"alienated": "Not the working class alone is alienated . . .
but everybody is." (BC, 62) At other times he suggests that
his assertions are to be taken as applying to the *typical* person
today; thus he says that he is concerned with "the character
structure of the average individual." (SS, 103) But this notion too is very nebulous—all the more so because Fromm
relies largely on his general impressions in deciding what is
average or typical and what is not. Consequently, his discussion is frequently characterized by an indeterminateness
as to who is being termed "alienated," and what he is "alienated" from.

Fromm's Relation to Hegel and Marx

Fromm acknowledges that "the thinker who coined the
concept of alienation was Hegel" (MC, 47); and he states
that Hegel, together with Marx, "laid the foundations for
the understanding of the problem of alienation." (EF,
140 n.) It is Marx, however, with whom he is most directly
acquainted, and to whom he is most indebted. His contribution, as he would appear to view it, is to have adapted Marx's
conception of alienation to the contemporary situation. The
only point of difference he recognizes between his position
and Marx's is that, in his view, alienation is even more per-

vasive than Marx thought. (*MC*, 56) Conceiving his task to be that of working out and elaborating upon Marx's insights into the alienation of modern man, Fromm proceeds to apply the term in connection with virtually every sphere of contemporary life.

II. Man's Relation to Nature

Alienation and the Transcendence of Nature

Fromm is very much concerned with man's relation to "nature." He never spells out precisely what he means by this term, apparently considering its meaning to be intuitively obvious. Unfortunately, he seems to construe it differently at different times. Sometimes it would appear to refer to life on a purely physical plane; here one is "at one" with it when one is completely absorbed in it. At other times it seems to mean something like man's natural environment; here one would be said to exist in unity with it when one is an integral functioning part within it. And at still other times, it would seem to refer to the world of physical objects, unity with which presumably would have something to do with a lack of the distinction of oneself from these objects.

Fromm fails to note these differences, speaking simply of "nature" in each case. This ambiguity in turn introduces a certain ambiguity into his concept of man's "essence"; for he conceives man's essence in terms of his relation to nature. He states: "The essence of man consists in the . . . contradiction inherent in his existence," namely, "that he is a part of nature and yet transcends it, being endowed with reason and self-awareness." (*BC*, 189) He refers to man's "emergence from a state of oneness with the natural world to an awareness of himself as an entity separate from surrounding nature and men," as "the process of individuation." (*EF*, 39–40) This process results in a loss of the "harmony" with nature which characterizes "animal existence." (*SS*, 30) Fromm characterizes this separation from nature, or "transcendence" of it, as the "alienation" of man from nature. Thus he can say, for example, "To transcend nature, to be alienated from nature . . . finds man naked, ashamed." (*EF*, 50)

He is not completely consistent with regard to the origin of this separation, and therefore also with regard to the question of its inevitability. At times he attributes the separation simply to the emergence of self-awareness; man is said to be "torn away" from nature as soon as it develops. (SS, 35) As a concomitant of man's reason, it develops "automatically" (EF, 47) and is something of which man "cannot rid himself." (SS, 30) It would thus seem that the alienation of man from nature is inevitable and inescapable.

At other times Fromm locates its origin in a very different quarter: "[Man] invents tools and, while thus mastering nature, he separates himself from it more and more." (EF, 49) Here the separation of man from nature is suggested to be a concomitant of man's achievement of *mastery* over it—something quite different from the attainment of self-awareness. And when Fromm speaks of "the unalienated man . . . who does not 'dominate' nature, but who becomes one with it" (MC, 63), he implies that the alienation of man from nature is *not* inescapable. Indeed, he even tells us how it is to be overcome. At the level of action, it is "by productive work" that man "relates himself to nature, becoming one with her." (SS, 68) And at the level of thought, man can achieve "an active and creative relatedness" to nature through "the proper grasp of the world by reason." (SS, 37)

There are several curiosities in this proposed procedure for overcoming alienation from nature. First: In one view of its origin, this alienation occurs precisely because man uses his reason to apprehend nature as "an object" distinct from him. Thus the problem, according to Fromm, is "to overcome this split in the activity of his reason." (BC, 60) But he also asserts that a distinguishing feature of the unalienated person is that he "uses his reason to grasp reality objectively." (SS, 241) In other words, Fromm suggests that the split between man and nature may be overcome by the same employment of reason which he contends produces the split in the first place.

Secondly: In Fromm's other view of the origin of man's alienation from nature, it results from man's achievement and exercise of "mastery" over nature. As has been seen, however, he suggests that a new unity with nature may be achieved through "productive work." (SS, 68) Yet what is "productive work," if not (in Marx's phrase) a "molding and working of nature," involving its subjugation and mastery?[5] Here again, the form of activity which is supposed to enable man to overcome his alienation from nature is the very one which is elsewhere said to give rise to it.

Three Types of Alienation from Nature

A number of these difficulties derive from the fact that Fromm conceives of alienation from nature in three different ways. The separation from nature which accompanies man's mastery over it has a character different from that which accompanies the emergence of self-awareness. In the first case, man is presented as assuming a very *active* stance toward nature—as it were, making a *slave* of it. In the second, on the other hand, the idea suggested is that of a *disengagement* from immediate immersion in nature, as a result of which it becomes remote and a *stranger* to one. Of course, to enslave is generally thereby also to estrange; and it is perhaps for this reason that Fromm speaks of alienation in the former case as well as in the latter. But it clearly is to estrange in a quite different way.

Fromm also speaks of alienation from nature in connection with another sort of separation. Here to be alienated from nature is to lack the "capacity to relate [one-]self fully . . . to nature." (MC, 5) This inability to "relate fully" to nature is not at all an inevitable concomitant of self-awareness and reason for Fromm; for, as has been seen, he holds that one can come to relate himself fully to nature without losing his self-awareness and reason. This inability is also to be distinguished from the kind of separation from nature associated with the mastery of it; for in that case nature is experienced not "passively," but rather as so much raw material to be utilized and *acted* upon.

In short, we are dealing here with three distinct kinds of

[5] It should be observed that, far from holding that man's mastery of nature brings about his alienation from it, Marx regarded the "humanization" of nature with approval, feeling that it involves the transformation of nature from something alien to man into a world in which he can feel truly at home.

separation from nature; and because Fromm employs the term "alienation" in connection with all three, it is necessary to distinguish three kinds of alienation from nature in his writings.

Alienation and Submergence in Nature

Fromm speaks of alienation in connection with yet another possible relation of man to nature. As has been observed, he holds that man "cannot rid himself" of his self-awareness and reason. Yet one of his major worries is that man will "submerge" himself completely in his environment. "Man attempts to find again harmony with nature by regression to a prehuman form of existence, eliminating his specifically human qualities of reason and love"—and, presumably, with his reason, his self-awareness. (*BC*, 189–90) Thus it appears that man *can* rid himself of his reason and self-awareness, after all. Or rather, Fromm is inconsistent on the matter.

Assuming that it is a possibility, however, one wishes to know what Fromm means when he speaks of a new "submergence" in nature, and of a "prehuman form of existence" to which it is possible for man to "regress." One would think he has in mind regression to the plane of simple animality; but for the most part, his thoughts run along other lines. "Nature" becomes "the world," and "the world" takes on overtones of "society." Fromm's basic concern is with the possibility of complete submergence in the *social* world, or "automaton conformity." This, he suggests, is "the solution that the majority of normal individuals find in modern society," when confronted with "the discrepancy between 'I' and the world." (*EF*, 208 f.)

Still, it is quite possible that Fromm does at times conceive of man's attempt to "find again harmony with nature" in terms of a regression to the plane of animality. In cases of such regression, no less than in cases of "automaton conformity," man would lose his self-awareness. For Fromm, one who has lost his "sense of self" cannot be said to *be* a "true self"; it is in these terms that he conceives of "alienation from oneself." Thus a further type of alienation is possible in man's relation to nature, arising not out of separation from it, but rather from the lack of separation from it.

III. Man's Relation to Others

It is part of "the essence of the concept of alienation," according to Fromm, that "others . . . have become alien to man." (*BC*, 46) There is an intimate connection in his mind between man's alienation from nature and his alienation from others. Indeed, at times he seems to identify the two. He says, for example: "To transcend nature, to be alienated from nature and from another human being, finds man naked, ashamed." (*EF*, 50) It is not at all clear why the transcendence of nature should involve "alienation" from others. On any ordinary view of "nature" and "others," the two are quite different. For Fromm, however, they are connected; and this connection is reflected in his discussion of alienation in the two contexts. He speaks of "alienation" in connection with four kinds of relation to others, which are closely analogous to the four kinds of relation to nature distinguished above.

Alienation and Distinctness from Others

Fromm holds that one "aspect of the process of individuation" is that one "becomes aware of being an entity separate from all others." (*EF*, 44–45) This process, once again, is supposed to take place "automatically" in the course of human development. (*EF*, 47) Initially, at the stage of "pre-individualistic existence," man is purportedly bound to his fellow men by "ties . . . regulated by instincts." (*SS*, 35) He is held to lack any sense of separateness at this stage; his unity with others is immediate and complete. Once he recognizes them to be "other," however, and acquires an awareness of his distinctness from them, he ceases to be united with them in this fashion.

Fromm considers a person in this situation to be alienated from others. It causes most people very little anguish to recognize that the other is "other," and that their fellow men are beings separate from themselves. Indeed, Fromm himself holds that this recognition is the presupposition of the richest of human relationships—love. "Love presupposes alienation," he states, because "in order to love, the 'other' must become a stranger." (*BC*, 60) The kind of separation presupposed by love is minimal in comparison with the kinds in connection with which the term "alienation" is ordinarily employed. Fromm, however, does use the term in this connection.

Alienation and "Relatedness" to Others

He does feel it to be quite possible for one who has become aware of his separateness from others to "find new ties with his fellow men which replace the old ones, regulated by instincts." (*SS*, 35) These new ties do not eliminate the experience of distinctness; but they make that kind of alienation from others endurable. It is one of Fromm's aims to describe how one may "reach a new harmony with his fellow man" in spite of it. (*BC*, 190) And he also speaks of alienation from others in connection with the lack of this "new harmony." In this context, one is alienated who fails to "relate himself fully to [his fellow] man." (*MC*, 5)

In order to determine precisely what this second type of alienation from others involves, the notion of "relating oneself fully" to one's fellow man must be explicated. Fromm uses this expression to refer to one form "among the various forms of relatedness": namely, "the productive one, love." (*SS*, 41) He is not willing to settle for *any* form of "unity and oneness with one's fellow men." It follows, however, that one can be alienated from others in the sense in question, and yet be quite unaware that anything is lacking in one's relations with others. For the definitive criterion of such alienation is not the *feeling* of remoteness from others, but rather the existence of a form of "relatedness" (or non-"relatedness") which is not the *proper* one "among the various forms of relatedness." And one might very well be "related" to others in some *other* way, quite without realizing that it was not the proper one.

This is not merely a hypothetical case for Fromm. The "conformist," with whom he is so concerned, is an example of such a person. The conformist has "reached a new harmony" with others; but to Fromm he very definitely is *not* properly "related" to them. Thus Fromm speaks of his "alienated conformity." (SS, 142) And one of the things Fromm finds most disturbing about the conformist is that he tends to *think* his relationships leave nothing to be desired. (SS, 145)

To say that the proper form of relatedness to others is "love" is not to say very much. More concretely, it would appear to involve both intimacy and the maintenance of individuality. It may be understood best if it is contrasted with those kinds of relation to others in which these characteristics are missing. One can imagine a person who cares nothing about others, who is unwilling to do anything for them, and who generally acts as if they did not exist. His is a privative form of relatedness to others; it is the very absence of any active or positive relation to them. On the other hand, one can imagine a person who cares about the others with whom he comes into contact, who is friendly toward them, and who takes an unselfish interest in their well-being. This is one side of what Fromm regards as the proper form of relatedness to others.

The other emerges if one thinks of that contrasting form which he associates with conformity. He contends that one cannot "relate oneself fully" to others unless he has a genuine "self" to relate. If this is lacking, one may be related to others; but his relatedness to them will lack depth and significance. For example, a person might be so eager to get along with others, to please them, to befriend them, that he "becomes exactly as all others are and as they expect him to be." (EF, 209) He achieves a very extensive unity with others; but he is not related to them as a unique individual. On the other hand, one can imagine a person who enters into each interpersonal encounter with a sense of his own identity, grounded in detached inwardness, critical reflectiveness, etc.[6] His concern for others, his interest in them and his contacts with them always have a personal quality, and always reflect his individuality. Only such a person, Fromm feels, can "relate himself fully" to others.

[6] I do not know if these expressions can be given a satisfactory explication. Fromm certainly gives none. I use them because he does, and because if he has anything more specific in mind, it is not clear to me what it is.

The proper form of relatedness to others, as Fromm conceives of it, has these two sides. In the absence of this form of relatedness, one is held to be alienated from others. This type of alienation exists, therefore, whenever either the element of active concern or that of genuine "selfhood" is lacking in one's relations with others.

Alienation and Exploitation of Others

The absence of active concern, of course, does not entail the adoption of an exploitative orientation toward others. The latter constitutes yet another distinct relation to others which is characterized by Fromm in terms of "alienation." Here one regards others as means to one's personal ends. Fromm writes: "What is modern man's relationship to his fellow man? It is one between two . . . living machines, who use each other." Following Marx, he refers to this relationship as "the alienation between man and man." (SS, 126–27) Men have "become instrumentalized" in each other's eyes; they regard each other as things or instruments to be used for their own selfish purposes. Relations between men are said to have the "character of alienation," in that "instead of relations between human beings, they assume the character of relations between things." (EF, 140, 279)

Perhaps the paradigm case of alienation from others, where it is conceived purely in terms of the lack of all relatedness to them, is that of the person who looks passively upon the distress of another, neither offering nor summoning any kind of assistance. In the present context, on the other hand, the paradigm case might be that of the employer who is bent upon the exploitation of those he employs. Like the passive bystander, such a person is not properly related to the others in question. Here, however, this is not the crucial consideration. The crucial consideration is that his relation to them (unlike the bystander's) is an exploitative one. For Fromm, this exploitativeness is an essential feature of his alienation from them.

To be sure, Fromm no doubt would say that one who exploits others is *also* alienated from them simply by virtue of his lack of the proper form of relatedness to them. But the criteria of the term's application are different in the two cases.

Unfortunately, Fromm is not sensitive to the distinction which must be drawn here. He speaks of "the asocial and egotistical attitude"—singular—"which is the essence of alienation" (SS, 283), failing to see that asociality need not be accompanied by egotistical exploitation of others. They may often occur together; but they are distinct.

Alienation and Conformity

Fromm's assertion that "the essence of alienation" is "the asocial and egotistical attitude" comes as something of a surprise; for one tends to associate his use of the term with his notion of the loss of selfhood through conformity. And, in fact, it is more usual for him to speak of alienation in these terms. "Automaton conformity," of course, is not the proper form of unity with others for Fromm. But in addition, since the conformist has no "sense of self except the one which conformity with the majority can give" (SS, 309), Fromm also considers him to be "alienated from himself."

Obviously, the "essence of alienation" here cannot be conceived in terms of an "asocial and egotistical attitude." The person Fromm describes is not "asocial," but rather is indiscriminatingly social. And he lacks the fundamental prerequisites of "egotism": desires that are not determined by others, and a willingness to pursue them regardless of how others are affected.

Conclusion

As in the case of "nature," Fromm refers to every type of lack of unity with others as "alienation from others," even when—in the case of mere awareness of the "otherness" of others—the separation is relatively unobjectionable and has considerable advantages. And he employs the term "alienation" in connection with all of the major types of relation to others of which he disapproves: lack of all relatedness, egotistical manipulation, and conformity. Moreover, because he thinks of each as an instance of alienation, he is led to believe that they constitute aspects of a single phenomenon— "the alienated social character of our time"—to which he is thus compelled to attribute a highly improbable collection of qualities: "adjustment, co-operativeness, aggressiveness, tolerance, ambition, etc." (SS, 172)

Even if he had not taken this last step, and had properly distinguished the various types of relation to others which he characterizes in terms of "alienation," the fruitfulness of so characterizing all of them is questionable. Confusion cannot be avoided when the same term refers to so many different types of relation to others; and the impression is inevitably created that the different phenomena in question are more intimately connected than in fact they are. Asociality and egotistical exploitation may presuppose the perception of others as separate from oneself; but this perception is by no means invariably or even commonly associated with asociality and exploitation. Asociality and exploitation, while perhaps more frequently conjoined, are nonetheless distinct. And the improper form of relatedness associated with conformity is to be distinguished from all three. The term "alienation" conceivably could function usefully in this general context, but only if its employment served to reinforce these distinctions, or at least did not have the effect of obscuring them. (The same considerations obviously apply to his use of the term in discussing man's relation to nature.)

IV. Man's Relation to Society

Society as Productive of Alienation

Fromm frequently speaks of our "society" and "culture" as "alienated." However, he means something very different than Hegel does when the latter speaks of the "social substance" as "alienated." Hegel has in mind the situation in which the individual regards the "social substance" as something *alien to him*. And it is common today to hear certain individuals and groups characterized as alienated from the society in which they live. Fromm, however, does not characterize separation from society (i.e., the social, economic, political, and cultural order) in terms of "alienation." He characteristically speaks of "alienation *in* modern society," rather than *from* it. And what he desires is "a form of production and an organization of society *in which* man can

overcome alienation from his product, from his work, from
his fellow man, from himself, and from nature." (*MC*, 59;
emphasis added.)

When Fromm says that society is "alienated," he means
that it is so structured that it tends to *make* individuals alienated in these various ways. In *The Sane Society*, he follows
Marx in tracing the source of man's alienation to the "contemporary socioeconomic structure," contending that it is a
"socially patterned defect." In fact, "the phenomenon of
alienation" is said to be an "effect of Capitalism on personality." (*SS*, 111)[7] And with Marx, Fromm also holds that
man's alienation can be overcome "only by simultaneous
changes" in virtually every sphere of the social, economic,
political, and cultural order. (*SS*, 238) A new "organization
of society" must be "created," he contends, if this end is to
be realized. (*MC*, 59)[8]

For Fromm—as for Marx, and in contrast to Hegel—the
overcoming of alienation does not involve the achievement
of unity with society. Even when he envisages a kind of society that would not be "alienating," he does not think of it
as something with which it would be desirable for the individual to unite himself. For he does not think of it in terms
of its social and cultural *content*, as Hegel does, using the
expression "social *substance*" to refer to it. Rather, Fromm
thinks of it in terms of what he considers to be its essential
function: namely, that of facilitating (rather than obstruct-
ing) the individual's "realization of his self" through "spontaneous activity."

The Undesirability of Oneness with Society

Generally speaking, Fromm not only does not place a high
value on unity with the social order; he is emphatically op-

[7] This obviously cannot be true, however, of that type of alienation from nature and from others which Fromm presents as the
inevitable consequence of the process of individuation.

[8] It is difficult to reconcile this view with another of Fromm's
contentions, that the individual *can* overcome his alienation *on his
own*, "by the realization of his self . . . [through] spontaneous activity." (*EF*, 283–84) (Marx more consistently holds that such activity will become possible only *after* the revolution.)

posed to it. He does use the term "alienation" in discussing that relation of the individual to society of which he disapproves. However, this relation is not one of *disunity*, as for Hegel, but rather one of "conformity," or complete *unity*. It is precisely the person who is completely at one with the social order whom Fromm terms "alienated"; and his alienation is alienation *from himself*.

Fromm contends that while we do not live in an authoritarian society and are not compelled by anyone to act as we do, "we all conform as much or more than people in an intensely authoritarian society would." (SS, 138) In his eyes, this is the height of alienation from oneself. For when one "adopts entirely the kind of personality offered to him by cultural patterns," one "ceases to be himself." (EF, 208–09) Hegel seeks universality without coercion; Fromm feels it has become a reality, and abhors it. Hegel holds that man can realize his essential nature only if he achieves universality, which involves restricting his spontaneity and individuality. Fromm complains that modern man "suffers from a defect of spontaneity and individuality which may seem incurable" (SS, 24); and he argues that man can realize his "self" only if he abandons his universality or conformity to "cultural patterns," and recovers his spontaneity and individuality.

This difference is in part a reflection of the fact that Fromm is haunted by the specter of the Mass Man and "automaton conformity," while Hegel is preoccupied with the problem posed by the extreme individualism of the Romantics.[9] Hegel no less than Fromm is opposed to "completely submerging oneself in the outside world"; he too seeks "a relationship that connects the individual with the world without eliminating his individuality." (EF, 45–46) But he settles on the formula of an extensive universality or unity with the "social substance," within the limits of which room for a degree of individual particularity is provided. Fromm, on the other hand, is opposed to this ordering of priorities.

There is a curious point of agreement between Fromm and Hegel: Both suggest that unity with the social substance involves the alienation of the particular, individualistic self.

[9] See pp. 57–58.

Because of the high value Hegel places upon the universality attained through unity with the social substance, he views this alienation in a positive light. Because of the high value Fromm places upon the particular self, on the other hand, he views its alienation (and consequently also the unity with the social substance which requires it) in a very negative light.

Of course, he fully recognizes the possibility of nonconformity to social patterns, and thus of a lack of unity with the social order. But he (like Marx) does not speak of it in terms of "alienation." This is a separation of which he seems to approve; and, generally speaking, he only characterizes those separations of which he does *not* approve—or at least, which he considers to involve some drawback—as forms of alienation.

V. Man's Relation to Himself

The "Self" in "Alienation from Oneself"

Perhaps the most important of these separations, for Fromm, is that of the individual from himself. The separation here in question, however, would seem not to consist of a disparity between one's essential nature and one's actual condition. Fromm does consider man to have an "ascertainable essence." But in his view, "The essence of man consists in the . . . contradiction inherent in his existence," namely, that "he is part of nature and yet transcends it." (BC, 189) There can be no disparity between one's actual condition and his essence so conceived. Fromm does not even attempt to formulate his concept of alienation from oneself in these terms. The term "self" in this expression does not refer to this "essence."

As has been suggested, Fromm's notion of the "self" is similar to the Hegelian concept of the "particular self," and to the Marxian concept of the self which derives from it. Hegel characterizes the "particular self" in terms of idiosyncrasy, willfulness, and independence from external direction. Fromm characterizes the self in similar terms, such as "individuality" and "spontaneity." He urges the development of this self, and (in contrast to Hegel) the elimination of anything which might hinder this development. As he conceives it, "alienation from oneself" consists of something like the loss or lack of a "sense of self," and of spontaneity and individuality. This loss or lack has the significance of "self-alienation" for Marx too; but it does so in virtue of the fact that it implies a disparity between one's actual condition and one's essential nature. It does so for Fromm, on the other hand, simply because one who lacks these things fails to satisfy his criterion of selfhood.

Alienation from Oneself as an "Experience"

While the above characterization of Fromm's concept of alienation from oneself may suffice as a rough approximation of what he has in mind, a closer examination of his discussion reveals that matters are not so simple—or, rather, not so clear. In introducing the concept in *The Sane Society*, for example, he says: "By alienation is meant a mode of experience in which the person experiences himself as an alien." (*SS*, 111) He thus seems to be suggesting that to be alienated from oneself is to have a certain type of experience.

For the most part, however, in his actual discussion, Fromm is concerned with the *absence* of certain types of experience. The important thing seems to be not the exact nature of the way in which the individual *does* experience himself, but rather the fact that he *lacks* the *proper* "sense of self." While this would not exclude the possibility that certain kinds of experience characteristically accompany the absence of the proper "sense of self," it suggests that it is in virtue of the latter that a person is to be considered "alienated from himself." Thus Fromm's characterization of such alienation as a "mode of experience" is rather misleading, and does not reflect the way in which he actually uses the expression.

It is also unfortunate that, in the passage cited above, he asserts this "mode of experience" to be one in which "the person experiences himself as an alien." For this implies an *awareness* that one's "sense of self" is *not* the *proper* one. This would mean that it would be appropriate to speak of alienation from oneself only in connection with cases in which this awareness is present. This restriction, however, would conflict directly with Fromm's purposes. For he wants to be

able to say of one who is alienated from himself that, while
he is "driven by forces which are separated from his self," he
is often "under the illusion of doing what *he* wants." (*SS*,
114) Similarly, he holds that "automaton conformity" frequently is not accompanied by any feeling that something is
wrong. (*SS*, 145)

In such cases the individual does *not* "experience himself
as an alien." Indeed, the only actual "experiences" occurring
are considered not merely to be irrelevant, but moreover to
conceal the true state of affairs. Fromm cannot afford to
cease to regard cases of this sort as instances of alienation
from oneself; for they are among his prime examples of it.
Such alienation thus cannot be characterized in terms of an
actual experience of oneself as "alien."

A Lack of the Proper "Sense of Self"

A person who is "alienated from himself" would thus appear to be one "not having a sense of self except the one which
conformity with the majority can give." (*SS*, 309) He does
not "truly sense 'I am I.'" (*SS*, 175) Fromm characterizes
such a person in a number of ways. Most importantly, he
does not "experience himself as a unique individual entity."
(*SS*, 241) He "fail[s] to experience [his] identity," in all of
its particularity and uniqueness. (*BC*, 59) He has no sense
"of himself as a unique and induplicable individual." (*SS*,
130)

He also "does not experience himself . . . as a thinking,
feeling, loving person." (*BC*, 46) Furthermore, he "does not
experience himself . . . as the bearer of productive human
powers." (*SS*, 113) He apparently has no idea that it is within
his power to produce and create. More generally, "He does
not experience himself . . . as the creator of his own acts."
(*SS*, 111) This would seem to mean that he does not feel
that any of his acts are his own. The "sense of self" which
he lacks "stems from the experience of myself as the subject
of *my* experiences, *my* thought, *my* feeling, *my* decision, *my*
judgment." (*SS*, 130)

It is in these terms that Fromm most commonly speaks of
alienation from oneself. However, if his emphasis upon the
individual's "failure to *experience himself*" in the ways in

question is retained, serious difficulties arise. For Fromm also maintains that one can *feel* or *think* one *is* "the creator of one's own acts," "a thinking person," "the subject of one's own thoughts," and so forth, and *still be* alienated from oneself. He readily allows that many of those to whom this characterization applies do in fact *think* that they do what they really want, and *think* that they have thoughts which are really their own. Yet he admits that the self-alienated person frequently "is under the illusion of doing what *he* wants." (*SS*, 114) He further admits that when such a person agrees with things he reads or hears, "he believes that [they] express *his* thoughts." (*BC*, 58) And Fromm also grants that such people form friendships which they often find quite satisfying; thus they may *feel* themselves to be capable of personal relationships. (*SS*, 142 ff.)

In short, a person may be alienated from himself according to Fromm, and yet *not* fail to "*experience* himself" in the ways Fromm considers desirable. The real problem in such a case is that his experience of himself is not grounded in reality; it is an "illusion." Fromm often speaks as though his concept of alienation from oneself can be understood simply in terms of the absence of the requisite ways of experiencing oneself. The discrimination he desires to make, however, requires that the emphasis be shifted to the issue of the veracity of these experiences. His own development of the concept requires him to hold that one is not alienated from himself only if one not only has a "sense of self," but also *is* a genuine "self"—i.e., satisfies certain objective conditions of selfhood.

The Failure to Be a Genuine "Self"

Fortunately for Fromm, the revision of his explicit characterization of alienation from oneself along these lines may be accomplished relatively simply. One has merely to replace the question, "Does X experience himself as *p, q, r*, etc.?" with the question, "Is X *in fact p, q, r*, etc.?" One must ask: Does he *in fact* have a unique and induplicable identity? Is he in fact a thinking, feeling, loving person? Is he in fact a creating person, and the creator of his own acts? And is he in fact the subject of *his* experience, *his* thought, *his* decisions, and the rest? If so, Fromm would consider him to have achieved genuine selfhood. If not, he would fall short of it, and would thus be alienated from himself. It is only if alienation from oneself is so construed that it makes a difference—as Fromm wants it to—whether or not one is merely "under the *illusion* of doing what he wants," of thinking his own thoughts, of having his own convictions, of enjoying true friendship, and so forth. At times, Fromm does in fact slip into this more objective mode of speaking, which consistency should have led him to use throughout his discussion.

It has been observed that Fromm does not hold the self delimited by the above characteristics to be man's "essence," and that therefore his concept of alienation from oneself strictly speaking cannot be construed in terms of a disparity between a person's actual condition and his essential nature. But in a sense, it can be assimilated to this model; for Fromm does consider these characteristics to define what man *should be*. He quite obviously feels that one who is alienated from himself is *not* as he should be, and that existence as a genuine self is preferable to existence in a state of self-alienation. Thus he characterizes his position as a "normative humanism." (*SS*, 22) Because he does not suggest such selfhood to be required by man's essential nature, he lacks Hegel's and Marx's ready explanation of *why* men should be as he contends they should be. But for him, as for them, alienation from oneself may be construed in terms of a disparity between the way one is and the way one should be. This is the sense of the expression implicit in his employment of it. To be alienated from oneself for Fromm is to fail to be the kind of "self" one should be.

The Criteria of the Characteristics of "Selfhood"

If one looks more closely at the various characteristics which the person who is alienated from himself is said to lack, one finds that the criteria of most of them are very difficult to formulate satisfactorily. What, for example, are the criteria of "a unique and induplicable identity"? Fromm suggests that one must be an individual, rather than a conformist, in order to have one; but this is very vague, and sheds little light on the matter.

Again: What precisely is being "a thinking, feeling, loving person"? It cannot be enough simply to *think* that one thinks, feels, and loves, for Fromm must preserve the possibility of "illusion." But how is one to distinguish between "illusion" and "reality" in concrete situations?

One further example: How is one to determine that a certain person is not "the creator of his own acts," but rather is "driven by forces which are separated from his self"? Here too, Fromm must preserve the possibility of "illusion." But how is one to decide whether or not, in performing certain actions, a person who *thinks* "his actions are his own" is actually driven by such forces?

It may be that the criteria of these characteristics can be formulated satisfactorily. Fromm, however, does not even come close to providing the requisite formulations; and it is far from obvious how one might go about doing so. Until this is done, crucial distinctions like those just mentioned will remain elusive; and this constitutes a serious obstacle to the understanding and application of his notion of selfhood, and of the derivative notion of alienation from oneself.

The Criteria of Alienation from Oneself

Another problem would remain, even if the criteria of these characteristics were to be formulated satisfactorily. Even a crude intuitive grasp of the natures of these different characteristics is sufficient to reveal that they are not reducible to each other. For example, it obviously is one thing not to have a unique and induplicable identity, another not to be the creator of one's own acts, and still another not to be a thinking, or feeling, or loving person. A complete list of the various distinct traits in terms of which he conceives of alienation from oneself would be quite long.

The problem presented by this large number of traits should be obvious. Is it appropriate to speak of alienation from oneself only when all of them are present? Or is a person to be considered self-alienated whenever several of them are present? Or if even one of them obtains? Fromm would seem to incline toward this last position. He holds that alienation from oneself takes many "forms"; and he appears to feel that the presence of any one of these traits constitutes one form of it. He seems to think that, as a matter of fact, many of them are likely to be found together; but he does not establish that they are inseparable, or even indicate that he holds this to be the case.

But if each of these traits by itself is held to constitute a form of alienation from oneself, one cannot meaningfully employ the expression without specifying precisely which trait or traits are intended. And if one must always specify the traits intended in other terms, the point of introducing the expression is not clear. For as Fromm uses it, it would appear not to convey anything *more* than would the specifications of these traits themselves.

VI. "Alienation" in Other Contexts

The contexts in which Fromm most frequently employs the term "alienation" are those of man's relations to nature, others, society, and himself. But he also employs it in connection with man's relations to his work and to things, and in a variety of other contexts as well.

Alienation and Work

When Fromm states that "Alienation as we find it in modern society is almost total," the first instance he cites is that "it pervades the relationship of man to his work." (*SS*, 114) Most people are said to "assume that the kind of work current in our society, namely, alienated work, is the only kind there is." (*SS*, 261) But Fromm himself rejects this view. With Marx he contends that, essentially considered, work is something positive and desirable. (*EF*, 287) Yet he also follows Marx in taking the position that in contemporary society men have to do work which is not their own free and creative activity, which is not meaningful and satisfying to them, which bears no relation to their personalities—in short, which is "alien" to them. He expresses this, as Marx does, by saying that "work has become alienated from the working person" (*SS*, 161), or, alternately, that the individual is "alienated from the work he does." (*SS*, 125)

Alienation and Things

It is also part of "the essence of the concept [of aliena-tion]," according to Fromm, that "things . . . have become alien to man." (*BC*, 46) If one is not "alive and responsive toward objects, so that objects come to life for him," one is termed "alienated" from them. (*MC*, 63) This is rather ob-scure; but Fromm presumably has in mind the same sort of thing Marx does, when Marx speaks of the dealer in minerals who is blind to their "beauty and particular characteristics," and who sees in them only their "commercial value." (*FS*, 601/B162) For Fromm does indicate that he is thinking of the situation in which "things are experienced as commodi-ties, as embodiments of exchange value." (*SS*, 107) When he says that man is alienated from "things," therefore, with-out further specifying the kind of "things" in question, he would appear to mean that men lack the proper (rather aesthetic) relatedness to objects generally, and perhaps to natural objects in particular.

He considers somewhat different forms of relatedness to be appropriate to certain special categories of things, such as one's products, one's possessions, and the things one con-sumes. If they are lacking, he again speaks of one's "aliena-tion" from these things. If one is alienated from his work, he is held to be "alienated from his product," for the same basic reasons. (*SS*, 115) Fromm also uses the term to char-acterize the relation of both the "stockholder" and the "owner of the big corporation" to their property. The former is alienated from his property because he "exercises very little control" over it (*SS*, 119); and the latter, because "he has no responsibility for the enterprise and no concrete relation-ship to it in any way." (*SS*, 117) Finally, Fromm holds that "Alienation . . . pervades the relationship of man to . . . the things he consumes." (*SS*, 114) For "the way we acquire things is separated from the way in which we use them." (*SS*, 120) And: "There is another aspect of alienation from the things we consume. . . . We are surrounded by things of whose nature and origin we know nothing." (*SS*, 122) In all these cases, the term "alienation" is used to indicate the lack of what Fromm considers to be the proper relation to the things in question.

Other Instances of Alienation

In other cases the term seems to be used simply to indicate that something is not as it should be. For example:

(1) Fromm contrasts "the productive and the alienated ways of life" (SS, 157), and elsewhere refers to "the alienated way of living." (SS, 137) One would make reference to the absence of a number of proper forms of relatedness if one were to characterize "the alienated way of life"; but the term "alienated" here serves simply to indicate that something is wrong with "the way of life" in question. It performs a similar function when Fromm says that from culture to culture "the specific spheres which are alienated" may differ (SS, 114); and when he terms our society "alienated."[10]

(2) When he speaks of "the alienated *kind* of interpersonal relationships" and "alienated friendships" (SS, 144, 145), it is obvious that he is using the term "alienated" to convey the idea that the relationships and friendships in question leave something to be desired.

(3) Fromm speaks of "the alienation of language" when discussing the situation in which one comes "under the illusion that the saying of the word is the equivalent of the experience." In this situation, language "substitutes itself for the living experience," and thereby ceases to be what it ought to be ("a symbol of the fact"). (MC, 45 f.) It is for this reason that he terms it "alienated."

(4) The term functions in the same general way when he discusses the "alienation of thought." He uses this expression to characterize the situation in which "one believes he has thought through something, that his idea is the result of his own thinking activity"; whereas "the fact is that he has transferred his brain to the idols of public opinion, the newspapers . . . or a political leader." (BC, 58) Thought is "alienated" when it is not true "thinking activity," but rather unquestioning acceptance of the views of someone else.

Other cases could be cited; but these should suffice to il-

[10] See pp. 135 ff.

lustrate Fromm's tendency to resort to the term "alienation" whenever he comes across something which is not as he feels it should be. Some precedent for this use of the term is to be found in its employment by Hegel and Marx in connection with a disparity between a man's actual condition and his essential nature. Marx does use it in a similar way to indicate that labor as it presently exists is not what it should be. The fruitfulness of his doing so, however, is questionable.[11] Fromm's extension of the employment of the term to a wide variety of other contexts can hardly be said to redeem Marx's, or to constitute any sort of advance. At least, the results are not particularly illuminating insofar as our understanding of thought, language, interpersonal relationships, etc., is concerned.

VII. Concluding Remarks

Fromm seems to refer to almost everything of which he disapproves as an instance of "alienation." He disapproves of a great deal; so it is not surprising that he finds alienation to be "all-pervasive." He uses the term above all to characterize various sorts of disunities or separations. It is not simply synonymous with "separation," however, because separations of which he does *not* disapprove—such as nonconformity to social or cultural patterns—are *not* termed instances or forms of alienation.

Any expression used over so wide an area can do no more than convey a very general idea. Thus when Fromm tells us that man, work, the process of consumption, our society and way of life, the predominant types of interpersonal relationships, language, love, and thought are all "alienated," he conveys nothing more than that he feels there is something wrong with these various things. And whatever may be wrong in one case is likely to be quite different from what is wrong in another. By being used in so many different contexts, the term loses all specific conceptual content, and serves merely to suggest dissatisfaction. Under these circumstances it is meaning-

[11] See pp. 101–02.

less to speak of "the phenomenon of alienation" and "the concept of alienation," as Fromm does.

It is not my intention to deny that Fromm attempts to come to terms with serious problems, or even that he says some sound things in discussing them. Nor do I mean to deny the attractiveness of his characterization of the normative condition of man, or the validity of his distinction between it and the actual condition of many men. But it would not seem that his employment of the term "alienation" improves his discussion. On the contrary, he uses it so freely and loosely that the results are much more confusing than illuminating. He may have helped make "alienation" a household word; but in his hands it ceases to be helpful in serious discussion of the problems which concern him.

KAREN HORNEY

The expression "alienation from self" enjoys some currency in the writings of a number of psychoanalytical theorists. An indebtedness to Fromm is acknowledged by some of them; but the influence of Karen Horney upon them is considerably greater. The use of the expression in psychoanalytical literature would appear to be confined to the writings of members of the Horney school; and an examination of the way in which they use it reveals quite clearly that it is her use of it which has shaped theirs. Generally speaking, their departures from her use of it are small; they tend to confine themselves simply to explication of her discussion and to examination of concrete instances to which the expression might apply. It is her own discussion, therefore, which is of the greatest interest.

I. *New Ways in Psychoanalysis*

The first of Horney's books in which she speaks of "alienation from self" was *New Ways in Psychoanalysis* (9).[12] This

[12] Published in 1939. Henceforth referred to as "*New Ways*," and identified as "NW" in references.

condition is here suggested to involve the stifling of spontaneity, or spontaneous individuality. If a person's "spontaneous individual self" has been "stunted," "warped," or "choked," he is said to be in a condition of "alienation from himself" or "alienation from self." (NW, 189, 252, 278) Horney conceives of the "spontaneous individual self" in terms of the "spontaneous assertion of [one's] individual initiative, feelings, wishes, opinions." (NW, 252) The "ultimate goal" of psychoanalysis, in her view, is that of "having the patient retrieve his spontaneity and his faculty of judgment" (NW, 190)—or, in other words, helping him to overcome his "alienation from self."

This characterization of "alienation from self" presents an obvious parallel with Fromm. Unfortunately, the parallel extends further. Difficulties comparable to those encountered in Fromm arise when one attempts to determine precisely what this alienation involves. The verbs "stunt," "warp," and "choke" all suggest a failure to develop a capacity beyond a rudimentary level, rather than a loss of a capacity previously acquired. Thus, "alienation from self" here is apparently to be understood in terms of a certain type of "selfhood" remaining remote or unrealized: namely, one conceived in terms of the "spontaneous assertion" of one's "individual initiative, feelings, wishes, opinions."

But it is not clear how this is to be understood. Consider, for example, the matter of one's "opinions." Horney conceivably could be thinking of the individual's formation of his own opinions (his capacity to make up his own mind), his expression of his opinions to others, or his actions in accordance with his opinions. But it is hard to see what she has in mind in speaking of "spontaneous assertion" on any of these interpretations. The normal functioning of the "faculty of judgment" is not usually characterized in terms of "spontaneity"; and making up one's mind as such need not involve any form of "expression." With regard to the second possible interpretation, Horney surely is not thinking of the impulsive blurting out of one's opinions; but it is hard to see what else "spontaneous assertion" might mean in connection with the expression of one's opinions to others. Finally, perseverance in conduct consistent with one's opinions would be more accurately characterized in terms of self-discipline than "spontaneity"; indeed, it would seem quite often to demand a checking of "spontaneous" tendencies.

Similar problems arise in connection with feelings and wishes. Whether Horney is construed as referring to expressing them to others, acting in accordance with them, or simply having them in the first place, it is difficult to see what she means in advocating their "spontaneous assertion." If a person happens to *lack* all feelings and wishes, his problem cannot appropriately be characterized in terms of an inability to assert them spontaneously. If he has them but is reluctant to acknowledge them *to himself*, the applicability of the term "assertion" is again questionable. Moreover, as the term is ordinarily understood, it conveys the idea of the expression of one's feelings and wishes in either word or deed in an interpersonal context. So understood, however, there are many cases in which their "spontaneous assertion" would have consequences few would regard as desirable, if "spontaneous" is taken in its usual sense. And it is not clear that the term can be given another sense which would avoid this difficulty without altering its meaning beyond recognition. Horney, at any rate, does not show how the problem may be resolved.

In short, Horney does not adequately explicate the concepts in terms of which she conceives of the "self" in *New Ways*. This has obvious implications for her conception of "alienation from self," which is introduced in connection with it. Any obscurity attaching to the notion of the self will also attach to the notion of a failure to develop such a self. And since, in *New Ways*, Horney conceives of "alienation from self" in terms of such a failure, her use of this expression is similarly obscure. Its relations to such expressions as "self" and "spontaneous assertion" are clear enough; but none of them is comprehensible unless at least one of them is provided with a more adequate explication and more specific criteria of application than any of them are in *New Ways*.

II. *Our Inner Conflicts*

Six years after the appearance of *New Ways*, Horney published *Our Inner Conflicts*. (10)[13] In this book "alienation from self" is construed somewhat differently. The condition so characterized here is that in which "the person simply becomes oblivious to what he really feels, likes, rejects, believes —in short, to what he really is." (*IC*, 111) Horney refers to "what he really is" as his "real self"; and one who is "alienated from himself" is one who has "become oblivious" to his "real self."

She suggests that this condition occurs when one develops an "idealized image" of oneself so different from the way one really is that there exists a profound "gap between his idealized image and his real self" (*IC*, 110), and when one "clings to the belief that he is his idealized image." (*IC*, 111) For under these circumstances one loses sight of one's "real self." Horney cites as an example of such "alienation from self" a person who has attained a position of respect through the employment of dubious means, and whose "pride in his respectability alienates him from his unsavory past"—and thus, apparently, from a substantial part of his "real self." (*IC*, 144)

Problems of interpretation notwithstanding, the failure to develop the capacity spontaneously to assert one's feelings and wishes and opinions clearly is to be distinguished from the development of an attitude of obliviousness to them. In fact, in *Conflicts* Horney seems to suggest that the former is the *effect* of the latter. She here defines "neurotic inertia" in terms of "a paralysis of initiative and action." This would appear to be a reasonable approximation of the notion of a "stunting" or "choking" of the "spontaneous assertion of . . . feelings, wishes, opinions"—and thus of the "alienation from self" of *New Ways*. And she asserts that, "generally speaking," neurotic inertia "is the result of a strong alienation from self. . . ." (*IC*, 160) In *Conflicts*, once again, "alienation

[13] 1945. Henceforth referred to as *"Conflicts,"* and identified as *"IC"* in references.

from self" has the sense of obliviousness to the "real self." And obviously, if "paralysis of initiative and action" is the *result* of this "alienation from self," the two cannot be one and the same in meaning.

Since Horney speaks of "what one really feels, likes, rejects, believes," the type of person in question apparently is to be understood actually to have certain definite feelings, likes and dislikes, and beliefs and opinions. He has them—but he is said to be "oblivious" to them. The term "oblivious" commonly suggests a casual disregard; but Horney quite clearly does not intend it to be understood in this way. It is less clear, however, how she *does* intend it to be understood. Her brief gloss is of little help; she merely tells us such things as that the kind of person in question is in a "permanent condition of being unreal to himself." (*IC*, 111)

The expression "to be oblivious to" means "to be unmindful or forgetful of," or, more informally, "to be unaware of," or possibly, "to pay no attention to," "to fail to recognize," or "to ignore." The first question one wants to ask is whether a person can legitimately be said to *have* feelings, likes, wishes, and opinions of which he is unaware. We have become accustomed to this idea in connection with the notions of repression and self-deception; but it would not seem that either of them is what Horney has in mind. The idea may be a defensible one, but only if the problem of the criteria of such feelings, opinions, etc., is dealt with satisfactorily; and this is a problem to which she does not address herself.

The issue is further clouded by a statement she makes which raises doubts about whether she really is committed to this idea. She states that the type of person in question "does not know what he really wants." (*IC*, 111) This description is sometimes used to suggest that someone really does want something, but is unaware that *that* is what he wants. But it is also often used to suggest that there is *no* specific thing he really wants: A decision, rather than a discovery, may be what is needed. Should the latter be the proper interpretation of this passage, and of the one initially under consideration as well, the problem of how feelings and opinions of which one is unaware disappears; but then the use of "oblivious" becomes incomprehensible.

Assuming the former interpretation to be the proper one, a further problem arises. It is not clear whether the type of person Horney is describing is to be understood as completely unaware of his "real self," or as engaged in a continuing struggle to put it out of his mind—thereby retaining at least some degree of awareness of it. The term "oblivious" is noncommittal on this score, while the description "does not know what he wants" suggests the former. Horney's example of the man whose "pride in his respectability alienates him from his unsavory past," however, suggests the latter; for one rarely succeeds in completely blotting his past from his memory. It would be inappropriate to say of someone who has succeeded in doing so that he "desperately . . . clings to the belief that he is his idealized image." (IC, 111) This characterization in turn gives rise to further problems. Could a person who "desperately clings" to such a belief be described as "oblivious" to his "real self"?

In short, Horney's discussion of "alienation from self" in *Conflicts,* while differing from that in *New Ways,* is no less free from difficulties and perplexities. This may be explained by the brevity of her discussion of the issues in question in each case; but an explanation of this sort does nothing to resolve the problems which arise.

III. *Neurosis and Human Growth*

In Horney's last book, *Neurosis and Human Growth* (8),[14] both of her earlier conceptions of "alienation from self" reappear. They are explicitly distinguished and defined on the basis of a distinction between two types or dimensions of the "self": the "actual self" and the "real self."

> The actual self is an all-inclusive term for everything that a person is at a given time. . . . The real self . . . is the "original" force toward individual growth and fulfillment, with which we may again achieve full identification when freed of the crippling shackles of neurosis. (NG, 158)

The "actual self" is further characterized in terms of one's

[14] Published in 1950. Henceforth referred to as *"Neurosis,"* and identified as *"NG"* in references.

"feelings, wishes, beliefs, and energies," and also "his past." (NG, 156–57) The "real self," on the other hand, is to be conceived as "that most alive center of ourselves," which "engenders the spontaneity of feelings," and "is the source of spontaneous interest and energies." (NG, 157) Clearly the "real self" here is to be identified with the "spontaneous individual self" of *New Ways*; while the "actual self" is to be identified with the "real self" of *Conflicts*. Thus the expression "real self" here takes on a meaning very different from that which it has in *Conflicts*. Having distinguished these two types or dimensions of "self," Horney then introduces two types of "alienation from self": "alienation from the actual self" and "alienation from the real self." The former roughly corresponds to the type discussed in *Conflicts*, while the latter approximates that discussed in *New Ways*. She states that "one cannot always distinguish neatly between alienation from the actual self and that from the real self." (NG, 158) It is not clear whether this means anything more than that one rarely comes across pure cases of either type. But it obviously must be possible to specify some sort of difference between them if it is to be meaningful to employ the different designations.

"Alienation from the Actual Self"

"Alienation from the actual self" is said to consist of the "blotting out or dimming" of "all of what a person actually is or has, including even his connection of his present life with his past." Its "core" is "the remoteness of his own feelings, wishes, beliefs, and energies." (NG, 156–57) It is presumably this type of "alienation from self" which Horney has in mind when she uses this expression in connection with a person's "unawareness of his own feelings, thoughts, or actions" (NG, 123), his failure to "own up to the existence of his own wishes" (NG, 115), and the tendency he may have to "override his genuine feelings, wishes, and thoughts," to the extent that they are "silenced and have become indistinct." (NG, 21)

These characterizations imply that the type of person under consideration actually has feelings, wishes, beliefs, etc. "of his own." For one cannot be "remote from" them or fail

to "own up to" them if they do not exist. The problem thus
is to determine the degree of awareness of them which this
type of person is supposed to have. In one passage Horney
explicitly states that he is "unaware" of them. This, together
with her assertions that they are "blotted out" and "silenced,"
would appear to indicate an answer incompatible with the
suggestion that such a person *is* aware of them, though only
"dimly," "remotely," and "indistinctly." But perhaps she
means to suggest that there are different degrees of severity
of such alienation; and that dim awareness characterizes the
milder cases, while unawareness characterizes the more severe.
This interpretation would take care of the difficulty which
seems to arise here, and the similar one which arises in her
discussion in *Conflicts*.

Shortly after she introduces the notion of "alienation from
the actual self" in these terms, however, she presents a quite
different picture of what it involves. It now is characterized
as "the subjective feeling of the neurotic of being removed
from himself." And, describing "moves" which have it as
their result, she speaks of one's becoming "ashamed of what
he actually is—of his feelings, resources, activities," and coming to feel "self-hate." (NG, 160) But this is quite different
from being unaware or only dimly aware of what one actually is and feels. For hating and being ashamed of what one
is and feels involves a vivid awareness of the things in question. The same formal description—"being removed from
oneself"—can be employed in both types of cases; but this
formal similarity conceals a very real and important difference
between the kinds of phenomena or mental states involved.
Horney also says of the self-alienated person that he "talks
about his most intimate personal life experiences," and often
shows considerable insight in doing so. "Yet they have lost
their personal meaning. . . . *His relation to himself has become impersonal. . . .*" (NG, 161; Horney's emphasis.) Setting aside the fact that one might want to distinguish cases
of this sort from cases of hating or being ashamed of oneself,
the problem here obviously is not that the person is unaware
or only dimly aware of his "actual self."

In these passages a set of criteria quite different from that
specified above is indicated, relating to the degree of accept-

ance and affirmation of what one recognizes one's "actual self" to be; and the personality disorder it reflects would seem to be rather different from the one initially specified. Horney states that she is here describing "only one aspect of the phenomenon" of "alienation from the actual self." But she cannot be describing an aspect of the *same* phenomenon so labeled previously, because it is characterized in terms of traits (pertaining to self-awareness) which are incompatible with certain essential traits of the latter.

Another difficulty arises because Horney sometimes speaks of "alienation from the actual self" in such a way that she blurs the distinction between it and "alienation from the real self," even while attempting to distinguish them. She says of the former:

> It is the loss of the feeling of being an active determining force in his [i.e., the neurotic's] own life. It is the loss of feeling himself as an organic whole. These *in turn indicate* an alienation from that most alive center of ourselves which I have suggested calling the *real* self. (NG, 157; first emphasis added.)

Her explicit statement that the traits in question "in turn indicate" the existence of "alienation from the real self" shows that, while she feels there is a connection between the two, she does not intend the distinction between them thereby to collapse. But if "alienation from the actual self" is to be conceived in terms of a "loss of the feeling of being an active determining force in one's own life," the only visible difference between the characterizations of the two lies in the reference to "feeling" in the "actual self" case. For the failure to *be* "an active determining force in one's own life" (whatever that may mean) would seem to differ little from the failure to develop "a spontaneous individual self" which is definitive of "alienation from the real self." This, however, would reduce the difference between the two types of "alienation from self" to the difference between an objective condition and its subjective counterpart. It is clear from her remarks elsewhere that Horney considers the difference to be more substantial than this. But if the above passage is taken seriously, it is difficult to see just what this more substantial difference might be.

"Alienation from the Real Self"

The situation is further complicated by the fact that she sometimes uses the expression "alienation from the real self" in such a way that the distinction seems to collapse from the other end. The "real self," once again, is characterized as "that most alive center of ourselves" which is the "source" of "spontaneous interest and energies" and "the spontaneity of feelings." (NG, 157) Horney also refers to it as "the spring of emotional forces, of constructive energies, of directive and judiciary powers" (NG, 173–74), and "the 'original' force toward individual growth and fulfillment." (NG, 158) "Alienation from the real self" involves ceasing to be animated by the energies springing from this "spring" or "source," which Horney also refers to as "the core of our being." (NG, 165) Here the "real self" becomes "inactive." (NG, 173) To be "alienated from the real self" is to be "alienated from that most alive center of ourselves." (NG, 157) It is to be cut off from or deprived of access to this source of energy.

The "real self" here would seem to be the analog in Horney's system to Freud's libido; and "alienation from the real self" would appear to be analogous to Freud's repression of libidinal energies. The basic idea is thus relatively comprehensible. But it is less clear why the use of the term "self" is appropriate in this connection. For while the source or force in question may plausibly be characterized as "the core of our being," the "self" is usually conceived to be something essentially more individuated than is a basic dynamic principle of this sort.

Horney appears to have used the term because she wants to refer not only to this force or source as such, but also the general type of selfhood which she associates with animation by it, and moreover to the particular self which the individual would have (or be) if he realized this type of selfhood. This modification or extension of the notion of the "real self" is implicit in her further remarks concerning what is involved in "alienation from the real self." For she goes on to speak of the "real self" in such alienation as being "abandoned," "exiled" and "disavowed," "eliminated," "locked out," and "shut away," so that one "cannot consult with it."

Even if due allowance is made for the fact that these expressions are rather metaphorical, it is clear that the "real self" cannot be construed along the lines of the basic source or force of Horney's initial characterization, when such metaphors are used in connection with it. It would make no sense to speak of "abandoning," "disavowing," or being unable to "consult with" one's "real self" if it is so conceived. It is only if the notion is modified along the lines suggested above that such statements become intelligible.

Much more needs to be said in order to render both the initial and the modified notions of the "real self" sufficiently clear. But it should already be obvious that it makes a considerable difference whether the expression is understood one way or the other, when one is attempting to understand what is involved in "alienation from the real self." For if it is understood in one way, such alienation would appear to consist in being cut off from a source of energy which in some sense actually exists within one, as "the core of one's being." (How could this be "eliminated"?) Whereas, if it is understood in the other way, such alienation would seem to consist in failing or ceasing to realize a certain type of selfhood, which therefore cannot be conceived actually to exist. Whatever the fruitfulness of the notions of such alienation deriving from the different uses of "real self" taken singly, Horney's use of the expression in both ways only invites confusion.

Even more unfortunately, she at times also uses the expressions "real self" and "alienation from the real self" virtually interchangeably with "actual self" and "alienation from the actual self." In her most systematic discussion of what is involved in alienation of the former sort, she suggests that it is characterized initially by "active moves away from the real self," in an attempt to be "something different from what [one] is or could be." (NG, 159) To identify the "real self" with "what one is or could be," however, is to identify it with the "actual self," which Horney explicitly defines as "everything that a person is" (NG, 158)—including, presumably, the actual capabilities to which she is referring with the words "could be." She thus fails to maintain the distinctions she proposes between types or levels of "self" and alienation.

Conclusion

At this point one might be inclined to abandon the distinctions she has such difficulty maintaining, and to allow the term "self" and the expression "alienation from self" to comprehend all of the things she tries to distinguish. But this would decrease rather than increase their utility. Horney deserves credit for recognizing that the domain with which she is concerned is too complex for them to be employed so generally without thereby obscuring important distinctions. She does not draw all of those which should be drawn, and she often fails to maintain those she does draw; but this does not detract from the soundness of her judgment concerning the need for something like the differentiations she attempts.

Her own discussion, while suggestive, falls short in that it does not adequately meet this need. And so, unfortunately, do those of subsequent writers who have taken her discussion as their point of departure. Some simply adopt one or the other of her conceptions of "alienation from self," and then go on to discuss some specific problem in terms of it.[15] Others devote themselves to the detailed exposition of Horney's discussion; but they tend to be so faithful to it that they merely perpetuate the problems it raises, and make no progress in the direction of their resolution.[16] The few who go further than this do so only to the extent of giving a somewhat different twist to some particular detail of Horney's theory, without substantially affecting the problems suggested above.[17]

The term "alienation" does not become virtually meaningless through indiscriminate use in Horney's hands, as it does in Fromm's. She is considerably more selective and rigorous in her employment of it than he is, even in his discussion of "alienation from oneself." Nonetheless, serious problems

[15] E.g., Kelman (11), Martin (12), DeRosis (3), Becker (1, 2).
[16] E.g., Weiss (17), Vollmerhausen (16).
[17] E.g., Schachtel (15), Wenkart (18), Rubins (13).

of both clarity and consistency arise in connection with her use of the term and her explications of its meaning. It is unclear whether these problems reflect basic inadequacies of her psychoanalytical theory, or simply inadequacies of presentation and elaboration. Unless they can be resolved, however, the fruitfulness of her notion of "alienation from self" will remain questionable.

5 The Sociological Literature

To say the least, such opposing conceptualizations of alienation make for serious communication problems as well as for conceptual and methodological difficulties in theory construction.

NEAL AND RETTIG (23, 62–63)

I. Introduction

In recent years American sociological journals have carried a large number of articles on the subject of alienation. This is one of the manifestations of what Robert Nisbet terms "the central place occupied by the hypothesis of alienation in contemporary social science." (25, 15) Books have appeared on such topics as "Alienated Youth in American Society" (13) and "The Alienated Voter" (14); and Talcott Parsons's and Edward Shils' concept of alienation figures importantly in their analysis of "the dynamic problems and processes of the social system." (27, 157) The use of the term in this literature constitutes the background in terms of which many recent references to alienation in popular social analysis and criticism must be understood. Moreover, many sociologists seem to share the assumption that in "alienation" they have found a scientifically fruitful concept.

Few generalizations can be made concerning the use of the term by sociologists. One general point that can be made is that their use of it is quite different from Fromm's (and Horney's). Generally speaking, they do not use it in any of the major contexts in which Fromm does. Only a few do so in connection with work and interpersonal relationships; and few, if any, speak of man's "alienation" from nature, things, or himself. For Fromm, virtually the only thing from which "modern man" is *not* alienated is society. His concern is that man today is an "automaton conformist," all too completely at one with society. Many sociologists, on the other hand, conceive alienation precisely in terms of some form of separation of the individual from some aspect of society. In Fromm's view, conformity goes hand in hand with alienation, as that through which man *becomes* alienated (from himself). Whereas for Parsons, for example, alienation is the very *opposite* of conformity, or at any rate is at the opposite end of a "conformity-alienation" continuum. (26, 32)

Sociologists differ from Fromm, and also from Marx, in another respect. The latter both hold that it is possible, and even common, for men to be unaware of their alienation. They take the position that it is a fact about many men that they are alienated from themselves; and that this fact is ascertainable in particular cases by contrasting the individual's actual condition with his essential nature or an ideal of selfhood. For sociologists, on the other hand, "alienation is a psychological state of an individual." (4, 849)[1] It is conceived solely in terms of the presence of certain attitudes and feelings; the question of an essential nature of man or an ideal of selfhood does not even arise. Moreover, an appropriate response to questions or statements designed to "tap" these feelings and attitudes is regarded as both necessary and sufficient to determine their presence. Thus there is no question of alienated individuals who are not aware of their alienation (though of course the alienated individual need not actually apply this term to himself).

Beyond this, it is difficult to generalize about the use of the term in recent sociological literature. Its use in connection with some form of separation of the individual from some aspect of society is its most common one, and is perhaps the one that is most uniquely sociological; but it is by no means its only one. At least some writers do use the term in con-

[1] See also 13, 465; 14, 59; 25, 245; 34, 457.

nection with work and interpersonal relationships. And more importantly, a number use it in connection with the phenomena of "powerlessness" and "meaninglessness."

This suggests that uses of the term from a number of different historical sources come together in the body of literature under consideration. Its use in connection with separation from society is reminiscent of Hegel. Marx's early writings are recalled by its uses in connection with work, powerlessness, and perhaps also (in the special sense intended) "meaninglessness." And the use of the term in connection with separation from other people has long been a common one.

While sociologists are quite willing to make these distinctions, many of them seem to assume that a connection between the different phenomena mentioned is indicated by the fact of their common designation. One often finds a writer listing a number of different uses of the term, then referring to the corresponding phenomena as different "types" of alienation, and subsequently speaking of them as so many "dimensions," "aspects," or "elements" of alienation. The implication—that the term "alienation" designates a single (albeit complex) phenomenon—is frequently affirmed explicitly. The apparent diversity of the things subsumed under the term—when it is discussed at all—is usually handled simply by adopting the expedient of suggesting "the concept of alienation" (and the corresponding phenomenon) to be "multidimensional."

But of course, no significant relation between phenomena is established by the mere fact that the same term is used to refer to them severally. The example of the three traditional uses of "alienation"—in connection with the transfer of property, mental derangement, and separation from others —is sufficient to illustrate this point. In each case something becomes "alien" in some way; but while this formal similarity accounts for the use of the term in all three contexts, it would be absurd to conclude that it warrants regarding the three things as three "aspects" of a single "multidimensional" phenomenon: "alienation."

The attempts of sociologists to deal in this way with the various instances of "alienation" with which they are concerned may not be so patently absurd. But the term is used in so many different connections in their writings that it cannot plausibly be viewed as designating a single (unidimensional or multidimensional) phenomenon, or even a syndrome of such phenomena. Some of the phenomena in connection with which it is used may plausibly be associated. Others, however, have nothing at all to do with each other; and some even preclude each other.

II. Alienation and Others

Sociologists' use of the term in connection with the relation of the individual to others is traceable in some cases to the influence of Marx, and in other cases simply to the ordinary use of the term in this context. But the particular interests of different writers lead them to modify the Marxian and ordinary conceptions of alienation from others in various ways. The conceptions of such alienation to be found in their writings must thus be distinguished from both, and frequently from each other as well.

Alienation as Loneliness

For some writers, *loneliness* is conceived as a type of alienation. Middleton, for example, considers the term to be applicable in the event of agreement with the statement, "I often feel lonely." (20, 974) Similarly, McClosky and Schaar use the term to refer to "the feeling of loneliness and yearning for supportive primary relationships." (17, 30) To be alienated, they contend, is to feel a lack of meaningful relationships with other people, and to feel unhappy about this lack. One does not exemplify this type of alienation, therefore, if one either (1) does not feel that he lacks such relationships, or (2) senses their absence, but does not feel unhappy about it, or (3) feels related meaningfully to *some* other people, even if not to all. For if any of these conditions obtains, one cannot properly be said to "feel lonely."

This type of alienation from others must thus be distinguished from Fromm's central, much broader type, which is so conceived that it obtains whenever a certain particular kind of relatedness to others is lacking, whether or not this lack is regretted or even recognized. It must also be distinguished from Marx's, which is to be construed in terms of such quite different criteria as the lack of respect for others and the willingness to exploit them. And it must further be distinguished from ordinary estrangement, which involves a *loss* (rather than the mere absence) of closeness, and which need not be general before it can be said to obtain.

Some writers characterize this type of alienation from others in terms of "social isolation." The term "social" is ambiguous, however, and can mean both "societal" and "interpersonal." "Social isolation" can thus be construed both in the sense of the absence of positive interpersonal relationships, and in the sense of disassociation from the norms, values, and culture of one's society. The distinction is important; but as the examples of Dean (7, 755) and Struening and Richardson (36, 769–70) show, it tends to be obscured when the type of alienation under consideration is characterized in these terms. As long as the reference is to interpersonal relationships, the term "loneliness" is better suited to its explication.

The writers who speak of alienation in connection with loneliness seem not to recognize that two types of it must be distinguished. An individual who tries unsuccessfully to establish meaningful contact with others is in a different situation from one who *chooses* to live alone, in order (for example) to achieve some special purpose. The latter may feel lonely, and may long for the companionship he denies himself; but the fact that his isolation is of his own choosing gives his alienation a quality that sets it apart from that of one whose isolation is not chosen.

Alienation as Lack of Solidarity

The conception of alienation from others presented by Hajda is easily confused with both simple loneliness and disassociation from the values and culture of one's society; but it is distinct from them. Hajda characterizes it in terms of the feeling of a lack of that solidarity with others which derives from the knowledge that one shares their views, interests, and tastes. For him, to be alienated is to feel "*uncomfortably*

different in the presence of [others] because of [one's] views
. . . interests . . . personal tastes, [etc.]." (10, 764)

Hajda rightly takes pains to distinguish this feeling from
the feeling of the alienness of the views, interests, and tastes
in question themselves. Alienation, as he conceives it, is an
awareness of "non-belonging or non-sharing" which "reflects
[one's] exclusion or self-exclusion from social and cultural
participation." (10, 758) As a "reflection" of this disassociation, it presupposes the latter, but "is not identical with [it]."
(10, 762) Its definitive characteristic is the feeling of difference from *others* which *results* from the perception of a
difference between their views, interests, and tastes and one's
own.

Alienation from others, so conceived, must not be confused
with alienation conceived in terms of loneliness. The latter
exists only when one feels that one has *no* close interpersonal
relationships; but the former does not require that one feel
uncomfortably different from everyone before it can be said
to exist. Moreover, neither feeling implies the presence of
the other. A person may have a warm relationship with his
parents, for example, yet feel uncomfortably different from
them insofar as their views, tastes, and interests are concerned. On the other hand, a person who feels that he lacks
close relationships with others may still feel a general, impersonal solidarity with them by virtue of the way of life he
shares with them.[2] Both types of alienation are to be conceived in terms of one's relations to others; but they occur
on quite different levels of interpersonal interaction.

Alienation as Dissatisfaction in Social Relations

Aiken and Hage's "alienation from expressive relations" is
a type of alienation from others which would appear to be
distinct from both of the types discussed above. They characterize it in terms of "dissatisfaction in social relations." (1,
497) Their criterion for the existence of such alienation consists simply in asking for a Yes-or-No answer to the question

[2] The difference between the types of unity in question here is
similar to that between the solidarity which is the concomitant of
Hegelian universality and the community of Marxian sociality. See
pp. 89–90.

of whether one is "satisfied" with those with whom one associates. In their case, this means one's "supervisor" and one's "fellow workers," since it is the work situation with which they are concerned. (1, 501)

This criterion—unfortunately, all too typical of the measures employed by the writers discussed in this chapter—is obviously extremely crude. Still, it does enable one to form at least a general idea of Aiken and Hage's concept of alienation. They claim that it "can be compared" with Marx's concept of "alienation from fellow workers" (1, 497); but the two are hardly identical. Dissatisfaction with those with whom one associates neither implies nor is implied by the kind of antagonism Marx has in mind. And whereas dissatisfaction suggests that a change of associates might result in a different attitude, the antagonism of which Marx speaks is a function of the egoism of the individual, and persists so long as this egoism does.[3]

Dissatisfaction with one's particular group of associates is quite compatible with a feeling of solidarity with them by virtue of shared tastes and values, and is thus distinct from Hajda's type of alienation. For it need reflect no "exclusion from social and cultural participation" with them, but may have quite other sources; and it is only if one's discomfort in their presence derives from this exclusion that alienation in Hajda's sense exists. Dissatisfaction with one's associates is also distinct from alienation conceived in terms of loneliness. For the problem giving rise to the dissatisfaction may be, not that one feels unable to enter into close relationships with one's present associates (these may exist), but rather (for example) that one wishes one had some more interesting and exciting friends as well. In short, the use of the criterion of dissatisfaction yields a different conception of alienation from others than does the use of the criterion of either loneliness or the "non-sharing" of interests, values, and tastes.

Concluding Remarks

The term "alienation" is employed in connection with the relations of the individual to others by relatively few sociolo-

[3] See pp. 102–08.

gists. Even so, however, there is considerable diversity in its employment in this connection. This exemplifies, on a small scale, one of the basic problems associated with the use of the term in recent sociological literature. Its employment by some writers in a certain general context seems to lead others to follow suit; but the tendency to do so is not powerful enough to produce uniformity in the employment of the term. On the contrary, different writers tend to use it in different ways, resulting in a proliferation of conceptions of alienation. The writers in question, however, seem to be unaware of this result. Indeed, one gets the impression that they think they are all discussing the same thing. This may be understandable, since the same term is employed in the same general context in each case; but they are, in fact, discussing quite different phenomena. And in addition to being mistaken, the assumption that the same thing is being discussed has unfortunate results, in that it suggests a pooling of correlations between the different types of alienation and other phenomena, which is unwarranted.

The use of the term "alienation" in the context under consideration is one of its best-established and most appropriate uses. If it is to be fruitful in sociological discussion, however, rather than a source of confusion and misunderstanding, it must either be employed in connection with a single type of interpersonal disunity (in which case it would be proper to speak of such alienation as a phenomenon to be correlated with other phenomena); or it must be employed as a general term which comprehends a variety of types of interpersonal disunity, but which is recognized not to refer specifically to any one of them.

III. Alienation and Work

Another context in which the term "alienation" is sometimes employed in recent sociological literature is that of the relation of the individual to his work. Here again, however, there is no uniformity in the way in which "alienation from work" or "alienated work" is conceived, in spite of the fact that virtually all of those who use the expressions acknowledge that they do so under the influence of Marx.[4] Such "alienation" is variously conceived in terms of dissatisfaction with one's job, the experience of one's work activity as not being intrinsically rewarding, and its experience as being insufficiently self-directed, meaningful, and self-expressive.

Alienation and Job Satisfaction

Aiken and Hage conceive of "alienation from work" in terms of the existence of a "feeling of disappointment" concerning one's position of employment. (1, 497) They consider it to exist to the extent that one is not "satisfied" with such things as one's position relative to other workers, the recognition extended to one by one's superiors, and the degree to which one's job measures up to one's "career expectations." (1, 501) They are thus concerned less with the nature of the work performed than with considerations pertaining to professional status. "Alienation from work" here is conceived in terms of dissatisfaction with the limitations associated with the occupation of one's position in the hierarchy of employment.

Aiken and Hage suggest that their conception of "alienation from work" is similar to Marx's conception of "alienation from the process of production." (1, 497) In fact, however, it is considerably different. The crucial consideration for Marx is that of whether or not one's productive activity is spontaneous and self-directed, and has no end other than the expression and development of one's personality. But it is quite possible for this not to be the case, and yet for one to be quite content with one's job. Indeed, cases of this sort would seem to be quite common today. A chief postal clerk may be quite satisfied with the authority he has, with his position in relation to his fellow workers, and with the way in which his superiors regard him; and his position may satisfy his initial and career job expectations completely. Such a person would not be "alienated from his work," given the criteria employed by Aiken and Hage. But it would be quite appro-

---

[4] The use of the term "labor," rather than "work," to translate Marx's term *Arbeit*, is largely a matter of convention. Both are standard renderings of the German word.

priate to speak of the "alienation of labor" here as Marx conceives of it.

Alienation and the Intrinsic Reward of Work

A number of other writers remain at least closer to Marx, by focusing upon the issue of the degree to which an individual finds the work he does intrinsically rewarding or enjoyable. Seeman, for example, conceives of "alienated work" as "work which is not intrinsically satisfying," and measures "work alienation" in terms of negative responses to questions which "ask essentially whether the respondent finds his work engaging and rewarding in itself." (31, 273, 275) Similarly, Middleton considers a person "alienated" from his work if he would concur with the statement, "I don't really enjoy most of the work that I do, but I feel that I must do it in order to have other things that I need and want." (20, 974)

Miller explicitly distinguishes between job satisfaction and satisfaction taken in the work done on the job, and observes that it is quite possible for the former to exist and at the same time for the latter to be lacking. (21, 759) And in fact it is not at all unusual to hear someone say something like, "It's a decent enough job, as far as that goes, but I couldn't be less interested in the work I have to do." For Miller, as for Seeman, "The measure of work alienation . . . [consists] of statements referring to the intrinsic pride or meaning of work." One is considered alienated from his work if he fails to find it "self-rewarding," and "works merely for his salary." (21, 759)

The idea that work is to be considered alienated if it is not felt to be intrinsically rewarding recalls Marx's characterization of "alienated labor" as labor which is not performed for its own sake, as an end in itself. And Marx too refers specifically to labor which is performed merely for the sake of the wages received for it. The conception of "alienated work" under consideration does differ from Marx's, however, in that it is subjectivized, so that the expression becomes applicable only in cases in which the individual actually *feels* that his work is not intrinsically rewarding.

Alienation and Control, Meaning, and Self-expression in Work

Robert Blauner also conceives of "alienation in the work process" as a "quality of personal experience." (2, 15) He purports to be concerned with alienation more generally, which he characterizes in the following way:

> Alienation exists when workers are unable to control their immediate work processes, to develop a sense of purpose and function which connects their jobs to the overall organization of production, to belong to integrated industrial communities, and when they fail to become involved in the activity of work as a mode of personal self-expression. (2, 15)

If the third factor mentioned (which refers to interpersonal relations) is set aside, however, the alienation Blauner has in mind emerges as a condition to be conceived fundamentally in terms of the relation of the individual to his work.[5] The first "aspect" or "dimension" of this alienation is characterized in terms of the absence of *personal control* over what is to be produced, how it is to be produced, and what is to be done with it once it is finished. (2, 16–22) The second concerns the *meaninglessness* of work to the worker: He makes so small a "contribution to the final product," by virtue of the division of labor and the standardization of production, that what he does seems meaningless to him. (2, 23) And the last is conceived in terms of the absence of any opportunity for *self-expression* in the work he does, so that it "does not express the unique abilities, potentialities, or personality of the worker." (2, 26)

Work of this sort is very much like Marx's "alienated labor." There is one difference, however, in addition to

[5] Justification for separating the third factor from the other three is provided by Blauner himself, when he observes that it and they are independent of each other: ". . . there is no necessary causal relation between social alienation and self-alienation. A worker may be integrated in the plant community and loyal to the company and still fail to achieve a sense of involvement and self-expression in his work activity itself." (2, 28) And, one might add, vice versa.

Blauner's subjectivization of the notion, which is also a further difference between Blauner's conception and that discussed immediately above. The feature he mentions most
closely approximating the "lack of intrinsic satisfaction" which
is central for writers like Seeman and Miller, is "meaninglessness." But the two are not identical; for work apparently
can have "meaning" in Blauner's view—and therefore may
not be "meaningless"—without being *intrinsically* meaningful.
All he requires is that one feel that his work contributes
significantly to a meaningful result. If it derives its meaningfulness solely from the result to which it merely contributes, however, it is not meaningful *in itself*.

Miller, on the other hand, together with Seeman and Middleton, considers anyone alienated from his work who does
not find "intrinsic meaning" in it. (21, 759) Miller's actual
use of the term "meaning" allows the issue to be posed
squarely. Many people who can be characterized as alienated
from their work if the criterion of "intrinsic meaningfulness"
is employed, cannot be so characterized if the criterion is
simply that of the "meaninglessness" of their work to them
generally. Blauner contrasts work which is "an end in itself"
with work which is "a means to an end" (2, 32); but the
consideration he has in mind is simply that of whether or
not the work is done solely for the wages received. Work
that is more meaningful *than this* is not necessarily work
that is *intrinsically* meaningful or satisfying.

Concluding Remarks

"Alienated work" or "alienation from work" is thus conceived by the various sociologists who speak of it in at least
three different ways: in terms of (1) job dissatisfaction, (2)
the feeling that one's work is not intrinsically satisfying, and
(3) dissatisfaction with the degree to which one's work is
self-directed, meaningful to one, and self-expressive. Common
to all three conceptions is the idea of conscious dissatisfaction
in the work situation, which alone suffices to distinguish
them from Marx's conception; for Marx does not hesitate
to speak of "alienated labor" even in the absence of actual
worker dissatisfaction. The three conceptions differ from

each other with reference to the condition in the work situation on which the dissatisfaction focuses.

A case can be made for using the term "alienation" in connection with each of the dissatisfactions mentioned. If it is to be used in connection with *all* of them, however, "alienation from work" cannot be construed merely as "a multidimensional, rather than a unitary, conception," as Blauner suggests. (2, 15) Rather, it would have to be conceived even more loosely, as a category subsuming a variety of phenomena some of which are quite independent of others.

IV. Alienation, Events, and Structures

In speaking of the existence of a relation of alienation between the worker and his product, Marx has in mind, among other things, the domination of the product—and thereby of the worker himself, by virtue of his dependence upon it—by "alien and hostile" economic forces. This has given rise to the employment of the term by a considerable number of sociologists in connection with the feeling that one is unable to control or even understand the social, economic, and, above all, political events and structures which affect him. This represents a substantial departure from Marx, who restricts his employment of the term in this context to the worker-product relation, and does not even use it to refer to the relation of the worker to the forces which control his product—let alone to social, economic, and political forces and events generally. Still, it would appear that it is in Marx that the historical impetus for this use of the term is to be found.

Most of the writers who employ the term in this general connection recognize that alienation conceived in terms of the feeling of "powerlessness" in the face of existing structures and events is to be distinguished from alienation conceived in terms of a sense of their "meaninglessness." The precise conditions under which the different writers consider the term to be applicable vary considerably, however; and an examination of the literature reveals that there are at least six different conceptions of alienation in operation, rather than just two.

Alienation and the Feeling of Powerlessness

While some writers fail to distinguish between the fact and the feeling of "powerlessness," it is plain from their remarks that it is the latter with which those who conceive of alienation in terms of "powerlessness" are concerned. Seeman explicates this conception of alienation as follows: "This variant of alienation can be conceived as the expectancy or probability held by the individual that his own behavior cannot determine . . . the outcomes . . . he seeks." (30, 784) Similar formulations are given by many others.[6] Some do not place any explicit restrictions on the types of "outcomes" with which these expectancies may be concerned. It seems to be a matter of general agreement, however, that they are primarily those which "have to do with the individual's sense of influence over sociopolitical events." (30, 785)

One is considered alienated in the sense under consideration to the extent that one expresses agreement with such statements as, "There is not much that I can do about most of the important problems that we face today." (20, 973) In some cases it would appear that the requisite sense of powerlessness need not be very unrealistic. Neal and Rettig, for example, test for this type of alienation by devising statements which elicit the individual's feeling of influence in relation to "some of the major political and economic concerns of the contemporary period," such as war and inflation. (22, 601) Other writers focus upon the issue of perceived political influence. Thus Seeman considers such alienation to be indicated by agreement with the statement, "This world is run by the few people in power, and there is not much the little guy can do about it." (30, 775)

In short, the type of alienation under consideration is to be conceived solely in terms of the felt *inability to influence* social, political, and economic events and structures significantly. It is the sense of powerlessness itself, rather than any attitudes which might be associated with it, which is definitive of alienation here. Thus Seeman is careful to distinguish it not only from the fact of powerlessness, but also from both

[6] E.g., Middleton (20), Levin (14), and Neal and Rettig (22).

the feeling that one's powerlessness is *wrong*, and the feeling that it is otherwise *objectionable*. (30, 784–85; 33, 775) And he and others also distinguish this feeling of impotence from the feeling that one is unable to *understand* these events and structures adequately.[7]

Alienation and the Wrongness of Powerlessness

The term "alienation" also is frequently used to refer not to the feeling of powerlessness itself, but rather to several of these related phenomena, and to certain others in this general area as well. For Thompson and Horton, the feeling of powerlessness gives rise to, rather than itself constitutes, what they call "political alienation." "Political alienation is most accurately understood as . . . *a reaction to* perceived relative inability to influence or to control one's social destiny." (37, 191; emphasis added.) Thompson and Horton do not consider a person alienated if he merely feels that he lacks this ability. For them, the term becomes applicable only if, in addition, "this powerlessness is regarded as in some sense illegitimate." (12, 486)

Similarly, Levin's "alienated voters" do not merely feel politically powerless, but "feel angry [and] resentful" about their powerlessness. (14, vii) And Levin does not consider their belief that their powerlessness is wrong to be a mere concomitant of their alienation; he terms it "the essential characteristic" of their alienation. (14, 59)

Clark too defines "alienation" in terms of the feeling that the control which one feels one lacks is "rightfully his." He states: "A measure of alienation must be a measure of the discrepancy between the power a man believes he has and what he believes he should have." (4, 849) In short, alienation is conceived by these writers in terms of the presence of a feeling which Seeman explicitly (and correctly) distinguishes from the feeling of powerlessness itself, and thus from the type of alienation defined in terms of it: the feeling of the wrongness of one's powerlessness.

[7] This distinction is discussed further on pp. 177–78.

Alienation, Distrust, and Apathy

Yet another conception is employed by McDill and Ridley. They too conceive of "political alienation" in terms of a certain type of "response to" the feeling of powerlessness, rather than simply in terms of this feeling itself. The response they have in mind, however, is not the one discussed above. Rather, it is a twofold response, consisting of distrust of those in power and political apathy. According to them, "Political alienation involves . . . apathy as a response to political powerlessness [and] also a general distrust of political leaders who are the wielders of this power." (*18, 206–07*)

McDill and Ridley seem to make apathy and distrust jointly necessary as well as sufficient conditions for the use of the expression. As the studies of Levin, Thompson and Horton, and others show, however, distrust of political leaders not only is conceptually distinct from apathy, but also can give rise to political activism instead. If it is considered desirable to term both the apathetic and the distrustful "alienated," therefore, it is necessary to distinguish two different conceptions of alienation here.

Apathy and distrust not only need not accompany each other; they also need not accompany the feeling of powerlessness or the feeling that one's powerlessness is wrong. With regard to the former, it is becoming quite common to see people who feel powerless resorting to active protest against their very powerlessness, rather than submitting passively to it. And one can feel powerless without feeling distrustful of those in power, as have countless numbers of people who have trusted in political leaders upon whom they have realized they had no influence. With regard to the feeling that one's powerlessness is wrong, this can quite easily lead to activism or protest rather than apathy. And one can have confidence in one's leaders while at the same time feeling that one does not have the political influence one should have; this feeling by no means implies distrust.

Thus if all those are to be termed "alienated" who either feel powerless, or feel both powerless and that they are wrongly so, or are distrustful of those in power, or are apathetic in the face of the existing power structure, one must distinguish four different conceptions of alienation here.

Alienation and the Incomprehensibility of Events

Several other uses of the term in this general context remain to be mentioned. One has already been indicated, which is commonly but misleadingly characterized in terms of "meaninglessness." Those who speak of "alienation" in the sense of "meaninglessness" do not have in mind a feeling of the general "meaninglessness of life," or of over-all "purposelessness." The latter are explicitly distinguished from the former by Dean (7, 754) and Struening and Richardson. (36, 769–70)

Seeman explicates the type of "meaninglessness" in question in terms of "a low expectancy that satisfactory predictions about future outcomes of behavior can be made." The kind of alienation defined in terms of it is thus a matter of "the individual's sense of understanding the events in which he is engaged," or which affect him. (30, 786) Dean similarly considers a person to have this sense of meaninglessness, and thus to be alienated in the sense under consideration, if he feels he cannot "understand . . . the very events upon which [his] life and happiness [are] known to depend." (7, 754) And Middleton employs the following statement as an indicator of the existence of this type of alienation: "Things have become so complicated in the world today that I really don't understand just what is going on." (20, 973)

Characterization of this type of alienation in terms of feelings of "meaninglessness" is misleading, because the feeling with which these writers are concerned is not the feeling that the events which affect one *have* no meaning and cannot even in principle be explained. Rather, they are concerned with the feeling a person may have that *he* is *unable* to understand them; the question of the actual meaningfulness or absurdity of the events themselves is left open. Such alienation might better be characterized in terms of "incomprehensibility." A person is alienated in the sense in question if the events affecting him are incomprehensible to him.

This type of alienation clearly must be distinguished from that which is defined in terms of the feeling of powerlessness.

It is one thing to feel unable to understand the events and forces which affect one, and another to feel unable to control or influence them. An economist, for example, may understand how inflation comes about, and still feel powerless to do anything about it when it occurs. On the other hand, men who have occupied positions of power have often recalled the uneasiness they experienced upon realizing how inadequately they understood the social, economic, or political developments which they knew their decisions were likely to influence. Thus the feeling that one is unable to understand events and the feeling that one is unable to influence them can occur quite independently of each other.

It should be observed that it was not because of the worker's inability to *understand* the economic laws which affected him that Marx termed them "alien" to him. Marx did so because he held these laws to be insensitive to the needs of the worker's personality and to his well-being. Thus Marx considered them to have the character of "alienness" even in his own case, although he felt he understood them clearly. While the use of the term "alienation" under consideration is often traced to him, therefore, there is no precedent for it to be found in his writings. It derives from him only by way of a misinterpretation of the way in which he actually does employ the term.

Alienation and Meaningless Choices

Levin also speaks of "alienation" in connection with "feelings of meaninglessness." But the two kinds of feelings he has in mind are quite different from the feeling discussed above. While at first glance he would seem to be working with the same conception of alienation as are others who define it in these terms, therefore, he actually is working with a different one. The "feelings of meaninglessness" with which he is concerned are those one experiences (1) when he is forced to choose from among a set of alternatives (e.g., in an election) between which "there are no real differences"; and (2) when he is prevented from reaching an intelligent decision concerning some political or other such issue "because the information upon which, he thinks, such a decision must be made is lacking." (14, 62) One who experiences either of

these feelings—which seem much more appropriately characterizable as "feelings of meaninglessness" than does that discussed above—is said to be "alienated."

The feeling that one cannot understand certain political
or economic developments is obviously quite different from
the first feeling mentioned by Levin. One may feel that he
understands very well why the major political parties have
nominated the men they have in a given year, and still feel
that there is nothing to choose between the nominees. The
feeling of being unable to understand events is also to be distinguished from the feeling that one lacks the information
necessary to reach an intelligent decision about them; for
the former focuses upon one's inability to make sense out of
them, rather than the lack of information concerning them.
Indeed, one of the problems in the former case often is that
one is confronted with more information than one can handle.
In the latter case, on the other hand, one feels not over-
whelmed in this way, but rather deprived of information one
would be capable of handling if only one had access to it.

The feelings of which Levin speaks may accompany and
even give rise to a feeling of powerlessness; for one may feel
that he is powerless to secure a more meaningful set of alternatives from which to choose and a more meaningful basis
for his decisions. Still, the two must be distinguished. One
who has strong preferences among candidates, or who has his
mind made up on a given issue, may nonetheless feel powerless to secure the outcome he desires. In the one case the fundamental issue is that of perceived influence; while in the
other it is that of the way one views the choices one must
make. Thus if the feelings Levin discusses are construed as
constituting a kind of alienation, it must be distinguished
both from that which other writers characterize in terms of
feelings of "meaninglessness," and from that which is defined in terms of feelings of powerlessness as such.

Appropriateness of the Term "Alienation"

Not all of the various uses of the term "alienation" which
have been distinguished in this section are equally appropriate. In fact, there is a sense in which all of them are inappropriate; for the ending "-ation" suggests not merely that

some sort of "alienness" exists, but also that a process of "becoming alien" has occurred. This idea is present in all standard uses of the term; but none of the writers discussed above restrict their employment of it to cases in which a transition from "non-alienness" has occurred. Those who refer to feelings of "powerlessness" or "meaninglessness" or to "apathy" as types of alienation do so regardless of whether these feelings or states were preceded by feelings of influence or understanding or by a tendency to activism.

In considering the appropriateness of the different uses of the term in this context relative to each other, therefore, one is in effect considering the relative appropriateness of characterizing the various phenomena in question in terms of "alienness." Events one cannot understand may reasonably be termed "alien" to one, as may men in positions of power whom one distrusts. Indeed, the latter type of alienation may be viewed simply as a special case of interpersonal estrangement. This is a use of the term which enjoys some currency in ordinary speech. Apathy too may be said to involve feelings of "alienness," at least to the extent that it is grounded in a feeling of indifference; for something toward which one feels indifferent may be considered sufficiently remote from one's concerns to be termed "alien" to him.

The use of the term "alienation" to characterize feelings of powerlessness, however, is more questionable. It does not seem entirely appropriate to term an event or development "alien" merely by virtue of the fact that one feels unable to influence it. It would seem odd, for example, to refer to a political development as "alien" to a political scientist who had a clear understanding of it, even though he could not influence it in any way. It is true that Marx terms the economic forces which dominate the individual "alien" to him; but he has in mind less the powerlessness of the individual in relation to him than the fact that they are completely indifferent to his interests and detrimental to his well-being.

Powers and forces one cannot influence bear quite a different aspect when they are seen as benevolent, at least when the issue of dependence upon other men does not arise. One hears little about the "alienness" of sociopolitical developments from those who believe in the March of Progress, and thus in their essential (if not always immediately apparent) benignity. The same is true with regard to events which are attributed to Divine Providence. It seems to be only as men cease to believe that the impersonal forces and developments affecting their lives are benign, and come to regard them as hostile or at least indifferent, that they begin to view them as "alien." Ordinary usage provides some justification for the use of the term in *this* connection, by virtue of its standard use in connection with antagonism and indifference in interpersonal relations. Since indifference and hostility are not implied by uninfluenceability, however, the appropriateness of using the term "alienation" in connection with feelings of "powerlessness" as such is questionable.

A different problem arises when the term is used in connection with the feeling that one is not simply powerless, but wrongly so. Here the feeling of powerlessness itself is presupposed; but the term "alienation" is employed only if one further feels that one's powerlessness constitutes a deprivation of influence to which one is inherently entitled. This conception of alienation thus comes close to being a subjectivized version of the traditional conception of "self-alienation" as a disparity between one's actual condition and one's essential nature. Thus Levin says, "The alienated man is acutely aware of the discrepancy between who he is and what he believes he should be." (14, 59)

But while it would be reasonable, given this tradition of Hegelian and Marxian usage, to characterize one who feels this discrepancy to exist as "self-alienated" (at least in his own eyes), the sociologists who speak of "alienation" in this context are not really concerned with the relation of the individual to *himself*. Generally speaking, it is "political alienation" that they purport to be discussing, with the implication that their concern is with the relation of the individual to political events and structures. People do differ with regard to their conceptions of what they are by nature entitled to be; and this issue is an important one. But where "political alienation" is concerned, the appropriateness of making this issue decisive is questionable. In effect, this renders it legitimate to speak of "political alienation" only where it is also proper to speak of "self-alienation"; and the shift of emphasis involved is at variance with the actual fundamental concern of the writers in question.

The use of the term "alienation" to refer to a feeling of being confronted with meaningless choices or decisions may be dealt with more summarily. Its appropriateness is dubious simply because there would seem to be no feature of this situation that is properly characterizable in terms of "alienness." The term "alienation," in all likelihood, never would have been used in this context if it had not been used previously in connection with other phenomena (notably the seeming incomprehensibility of events affecting one) which are also commonly characterized in terms of "meaninglessness."

A "Multidimensional" Concept?

However inappropriate some of these uses of the term may be, one must reckon with the fact that it *is* currently employed in connection with the various phenomena distinguished above. In an attempt to eliminate the confusion generated by the use of the term in so many different ways without sacrificing its breadth of application, a number of writers have suggested treating the different phenomena as members of a general syndrome, and merging the various distinct conceptions of "alienation" under consideration into a single one with a variety of different "dimensions"—a "multidimensional" conception of "alienation."

At first glance, this suggestion may seem attractive. In fact, however, it is far from satisfactory. If followed, the term either would be employed only when all of the different phenomena in question obtain, or it would be employed whenever some subset of them obtains; and in either case, the result would be undesirable. If the first course were to be followed, the term would be applicable in a much smaller number of cases than any of the writers considered would find acceptable. For while there are considerable numbers of people who manifest several of the feelings in question, most of them manifest only some. Only a small number—which would exclude activists, intellectuals, and those who regard their powerlessness as natural or inconsequential—could then be termed "alienated." Following this course would so restrict the applicability of the term that it would cease to serve the purposes of most sociologists.

A different but no less serious problem would arise if the second course were to be followed: namely, the term would subsume phenomena which differ too considerably to be considered members of a single syndrome. The intelligent voter confronted with a meaningless choice of candidates, the apathetic slum dweller, the student activist who distrusts those in power, the average citizen who finds social and economic events incomprehensible, and the dropout from society have in common a feeling of remoteness of some sort from some aspect of the socio-politico-economic world. But the origin and character of their separations from it differ so considerably that these separations cannot plausibly be viewed as dimensions of a single syndrome. Characterization of them in this fashion implies a degree of interrelatedness which they quite obviously lack.

The term "alienation" could be used to comprehend all of them; but then it would not serve to denote a multidimensional concept at all. Rather, it would merely indicate that the different phenomena in question have a certain *formal* similarity. Used in this way, it would function neither as a concrete descriptive term nor as a theoretical term, but rather as a general, nontheoretical classificatory term, analogous to "separation." Indeed, this is the only level at which it is capable of functioning, unless its use is substantially restricted either to a single phenomenon, or to a group of phenomena among which one may at least reasonably expect to find some factual interconnectedness.

V. Alienation, Culture, and Society

By far the most common use of the term in recent sociological literature is in connection with separation from some aspect of the social or cultural life of one's society. This is also the most common nontraditional use of the term in ordinary speech. Whereas the expression "political alienation" frequently occurs in discussions of the phenomena dealt with in the previous section, the phenomena now to be con-

sidered are commonly characterized as types of "social alienation," or "alienation from society."

In addition to being the most common use of the term in
the writings of sociologists, this is also the one most uniquely
sociological in origin. Their other uses of it, in connection
with work, other people, and political and economic events
and structures, all derive more or less directly from external
sources (notably Marx). To find a precedent for the use of the
term in the present general context, however, one must go
back to Hegel's use of it in connection with the separation
of the individual from the social substance. And this precedent is quite unknown to most sociologists; they tend either
to regard the use of the term under consideration as their
own invention, or to attribute it mistakenly to Marx, in whose
writings it is not to be found.

The diversity of conceptions of alienation in this context
is greater than in any of those considered previously. This
may be in part precisely *because* the term is employed more
frequently in this context than in any other. However, it no
doubt is also partly due to the fact that so many different
things make up the sociocultural life of a society.

Alienation and Popular Culture

A number of writers construe alienation in terms of disassociation from "popular cultural standards." (30, 788) At
issue here is the individual's "acceptance of popular culture."
(20, 974) These writers consider one to be alienated from
popular culture if he does not "accept" it, but rather "rejects"
it, or has an attitude of indifference to or detachment from it.

Even though it is only the acceptance or rejection of "popular culture" that is in question, and not the fundamental
values or behavioral norms of the society, some writers in-
cautiously speak of "alienation from society" in this context.
For example, Nettler defines the "alienated person" as "one
who has been estranged from, made unfriendly toward, his
society and the culture it carries." (24, 671–72) But the questions he uses to test for alienation show that he has in mind
a rejection far less sweeping than this definition would seem
to indicate, comprehending such things as "the mass media
and mass taste," "popular education," and "conventional reli-

gion." (24, 674) Similarly, Middleton speaks of "cultural estrangement," but in fact has in mind a narrower rejection than this expression suggests; for his criterion of it is that one agree with the statement: "I am not much interested in the TV programs, movies, or magazines that most people seem to like." (20, 974) Other writers make reference to such things as a lack of interest in new cars and spectator sports. In all such cases, the expression "popular culture" would seem to indicate most accurately the domain of objects of disaffection in question.

Alienation from popular culture is always referred to as a "feeling," or something similar. The exact nature of this "feeling" of distance or separation from popular culture varies somewhat from writer to writer. For Middleton, to be alienated from popular culture is simply to feel "uninterested" in it. Similarly, Seeman speaks interchangeably of "alienation" from popular culture and "detachment" from it; the feeling involved is simply a feeling of indifference toward it, as opposed to a feeling that importance or value attaches to its various components. (30, 788) According to Nettler, on the other hand, to be alienated from it is to feel "unfriendliness" toward it, to feel "averse" to it, and to "resent" it. (24, 672–74)

It should be observed that individuals who satisfy the above criteria of alienation from popular culture frequently do not feel unhappy about their alienation. On the contrary, an awareness of it often gives rise to feelings of pride and superiority; for many of those in question view immediate involvement in popular culture with disdain. To the extent that affirmation constitutes a form of choice, therefore, this type of alienation may be said frequently to be chosen. The concomitant loss of solidarity with others who are involved in popular culture may at the same time be regarded with a certain sadness. But if this loss of *solidarity* is to be considered a type of alienation, it is a distinct type: namely, a form of alienation from *others*.[8]

8 See pp. 178 f.

Alienation and Societal Values

Disassociation from the popular culture prevailing in one's society must be distinguished from disassociation from the fundamental values of one's society. Popular culture and fundamental values may often be related, but they constitute quite different levels of the sociocultural life of a society. The distinction between them is indicated by Keniston when he observes,

> Standards of taste and cultivation are of course part of this surrounding environment, but more important are those usually implicit and unexamined assumptions about the nature of life, man, society, history, and the universe which are simply taken for granted by most members of a society. (13, 79)

When he refers to the young men who are the subjects of his study as "alienated,"[9] he is referring to "their generalized refusal of American culture" (13, 79); that is, to their rejection of these fundamental assumptions and assignations of value, rather than merely of popular American tastes and pastimes.

"Most young men and women in any society," according to Keniston, "are more or less 'acculturated'—that is, they have already accepted the basic shared values of their culture. . . ." (13, 196–97) When there is "a failure of acculturation," however, and an individual does not assimilate these basic values, a type of sociocultural disassociation exists which is distinct from that discussed above. Keniston is one of a number of writers who conceive of alienation in these terms. He recognizes that the term may be used in connection with other phenomena; but he chooses to "reserve the term 'alienation' for . . . an explicit rejection, 'freely' chosen by the individual, of what he perceives as the dominant values or norms of his society." (13, 455)

Merton and Parsons both construe alienation in a similar way. In his influential paper "Social Structure and Anomie,"

[9] The subtitle of his book *The Uncommitted* (13) is "Alienated Youth in American Society."

Merton speaks of "alienation from reigning goals and standards." (19, 155) Those who do not share "the common frame of values" of a society are said to be "*in* the society but not *of* it. Sociologically, these constitute the true aliens." (19, 153) "Alienation" is not a central category in Merton's discussion; but when he does speak of it, he does so in connection with this disassociation from fundamental social values.

The term figures more prominently in Parsons' discussion of the interaction between the social system and the individual personality. Parsons introduces the conception of "a 'conformity-alienation' dimension" in the individual's personality structure, "in the sense of a disposition to conform with the expectations of others or to be alienated from them." (26, 32) While this might seem to suggest that he has in mind a form of alienation from *other people*, rather than a disassociation from societal *values*, it is in fact the latter with which he is concerned. The "others" he refers to are viewed solely in their capacity as "role-models," through whom the values of the society are transmitted and in whom they are embodied. He states: "Alienation is . . . a possible product of something going wrong in the process of value-acquisition through identification." (26, 233) It is the individual's relation to the values in question, rather than to the others who accept and transmit them, in which Parsons is interested. "The phenomenon of interest here is the more generalized alienation from the value-patterns involved in the role-expectation." (26, 234) And the values Parsons is concerned with here are not those which may be assigned to such things as new cars, movies, and spectator sports. Rather, they are those which relate to the fundamental roles which define adulthood or membership in a given society.

A person's attitude toward the elements of popular culture may of course be discussed in similar terms. But this does not lessen the importance of distinguishing between alienation from them and alienation from societal values. The difference becomes clearer when one examines more closely the difference between the objects of the two types of alienation and their positions in the life of a society. Here it is instructive to compare the values rejected by Keniston's "alienated

youth" and Merton's "true alien" in American society, with
examples of popular culture cited by Middleton and Nettler.

According to Keniston, our society is one in which "playfulness, fantasy, relaxation, creativity, feeling, and synthesis
take second place to problem-solving, cognitive control, work,
measurement, rationality, and analysis." (13, 366) In other
words, "ego dictatorship" is a presupposition of "conventional
adulthood." (Cf. 13, 196) The young men Keniston discusses
refuse to place a high value on "ego dictatorship," and instead
value the other qualities he mentions. It is by virtue of their
refusal of this fundamental value, or the cluster of values
associated with "ego dictatorship," that he terms them
"alienated."

The fundamental value of "contemporary American culture" in Merton's eyes is the endless accumulation of wealth,
or "monetary success," together with its concomitant prestige.
He considers those who reject it to be "true aliens" in American society; for in doing so they are rejecting a value so
fundamental to the society that "they can be included as
members of the *society* (in distinction from the *population*)
only in a fictional sense." (19, 153) Merton speaks of
"alienation" only in connection with the rejection of a value
so fundamental that this may be said of those who reject it.

It is unimportant, for present purposes, whether or not the
values singled out by Keniston and Merton are actually so
basic to American society that acceptance of them is a presupposition or criterion of membership in it. The point to be
grasped is that they (and others) consider certain values to
occupy such a position; and that they speak of alienation in
connection with the rejection of these values precisely *because*, in their view, these values occupy this position of
special importance. They would not use the term in connection with the rejection of these values if they did not take
this to be so.

Middleton, on the other hand, is concerned with the individual's attitude toward "the TV programs, movies, [and]
magazines that most people seem to like." (20, 974) It is
things of this sort which constitute popular culture. But there
is no suggestion that one who is not interested in them is a
member of American society in a fictional sense only. The

same may be said of many of the examples in Nettler's "measure of alienation": e.g., "Do you read *Reader's Digest?*" "What do you think of the new model American automobiles?" "Do you like to participate in church activities?" And, "Do national spectator-sports (football, baseball) interest you?" (24, 675) These are not criteria of conventional adulthood in American society. Some of Nettler's other questions relate to more fundamental values. However, this does not indicate that there is no distinction to be drawn, but merely that he fails to draw it.

In short, quite different aspects of the sociocultural life of a society are in question here. And it should be obvious that a person can reject one without rejecting the other. Indeed, it is doubtful that the rejection of one even creates a strong presumption of the rejection of the other. There certainly is no obvious connection between a high valuation of popular television programs, new cars, and spectator sports on the one hand, and emphasis on monetary success and "ego dictatorship" on the other. Many of those most strongly oriented toward the latter have little interest in the former; and elements of popular culture of this sort are valued highly by large numbers of people in this country for whom the latter are not basic values (e.g., many of the "underprivileged"). Indeed, there would seem to be a certain degree of actual conflict between popular culture and these values. The kinds of activities which the former typically involves are associated with precisely those qualities ("playfulness, fantasy, relaxation, feeling") which are *suppressed* whenever Keniston's ego-virtues predominate; and they also involve taking time out from the pursuit of monetary success. Popular-cultural activities and interests, moreover, are generally viewed not as continuous with these values, but rather as a means of escape from the pressures the latter generate. Consequently, if the term "alienation" is to be used in connection with attitudes of indifference and antipathy toward both, one must distinguish between alienation from popular culture and alienation from fundamental societal values.

It should also be observed that there is often a difference between a society's "role-expectation structures" and basic values in Merton's and Keniston's sense, and the *cultural ideals* commonly affirmed by the members of the society. The two may coincide; but they may also diverge, and even conflict, as many social critics argue they have in American society. The basic values discussed by Merton and Keniston, for example, seem far from consistent with the ideals of self-realization, personal growth, and "the pursuit of happiness," in terms of which our cultural ideals are commonly described. Many young people, who are termed "alienated" by Merton, Keniston, and others by virtue of their rejection of the former, are deeply committed to the latter in a way many of their critics are not. Their charge that too many adults are hypocrites frequently derives from their feeling that the *real* basic values of these adults are quite at odds with the ideals they affirm. Whether or not this accusation is just, it illustrates the possibility of a divergence of the real and the ideal values of a society.

A divergence of this sort can result in a social crisis of considerable dimensions; for under such conditions membership in the society requires adherence to conflicting sets of values. To adhere to one is to reject the other, to the extent that they conflict; but this is something the individual member of the society may find it difficult to admit, or—if he does admit it—to live with. And while such a situation persists, a division of the membership of the society into mutually uncomprehending and hostile groups is a very real possibility. Where such a divergence occurs, the problem (in Hegelian terminology) is not simply that individuals are at odds with the social substance, but rather that the social substance is at odds with itself.

Alienation and Societal Behavioral Norms

A number of sociologists speak of "alienation" in connection with the rejection of yet another part of the "substance" of a society: "the common social expectations about the kind of behavior that is proper, appropriate, and legal." (13, 466) The expression conventionally used in sociological literature to refer to these expectations is "behavioral norms"; it comprehends both legal and extralegal (e.g., ethical) norms. Keniston observes that it is possible for an individual not only to reject the popular culture and the fundamental values

of his society, but also—even while accepting them—to reject
its behavioral norms; and he suggests that the rejection of the
latter might also be considered a type of alienation, distinguished from those discussed above by its difference of object or focus. (13, 466) Similarly, Lowry speaks of the individual's "alienation from the prevailing ethic and cultural
norms of the community" which constitute a "guide to his
inter-personal and group behavior." (15, 429) And Putney
and Middleton refer to the "failure to profess norms" as
"normative alienation." (28, 433)

The difference between behavioral norms and popular culture, and thus between the types of alienation conceived in
terms of their rejection, should be obvious. There is also a
difference between such norms and basic societal values, although it may not be as apparent. One statement of it is to be
found in Merton's paper on "Social Structure and Anomie";
indeed, it is basic to his entire conception of "anomie."[10]

> Among the several elements of social and cultural struc-
> tures, two are of immediate importance. These are analyti-
> cally separable although they merge in concrete situations.
> The first consists of culturally defined goals, purposes and
> interests, held out as legitimate objectives for all. . . .
> They are the things "worth striving for." . . .
> A second element of the cultural structure defines, regu-
> lates and controls the acceptable modes of reaching out for
> these goals. Every social group invariably couples its cul-
> tural objectives with regulations, rooted in the mores or
> institutions, of allowable procedures for moving toward
> these objectives. (19, 132–33)

For Merton, this distinction between values and norms is
an end/means distinction. It retains this character for a number of those who have incorporated it into their discussions of
alienation. Seeman, for example, contrasts societal goals with
"behaviors . . . required to achieve given goals." (30, 788)
Others, such as Keniston, do not contrast societal values
merely with norms of behavior relating directly to them, but
rather with behavioral norms generally.

[10] See pp. 194 f.

Merton is concerned with situations in which individuals adhere to societal goals or values, but reject and violate the corresponding behavioral norms in order to realize them. And clearly, one *can* accept either the former or the latter, while rejecting the other. One may relinquish all hope of attaining monetary success, for example, and at the same time conduct oneself in accordance with the norms governing both professional and private life in one's society. On the other hand, many people aspire to monetary success, and yet do not act in accordance with prevailing norms relating to its attainment. Consequently, one must distinguish between disassociation from societal goals and values and the rejection of societal norms of behavior. And if both are to be characterized in terms of "alienation," they must be recognized to constitute different types of alienation.

Some writers use the term "normlessness" to refer to the rejection of societal norms, and employ this term to identify the type of alienation under consideration. But "normlessness"—the lack of norms—comprehends not only situations in which recognized norms are *rejected*, but also those in which people are *unaware* of any clear norms governing behavior. This is a matter of sociological usage, as well as of the logic of the term. It follows, therefore, that alienation, in the sense of rejection of societal norms, is not to be identified with "normlessness" as such.

Indeed, it cannot even be considered a *type* of "normlessness." For the latter term cannot appropriately be employed in a number of significant kinds of cases of such alienation. A person cannot be considered "normless" as long as he acts in accordance with norms of some sort; and it is clearly possible for his actions to be governed by norms of some sort, even though he rejects those norms which are commonly acknowledged in the society in which he lives. Further, one may on occasion quite deliberately violate certain societal norms, and still be said to accept them; for norms can be "internalized," but subordinated to certain other considerations which on occasion require their violation. Thus the violation of societal norms as such cannot support a judgment of "normlessness," even with regard to the very norms which are violated.

A further distinction should be noted between the rejection of societal norms of behavior and what Dean terms "Conflict of Norms." The latter is said to obtain when a person "incorporates in his personality conflicting norms." (7, 755) But to *reject* norms and to "incorporate" them "into [one's] personality" are very different things; the existence of a conflict between certain "incorporated" norms does not alter this fact. It is not clear, therefore, why Dean considers "conflict of norms" to be a possible "component" of alienation. It is even less clear why he considers it to be a "subtype of Normlessness." (7, 755) For to *adhere to* norms (which conflict) is by the very nature of the case not to be norm-*less*.

It is important to observe that the term "rejection" covers two quite different kinds of cases. One may simply violate societal behavioral norms out of motives which have as their object a purely personal gratification. Here one intends to offer no open challenge to the norms in question; on the contrary, one seeks to elude detection when violating them, and accountability for doing so. This apparently is the kind of rejection sociologists have in mind when they speak (for example) of the adoption of "socially unapproved behaviors . . . to achieve given goals." (30, 788) People who commit crimes for profit (e.g., thieves, embezzlers) would seem to embody this kind of norm-rejection most clearly.

But one's rejection of societal norms of behavior may also be a *principled* one. One may openly violate certain laws which one considers unjust, accepting full responsibility for doing so; civil disobedience manifests this form of principled rejection. Or one may live in open disregard of certain conventions (e.g., those governing sexual relations, or acceptable language), which one considers unhealthy or otherwise undesirable. The rejection of conventional behavioral norms which Keniston found to prevail among the young people he studied (13) had this principled quality, and thus a special, quite distinctive character.

Unfortunately, the difference between these two sorts of cases is given little attention by the sociologists who speak of "alienation" in this general context. It has the consequence, however, that one should not talk about alienation from societal behavioral norms without either explicitly restricting the term to one type of rejection or the other, or distinguishing two forms of alienation from such norms.

Alienation and "Anomie"

A large body of recent sociological literature has been devoted to discussion of the societal condition of "anomie." The term "anomie" was first given a technical sociological sense of Émile Durkheim.[11] It is Robert Merton's reformulation of the conception, however, that has been definitive for contemporary sociology.[12] According to Merton,

> Anomie is . . . a breakdown in the cultural structure, occurring particularly when there is an acute disjunction between the cultural . . . goals and the socially structured capacities of members of the group to act in accord with them. (19, 162)

Merton has in mind the situation in which cultural goals for the most part can be achieved only through deviance from societal behavioral norms. Under these circumstances there emerges what he terms "a strain toward the breakdown of the norms, toward normlessness." (19, 163) It is in these terms that "anomie" is conceived.

In a part of the literature devoted to the discussion of anomic societies, a conception of alienation has emerged which is related to the one discussed in the previous section, but which must be distinguished from it. The term here is used, in Seeman's words, to refer to "the anomic situation, from the individual point of view." Seeman has in mind a person for whom "there is a high expectancy that socially unapproved behaviors are required to achieve given goals." (30, 787) Similarly, Middleton considers a person to embody this orientation if he believes that, "In order to get ahead in the world today, you are almost forced to do some things which are not right." (20, 973–74) To have this expectancy or to

---

[11] See his book *Suicide* (8), especially p. 253.
[12] See his "Social Structure and Anomie," in 19. For a discussion of the development of the concept of "anomie," see Marshall Clinard, "The Theoretical Implications of Anomie and Deviant Behavior." (5)

hold this belief is, according to Seeman and Middleton, to be alienated.

Neal and Rettig construe alienation in a similar way. "Normlessness" for them is one "form" of alienation. They do not define "normlessness" in terms of the rejection of norms, however, but rather in terms of an orientation which they characterize as follows: "Socially approved alternatives are viewed as relatively ineffective, and the consequent necessity of unapproved behavior in goal attainment is emphasized." (22, 605) Here again, one is considered to be alienated simply insofar as he *holds the view* that goal attainment presupposes unapproved behavior. It is this *belief*, rather than actual unapproved *behavior*, which is the defining criterion of this type of alienation.

Such a belief quite obviously need not be associated with actual deviant behavior. On the contrary, as Merton points out, a variety of types of "individual adaptation" are possible on the part of people who hold it. One *may* proceed to pursue the goals in question in unapproved ways; but one may also adhere both to these goals *and* to "institutionalized means" in spite of this belief, and simply hope for the best. Or one may adhere to the accepted behavioral norms, abandoning all real hope of achieving the goals. Thus the *expectancy* under consideration is to be distinguished from the actual *rejection* of behavioral norms discussed above. If such an expectancy or belief is made definitive of a type of alienation, therefore, it is yet another distinct type, which is not to be identified with any of those discussed previously.

This expectancy (and the type of alienation defined in terms of it) is also to be distinguished from "the feeling that the world and oneself are adrift, wandering, lacking in clear rules and stable moorings." This is how McClosky and Schaar characterize "anomy" (with a "y")—another psychological state suggested to be that which most typically accompanies a societal condition of anomie. According to them, "the anomic [person] feels literally *de*-moralized; for him, the norms governing behavior are weak, ambiguous, and remote." (17, 19) "Anomy" is defined in a similar way by MacIver. (16)

"Anomy" so construed is much more the subjective counterpart of "anomie" as conceived by Durkheim than as conceived by Merton; for it is only in the Durkheimian anomic society that there *cease to be* clear norms of behavior. (8, 253) In Merton's anomic society, on the other hand, behavioral norms are clear enough; the problem rather is that the types of action they permit do not enable most people to realize societal goals. (19, 136) These clearly are two quite different kinds of situation. And of the two, only the former may properly be characterized in terms of a condition of "normlessness."

Alienation conceived in terms of the expectation under consideration must also be distinguished from Srole's widely discussed concept of "anomia" (with an "*a*"), which designates yet another psychological state purportedly corresponding to a societal condition of anomie. Srole measures "anomia" in terms of agreement with five different statements, which express feelings of (1) being ignored by those in power; (2) lacking confidence in one's ability to fulfill one's life-goals; (3) going downhill in life—slipping backward on the treadmill; (4) despairing of life's being worthwhile; and (5) being unable to count on anyone. (35, 712–13) None of these items bears directly upon the expectancy that established goals can be attained only through deviation from accepted norms of behavior. The second one might seem to; but it says nothing about deviant behavior, and indeed seems to imply that nothing—including deviant behavior—will be of any avail. Consequently, as Neal and Rettig observe, the expectancy under consideration and Srole's "anomia" are conceptually quite distinct, as well as empirically "separate and unrelated." (22, 599, 605)

This distinction might seem too obvious to need mentioning. In his introductory remarks, however, Srole refers to "anomia" as a type of alienation; and since both "anomia" and the type of alienation presently under consideration are suggested to be *the* psychological state typically associated with a societal condition of anomie, some writers tend to confuse them.[13] This confusion is understandable; but its

[13] E.g., McDill and Ridley (18) and Putney and Middleton (28).

understandability does not diminish the importance of avoiding it.[14]

Appropriateness of the Term "Alienation"

Sociologists thus speak of "alienation" in connection with disassociation from popular culture, nonacceptance of the basic values of one's society, rejection of the behavioral norms prevailing in it, and the expectation that societal goals cannot be attained except through deviation from such norms. Here again, the term is employed not only in cases in which the phenomena in question were preceded by their respective opposites, but also in cases in which they were not—in spite of the fact that its construction suggests a process of "becoming alien," and thus an initial state of nonalienness.

The construction of a term is not necessarily decisive for its use; but where popular culture and societal values and behavioral norms are concerned, it does seem questionable whether a simple feeling of indifference or aversion should be regarded as a sufficient condition of alienation. For example, a foreigner residing in this country might have one or the other of these feelings toward American popular culture and societal values; and, while it might be appropriate to term them "alien to him," it is doubtful whether he should be termed "alienated from them." The appropriateness of the term "alienation" in cases falling within this general context thus would appear to depend partly upon the satisfaction of certain conditions pertaining to the individual's background and development, if not upon the occurrence of an actual transition from a state of acceptance to a state of nonacceptance. Unfortunately, this issue is given little attention by the writers under consideration. Accordingly, one may say either that their discussions of how the term is to be understood are inadequate, or that their uses of the term—insofar as they are not restricted in this way—are inappropriate.

[14] While Srole says that he speaks of "anomia" rather than "alienation" simply "for semantic neatness" (35, 711), he gives the impression of bringing in the latter term only to help stir up interest in what he is going to discuss. At any rate, he does not speak of "alienation" in the body of his discussion. His use of the term, therefore, does not warrant special attention.

It is also the case that here, as in the preceding section, the phenomena in question are too diverse and independent to be viewed as so many different "elements" or "dimensions" of a single "multidimensional" phenomenon of (sociocultural) alienation. For popular culture and fundamental societal values may come into conflict, so that disassociation from one may be in part a function of adherence to the other.[15] And the type of alienation associated with anomie presupposes an adherence to precisely those societal values which are the focus of another of the types of alienation discussed.

Such considerations rule out any suggestion that the various phenomena distinguished constitute an interrelated syndrome, on conceptual as well as empirical grounds. As an attempt to integrate the various discussions of alienation considered in this section, therefore, the introduction of the conception of "multidimensionality" is even less promising here than previously. Thus once again, it would appear that as long as the term retains the breadth of application which has been described in this section, it is capable of functioning only as a general classificatory term. For under these circumstances it comprehends too many different types of disharmony at the sociocultural level to be of any real descriptive or theoretical use.

Finally, it would appear that some of the uses of the term in this general context too are more appropriate than others. If the proper qualifications with regard to background and development are made, the uses of the term in connection with disassociation from popular culture and nonacceptance of fundamental societal values would seem to be quite appropriate. They not only are consonant with the root meaning of the term, but also find historical legitimation in Hegel's use of the term in connection with a disruption of the relation of the individual to the social substance. Resembling the term's earliest special employment, and constituting its seemingly most common special uses in ordinary speech, they may also be the most helpful of the many employments of the term to be found in recent sociological literature.

[15] See pp. 189–90.

There also is clearly some point in considering those whose rejection of societal behavioral norms is principled, to be alienated from these norms. For it can be said quite appropriately that they experience these norms as something "alien" to them and to what they believe. The matter is different, however, in cases of the nonprincipled type of rejection of such norms. It is one of the features of this type of rejection that, generally speaking, one violates the norms in question only when some further advantage is to be gained by doing so. Here there is no disaffection with these norms *as such*; when they are violated, it is because they seem to preclude or render inordinately difficult the attainment of some goal one is determined to attain. As long as this is the case, it is not the "alienness" of the norms in the eyes of the agent as such which is manifesting itself in his violation of them. And under these circumstances, he cannot appropriately be termed "alienated" from them.

With regard to the expectancy that "socially unapproved behaviors are required to achieve given goals," it is not clear why Seeman, Middleton, and others refer to this expectancy as such as a type of alienation. "Alienation" must be alienation *from* something; something must seem "alien" in some way if the term is to have any application. It is difficult to see, however, what the object of the implicit "from" clause in the present case could be. For, as has been observed, this expectancy need involve no form of disassociation from the behavioral norms in question. And the object of the "from" clause cannot be the *prevailing* mode of expectation (e.g., that socially *approved* behaviors *are adequate* to achieve given goals); for none of these writers make the characterization of this expectancy as a type of alienation contingent upon its being a minority view.

It has been suggested (by Merton and others) that this expectancy manifests disillusionment with the promise of virtue being rewarded by the attainment of cultural goals. If a person with this expectancy is to be termed "alienated," that from which he is alienated would seem to have to be something like this promise. To speak of it as "alien" to him, however, is awkward, to say the least. The term "disillusionment" is much more appropriate to the phenomenon than is the term "alienation." Since the phenomenon can be characterized in another less pretentious and more accurate way, therefore, it seems reasonable to suggest that it should be.

VI. Conclusion

Conceptions of Alienation and Their Operationalization

It was observed at the outset of this chapter that sociologists as a rule formulate their conceptions of alienation in terms of the occurrence of certain feelings or attitudes. This point by now has been amply illustrated. Different writers, or the same writers at different times, may focus on widely differing feelings and attitudes, but they always focus on some kind or other. They do not consider an individual to be alienated unless he has the appropriate feelings. He need not be conscious of them at all times; but he must have them when his attention is directed toward the proper matters.

Sociologists, self-consciously striving to be "social *scientists,*" are anxious to develop objective criteria for the phenomena with which they are concerned. They therefore generally try to "operationalize" their conceptions of alienation, and to develop ways of "tapping" the feelings in question. The commonly accepted procedure for doing this is to devise lists of statements or questions which seem to them to express these feelings, and which require nothing more of those tested than agreement or disagreement, or affirmative or negative answers (sometimes on a graded scale). A person is then considered alienated if and only if he makes the appropriate responses, or would do so if he were to respond to the test items.

The issue here is not whether the tests employed by different writers are devised well or poorly, or whether the results obtained from their use are interpreted properly or improperly. What is significant is the fact that, because of the importance attached to the operationalization of the conceptions of alienation involved, and because of the way in which they are operationalized, these conceptions in effect come to be construed in terms of the content of the test items employed. The question of whether or not various sociological conceptions of alienation *can* be operationalized is no real question at all. For these conceptions are operational in their very nature: The types of alienation discussed are *conceived* operationally. McClosky and Schaar are very candid on this point. They observe that their "anomy scale" is "valid" because, quite simply, "the [test] items define, by their content, our concept of anomy." (17, 24) The same is true, generally speaking, for the conceptions of alienation under consideration; although not all of McClosky's and Schaar's colleagues are so clear and frank about what they are doing.

The problem which looms so large in the case of Fromm, of formulating clear criteria for the types of alienation he discusses, is therefore no problem here. One question which does arise, however, is whether the conceptions of alienation so developed have any broad applicability. For if they are to be construed in terms of the content of the test items used, and if this content is too culture-specific, then the conceptions themselves become culture-specific to the point that the purposes for which they may be used are quite restricted.

This problem may be insoluble where operational conceptions of alienation are concerned; for it is questionable whether it is possible to construct tests which have the degree of sensitivity required to elicit the feelings with which the writers discussed are concerned, and which at the same time avoid culture-specificity. At any rate, whenever this is not possible, the same conceptions of alienation cannot be both defined in the above manner, and also applied across lines of significant cultural difference. Fromm's conceptions of alienation from nature, from others, and from oneself may be too vague to be *concretely* applicable; many of the conceptions of alienation discussed in this chapter, on the other hand, may be too particular to be *generally* applicable. Of the two limitations, however, the latter would seem to be preferable to the former, at least where analytical and scientific interests are concerned. (Of course, more is involved here than merely a contrast of relative concreteness of approach. The very phenomena in question in the two cases are also for the most part quite different.)

"Alienation": In Search of a Role

If one were to go by the various general contexts in which the term is used in recent sociological literature, it might seem that four different basic uses of the term, or types of alienation, emerge: interpersonal alienation, work alienation, politicoeconomic alienation, and sociocultural alienation. Closer examination reveals, however, that each of these designations comprehends a variety of different and often quite independent phenomena. Sometimes this is true even in the case of a single writer. More commonly, different writers use the same general designation to refer to different specific phenomena, thereby appearing to speak of the same thing, but in reality not doing so.

Confronted with this situation, some writers simply stipulate that the term is to be used only in connection with some one particular phenomenon. This procedure is unsatisfactory because of the apparent hopelessness of securing agreement with regard to the selection of the phenomenon to be so designated. If such agreement could be secured, the term could certainly function usefully; for its employment in any one of a number of the specific connections in which it is presently used would be quite appropriate. Precisely because of that fact, however, there would appear to be little prospect of a restriction of the use of the term to any one of them by sociologists generally. And as Neal and Rettig observe, "To say the least, such opposing conceptualizations of alienation make for serious communication problems as well as for conceptual and methodological difficulties in theory construction." (23, 62–63)

Neal and Rettig are among those who attempt to deal with this situation by proposing the construal of alienation as a "multidimensional conception" which would incorporate the various particular conceptions distinguished, while preserving the distinctions between them. Thus they feel it still is possible to speak of "alienation *in toto*," which they describe as "an abstract concept tying together common elements derivable from the lower-order structure." (23, 60) This approach is also unsatisfactory, in that it involves the suggestion of an interrelation between phenomena which simply cannot plausibly be viewed as interrelated to the degree required for their treatment in this manner. This has been seen to be so even when one considers only the uses of the term in one or another single general context. It is all the more true when one takes into consideration all of its uses in the literature.

Neal and Rettig suggest that these differences "should not lead to the abandonment of empirical research in this area . . . but should rather act as incentives for additional work." And they conclude that "careful empirical studies of alienation should eventually provide a basis for synthesizing numerous sociological and psychological concerns with man and society. . . ." (23, 64–65) But while "additional work" certainly should be done on the phenomena in question, and while empirical studies may show that certain of them are interrelated, it is clear from the outset that many are quite independent of each other, and moreover that some are actually incompatible with others. Neal and Rettig seem to think that the all-embracing synthesis of which they speak would require little more than "the development of additional measures of alienation by means of multidimensional techniques." (23, 63) In fact, however, the elimination of a considerable number of the present uses of the term would be necessary as well, before such a synthesis would even begin to become viable. The suggestion that the different writers who use the term are all somehow talking about different "dimensions," "aspects," or "modes" of the same thing is untenable; and it cannot help giving rise to serious misunderstandings and confusions on the part of those who accept it.

If the breadth of application of the term "alienation" cannot be markedly reduced, the capacity in which it is understood to function must be altered. For the only capacity in which this breadth of application leaves it capable of functioning at all usefully is that of a general term, which marks out a wide range of types of dissatisfaction, disharmony, and disaffection sharing the feature of deriving from or involving feelings of "alienness" of some sort. As such, it would be understood neither to designate a particular variable or pattern among other specific attitudinal and behavioral configurations, nor to stand as a theoretical construct such as might be used in their interpretation and explanation.

Of course, relations might be established between certain of the phenomena comprehended by it. No interconnection among these phenomena generally would be implied by the application of the term "alienation" to all of them, however, over and above a merely formal structural similarity.

This might appear to be too insignificant a role for a term with so spectacular a reputation. It is the only useful role, however, for which its present diversity of employment in the sociological literature renders it suited. If at some point in the future it should cease to be employed so widely, it might become possible for it to play a different role in sociological inquiry and theory. At the present time, however, the tendency would appear to be in the opposite direction.

6 Existential Philosophy and Theology

I. Introduction

Many people seem to be of the opinion that the idea of alienation occupies a position of great importance in the thought of "the existentialists." And discussions of alienation are in fact to be found in the works of several of the most important writers commonly so designated: Martin Heidegger, Jean-Paul Sartre, and Paul Tillich.[1] Heidegger and Sartre have attracted more attention by far than any of the other so-called "existential" philosophers; and Tillich is generally considered to be the leading "existential" theologian.

The common view of the matter, however, is largely mistaken. In their principal contributions to existential philosophy, neither Heidegger (in *Being and Time*) nor Sartre (in *Being and Nothingness*) speaks of "alienation" very extensively; nor, insofar as they do speak of it, do they do so in anything like the ways in which the term is popularly employed. And while the term is used extensively by Tillich, in his *Systematic Theology*, and by Sartre, in his recent *Critique of Dialectical Reason*, their uses of it in these works are not distinctively "existential," but rather derive from Hegel and Marx.

[1] The term Tillich actually uses is not "alienation," but rather "estrangement." To exclude him from consideration on this ground, however, would be improper; for he regards both terms as equivalent renderings of the German term *Entfremdung*, and does not intend any significance to be attached to his choice of the latter term as opposed to the former.

The common view is further mistaken with respect to the extent to which alienation is explicitly discussed by other Continental philosophers associated with existentialism. If Kierkegaard and Nietzsche are included among them, they constitute no exceptions. Nietzsche uses variants of the term *Entfremdung* in a few scattered passages, but only in passing, and in quite ordinary ways, which warrant no special attention. And Kierkegaard does not speak of "alienation" at all.

The more recent writers usually associated with existentialism, after Heidegger and Sartre, are Karl Jaspers, Gabriel Marcel, and Albert Camus. Jaspers makes frequent use of the terms *fremd* ("alien") and *Fremdheit* ("alienness"), as in the following passage:

> The world as *object of knowledge* is [something] alien. I stand at a *distance* from it. . . . To me it is the other. I am a matter of indifference to it. . . . I do not feel secure in it, for it does not speak the language of something related to me. The more decisively I grasp it cognizingly, the more homeless I feel in the world—which, as the other, as only that, is desolate. (8, 3)[2]

Some might find it natural to use the term "alienation" (*Entfremdung*) in this connection. Jaspers, however, does not; nor does he use it elsewhere. Rather, he confines himself to the employment of less pretentious terms, such as might be used in more ordinary ways of speaking about the experiences and phenomena with which he is concerned.

Marcel does speak of *aliénation*, in one passage in his book *Being and Having*, in which he is discussing the contrast between "the thinker" and "the ideologist." The former, he suggests, never makes an unconditional commitment to any particular idea; "the whole of his thought is always being called in question. . . ." Whereas the latter, in his devotion to one of his ideas, "is unconsciously enslaved to a [deadened] part of himself"—a condition which Marcel suggests might be viewed as an "alienation of the subject . . . in the face of the thing." (9, 180–81) His use of the term here, however, is neither novel—it derives directly from Marx—nor extensive,

[2] My translation.

being confined to a single paragraph. And he would not appear to use the term elsewhere in his writings, in this context or in any other, except on occasion in an ordinary sense.

One might expect that Camus, at least, would make extensive use of the term; for his name is commonly mentioned in popular discussions of alienation. In point of fact, however, he does not use the term at all. Consider the following passage from *The Myth of Sisyphus*, which resembles the one from Jaspers cited above:

> One step further—and alienness confronts us: the perception that the world is "dense," the realization of how very alien a stone is, how impenetrable it is for us, and of the intensity with which nature or a landscape denies us. In the depths of every beauty there lies something inhuman . . . , [which renders it] more remote from us than a lost paradise. (1, 107)[3]

Like Jaspers, Camus confines himself to the use of such ordinary terms as "alien" (*étrange*) and "alienness" (*étrangeté*). It would be an error to attribute to *étrangeté* the sense of "alien*ation*," for reasons of both ordinary linguistic usage and Camus' intent in using the term. He is concerned to characterize a *way* in which the world is seen, rather than the process of *coming to* (or having come to) see it that way. Others might find it desirable to speak of alienation in this connection; Camus does not.

Similarly, many have seen in Camus' character Meursault —in *The Stranger* (2)—an excellent example, and even a paradigm case, of a man extremely alienated from the people and the society around him. But however appropriate it may be to use this term to describe Meursault, it is not Camus' term. Camus refers to him simply as *l'étranger*—"the stranger" or "alien." This work belongs not to that body of literature in which the term "alienation" is employed, but rather to the related body of literature in which other terms are used to express similar ideas. The same holds true of Camus' other writings.

If the commonly held view linking alienation with ex-

[3] My translation.

istentialism has any justification, therefore, it is not to be found in the fact that all or most of the principal writers associated with existentialism make extensive use of the term; for they do not. It is to be found, if anywhere, in the fact that *some* influential existentialists do speak of it; and in the further fact that certain of the phenomena discussed by others lend themselves sufficiently readily to characterization in terms of "alienation" to enable such characterizations to catch on. Insofar as the term is associated with notions of the separation or isolation of the individual from nature (or the world), society, and other people, however, its use is completely unrelated even to the ways in which it *is* used by Heidegger, Sartre, and Tillich, as shall be seen.

II. *Entfremdung* in Heidegger's *Being and Time*

Heidegger's discussion of alienation (*Entfremdung*) occurs in his most famous work, *Being and Time*.[4] While the term appears no more than half a dozen times in the entire book, its occurrence is not without significance; for it is introduced into the discussion quite systematically, and is associated with such central Heideggerian concepts as "falling" and "inauthenticity."

Heidegger distinguishes what might be called two fundamental ways of living, one of which he terms "authentic" (*eigentlich*), and the other "inauthentic" (*uneigentlich*). These terms have strong evaluative overtones; but he would have them understood very literally and purely descriptively. "Authentic" existence is self-determined existence, shaped

---

[4] In my citations I follow the translation of Macquarrie and Robinson (4), with a few minor exceptions. My page references, however, are to the German edition (5); for while the German pagination is indicated marginally in the English edition, the reverse (quite naturally) is not true.

It is of some interest to note that *Sein und Zeit* was first published in 1927—five years before the first publication of Marx's "Economic and Philosophical Manuscripts" of 1844. Heidegger's use of the term *Entfremdung* is thus one instance of its use which is not to be traced to the publication of Marx's "Manuscripts." He might conceivably have been familiar with Hegel's use of the term in the *Phenomenology*; if he was, however, this is not explicitly indicated.

and given direction by decisions and choices which are truly one's *own* (*eigene*), and are made in full awareness of the fundamental conditions of human life (e.g., having to die, being responsible for what one is and does). And "inauthentic" existence is existence which is absorbed in the present, determined by impersonal social expectations and conventions, and which exhibits a systematic refusal to face up to the above-mentioned conditions. Heidegger would also have the term "falling" (*Verfallen*) understood nonevaluatively, as referring to an inherent human tendency to slip into or remain in the latter mode of existence.

Each of the types of existence indicated is characterized as a "potentiality-for-being" (*Seinkönnen*) for man (or, in Heidegger's terminology, for *Dasein*). That is, each type of existence is a potential way of "being" for man, which each of us may or may not actualize. And Heidegger refers to the former type as "Dasein's ownmost non-relational potentiality-for-being," reflecting the fact that it is that sort of existence which is not determined by one's relations to "the others," but rather by one's own decisions and choices. To exist "inauthentically" is to be divorced from one's "ownmost non-relational potentiality-for-being."

It is in this connection that Heidegger speaks of "alienation." He refers to such a case as one in which there exists "an alienation in which [Dasein's] ownmost potentiality-for-being is hidden from it." (5, 178) The term is not used to designate *any* state in which one or another of one's "potentialities-for-being" is not realized; Heidegger never terms "authentic" existence a state in which there exists "an alienation of Dasein from its fallen, public potentiality-for-being." Rather, his use of the term is restricted to cases in which one does not exist in an "authentic" manner: cases in which one is cut off or separated from one's potential "authentic" existence, and in which one's potential "authentic" existence is thus "alien" to one. It is no doubt the fact that cases of this sort can be characterized in this way, which accounts for the seeming appropriateness of the term "alienation" in this context.

Heidegger uses the term in connection with three specific (and presumably interrelated) phenomena associated with "falling" and "inauthenticity." The first is a certain way of thinking (or avoiding thinking) about death. Death for Heidegger is one of the individual's "possibilities-of-being" (*Seinsmöglichkeiten*)—a possibility which may or may not be realized in the immediate future, but which must be realized eventually and which might be realized at any moment. The full recognition of this fact is something to which Heidegger attaches great importance; for he considers it to be a necessary condition of "non-relational," "authentic" existence.

> If Dasein stands before itself as this possibility, it is
> fully referred to its ownmost potentiality-for-being. [For]
> when it stands before itself in this way, all its relations to
> any other Dasein are undone. (5, 250)

Heidegger observes, however, that people have a tendency not to face up to the fact that they themselves must die. They tend to consider the matter no further than to admit the truth of the general and impersonal proposition that "one dies"—something they can do with relative equanimity. He then goes on to say: "The cultivation of such a 'superior' indifference *alienates* Dasein from its ownmost non-relational potentiality-for-being." (5, 254) This way of viewing the matter keeps the fact that we ourselves must die at arm's length, and thus precludes the attainment of that personal recognition of this fact which is purported to be a necessary condition of "authentic" existence. It thus contributes to Dasein's alienation.

Heidegger also speaks of "alienation" in his discussion of the different temporal orientations which it is possible for us to adopt. "Authenticity" is not conceived simply in terms of "being-towards-death." It is also conceived in terms of self-directedness, or the structuring of one's life in accordance with *projects* one resolves upon. Both involve a relation to the future, as opposed to complete absorption with the past or in the present. The predominant temporal orientation of "authentic" Dasein is thus toward the future.

Heidegger suggests, however, that Dasein has a tendency to become absorbed in the novelties and distractions of the present. When it is so absorbed, its existence ceases to be determined by its recognition of its "having to die" and projects of its own undertaking, which are essential to its "authenticity." Consequently, Heidegger states, it is "alienated from its ownmost potentiality-for-being." (5, 348)

In the third context in which he speaks of "alienation," he is concerned with the fact that it is possible for Dasein to achieve a kind of superficial understanding of itself which does not lay the foundation for "authentic" existence, as does a profound, genuine self-knowledge, but rather has precisely the opposite effect: It "*closes off* from [Dasein] its authenticity and possibility." He has in mind those who occupy themselves with human cultural life, and who think that "understanding the most alien cultures and 'synthesizing' them with one's own may lead to Dasein's becoming for the first time thoroughly and genuinely enlightened about itself." (5, 178)

Heidegger considers this cultural-anthropological view to be mistaken, since reflection on this level cannot by its very nature yield the kind of vivid and personal recognition of such things as one's own "having to die" and one's responsibility for oneself, which constitute genuine self-knowledge. Moreover, he feels that this kind of orientation tends to lead to a preoccupation and satisfaction with a superficial cultural understanding of human life, and thus to a blindness to those more fundamental features of human existence which must be confronted and acknowledged if "authenticity" is to be attained. In such a case, he says, Dasein "drifts along towards an alienation in which its ownmost potentiality-for-being is hidden from it." (5, 178)

These are the only passages in *Being and Time* in which "alienation" is mentioned. Heidegger uses the term quite consistently. In each case he is concerned with some attitude or orientation which has the effect of removing some one of the necessary conditions of "authentic" existence, and thus of rendering such existence an unactualized possibility. And the term "alienation" in each case refers to this failure to actualize the possibility of "authentic" existence.

Heidegger's conception of alienation is thus somewhat similar to the Hegelian and Marxian conceptions of "self-alienation" construed in terms of a disparity between a person's essential nature and his actual condition; for that from

which "inauthentic" Dasein is alienated could be characterized as a possible type of "selfhood." But Heidegger differs
radically from Hegel and the early Marx, in that he at least
claims not to be assigning to any of man's "potentialities-for-
being" the status of "man's essence"—or even the status of an
objective ideal of human existence, in the manner of Fromm.
Rather, he purports merely to be *describing* different possible
types of existence, without assigning relative values to them.
This, he holds, is all that philosophy can do, if it aspires to
general validity; for two of his most basic contentions are
that man has no fixed essence over and above the basic and
inescapable conditions of his existence, and that there exists
no basis for value judgments other than personal decision.

While these basic views do dictate a restriction to the kind
of neutral descriptive program to which Heidegger professes
to confine himself, it may plausibly be argued that he in fact
is less than scrupulous in his observance of this self-limitation.
It has often been observed that terms like "authentic," "inauthentic," and "falling" are questionable choices if one's
program is simply that of nonevaluative description. Heidegger's use of the term "alienation" only raises further doubts
about his profession of confinement to this program. If one
merely wished to distinguish between and describe several
basic "potentialities-for-being," without granting one or another of them a privileged (essential or ideal) status, the
proper procedure would seem to be either to use the term
"alienation" to refer to states in which *any* such "potentiality"
is unrealized, or not to use it at all. Heidegger, however, does
use it, but only in connection with states in which *one* such
potentiality is not realized—one which it is plain he, in point
of fact, favors. This constitutes unequal treatment of the different potentialities; and where the term is employed selec-
tively, as it is here, it tends to impart a negative coloring to
that to which it is applied.

Heidegger does nothing to compensate for this inequality
of treatment, because he welcomes its result. Favoring a certain type of existence over others, but being unable to argue
that his preference has any objective basis, he chooses his
terms in such a way that, while he can claim simply to be

describing, their overtones and associations do the work of winning people over to his point of view. "Alienation" is one such term. Heidegger introduces it as a technical, descriptive term. Its value to him lies less in the purely descriptive function it performs in his explicitly developed scheme, however, than in the persuasive function it performs by virtue of its extra-systematic associations. For people tend to understand the term not simply in the sense of "separation," but rather in the sense of "a separation which ought not exist."

It need hardly be said that the legitimacy of such a procedure is questionable. It may be legitimate to employ a term which has come to have certain overtones and associations, in circumstances requiring that they be set aside; but only provided that one makes a special effort to neutralize them (and that they are weak enough to render the undertaking reasonable). Heidegger not only does not do this in the present case, but seems to have employed the term with its overtones and associations expressly in mind.

Given his basic views about essence and values, the state of "alienation from one's ownmost non-relational potentiality-for-being" cannot be construed as a state in which a disparity exists between one's actual condition and one's essential nature or an objective ideal of human existence. It can legitimately be understood only as a state in which one is *other than one might be*—just as is the case when one exists "authentically." If this is all that can be meant, however, the point of characterizing such a state as one of "alienation" is largely lost. For to have any point, it would seem to require that the unrealized type of "selfhood" in question be granted a privileged position. If so, Heidegger's use of the term derives what appropriateness it may appear to have from the fact that we tend to think in essentialist terms, which Heidegger himself requires us to reject.

III. Estrangement in Tillich's *Systematic Theology*

Tillich conceives of "estrangement" rather like Heidegger would seem to *want* Entfremdung to be understood; only Tillich does not have Heidegger's qualms about speaking in essentialist terms. In his *Systematic Theology* (15),[5] he speaks constantly of "man's essential nature" (or "being" or "state"); and he uses the expression in a very traditional way, to refer to what man, as such, "essentially is and ought to be." This places him in a much better position than Heidegger to defend his use of the term "estrangement," which he introduces precisely in terms of a disparity between man's actual ("existential") condition and his essential nature. "Existence is estranged from essence," he states. (II, 30) "Man's estrangement from his essential being is the universal character of existence." (II, 74)

Tillich's essentialism constitutes a rather significant departure from the position taken by most existential philosophers. He is commonly styled an "existentialist," and it is in considerable measure through his influence that the term "alienation" (through its synonymy with his term "estrangement") has come to be linked closely with existentialism. At least on these matters, however, he stands considerably closer to Hegel—whose influence he explicitly acknowledges (II, 45)—than he does to Heidegger and Sartre. He attempts to characterize the difference between Hegel and his existentialist critics in terms of his acceptance, and their rejection, of the view that man *can overcome* the disparity between his actual condition and his essential nature. But this way of presenting the difference between them obscures the fact that whatever they may do in their weaker moments, philosophers such as Heidegger and Sartre are united in their explicit and emphatic rejection of the view that man as such has an essential nature which defines how one ought to be, and which one may or may not actualize.

It remains a fact that Tillich is commonly linked with Heidegger and Sartre—an association which he himself encourages, both by his evident sympathy with them, and by his frequent use of the term "existential" in his presentation of his own views. (Indeed, in Volume Three of *Systematic*

[5] Since all references in this section are to this work, I shall not explicitly identify the work each time I refer to a passage in it. Because it is published in three volumes, whose pages are not consecutively numbered, I shall indicate the volume number by a Roman numeral, as well as the page number. E.g.: (II, 112)

Theology, "estrangement" is indexed not by itself, but rather as: "estrangement, existential.") This association explains why he is considered together with Heidegger and Sartre here. It should be clear, however, that profound philosophical differences separate him and them. And these differences directly affect the way in which "estrangement" or "alienation" is to be construed in their writings. The English, German, and French terms they employ may be equivalent; but this should not be taken to indicate the existence of a single "existentialist" conception of "alienation."

The importance of the concept of estrangement in Tillich's thought can be seen in two positions he takes. First, he argues that estrangement is virtually definitive of human existence as such: "The state of existence is the state of estrangement. . . . Man as he exists is not what he essentially is and ought to be. He is estranged from his true being." (II, 44–45) Tillich considers estrangement to be the basic "question" associated with the "human situation." And since, in his view, it is the task of theology to show what the "answers" to such "questions" are, the problem of estrangement becomes the central issue with which he has to deal.

Secondly, the whole significance of Jesus is conceived by Tillich in terms of the overcoming of this estrangement. Jesus' "greatness" is said to consist precisely in "his power of conquering existential estrangement." (II, 146) And Tillich characterizes him "as the bearer of the New Being or as the one in whom . . . man's existential estrangement is overcome." (II, 125) To identify a problem as the problem to which Jesus was the solution is, for a Christian theologian, to assign it the greatest possible importance.

As has been seen, Tillich presents his concept of estrangement in terms of a disparity between man's actual or "existential" condition and his essential nature. He sometimes speaks of the estrangement of *existence* from essence, and at other times speaks of the estrangement of *man* from his essential nature (or being or state); but his meaning is the same in both cases. And just as Hegel had used the expression *Entfremdung seiner selbst* to refer to one in this condition, Tillich often characterizes it as the condition of "estrangement from oneself."

Estrangement and Man's Nature

When Tillich writes, "Each expression of the estranged state contradicts man's essential being, his potency for goodness" (II, 59–60), it is natural to conclude that he intends man's essential being to be construed in terms of the "potency for goodness." When he writes, "Only what is essentially free can come under existential bondage" (II, 79), the implication would seem to be that man's essential nature is to be conceived in terms of freedom. And when he asserts that Jesus is "the one in whom the conflict between the essential unity of God and man and man's existential estrangement is overcome" (II, 125), the suggestion would seem to be that the defining characteristic of man's essential nature is unity with God.

It is far from clear, in the light of these and other comparable passages, precisely how man's essential nature is to be understood; for the characteristics mentioned display considerable diversity. Since "estrangement" is defined in terms of a disparity between existence and essence, however, any lack of clarity with regard to what constitutes man's essence results in a lack of clarity with regard to the precise nature of estrangement.

Tillich further refers to "the three concepts of 'unbelief,' 'concupiscence,' and *hubris*"[6] as "the marks of man's estrangement." (II, 47) The term "mark" is rather ambiguous, and does not clearly indicate the relation between these concepts and the concept of estrangement. It can be used to designate either a characteristic of something ("Fidelity is the mark of friendship"), or the effect or manifestation of something ("He bore the marks of many sorrows"). On some occasions, Tillich uses language which seems to indicate that the second interpretation is intended: as when, for example, he refers to the three phenomena in question as "expressions of estrangement." (II, 47) On other occasions, however, he seems to suggest that they are related to estrangement in a more intimate way—as phenomena in terms of which the concept of

[6] "*Hubris* is the self-elevation of man into the sphere of the divine." (II, 50) "Its main symptom is that man does not acknowledge his finitude." (II, 51)

estrangement is to be concretely conceived. Thus he asserts: "The characteristics of the New Being are the opposite of those of estrangement, namely, faith instead of unbelief, surrender instead of *hubris*, love instead of concupiscence." (II, 177)

On the whole, the evidence would appear to favor the latter interpretation. Perhaps most significantly, Tillich uses as section headings the phrases "Estrangement as 'concupiscence'" (II, 51), "Estrangement as 'Unbelief'" (II, 47), and "Estrangement as 'Hubris.'" (II, 49) His use of the word "as" here suggests that the three phenomena are meant to be understood not merely as the effects of estrangement, but rather as its constituents. It thus would seem that an explication of Tillich's concept of estrangement must make reference to the phenomena of unbelief, *hubris*, and concupiscence. And since estrangement is to be construed formally in terms of a disparity between existence and essence, it follows that the "opposites" of these phenomena—"belief," "acknowledgment of finitude" (II, 51), and "love"—are also elements of man's essence.

Nor is this all; for there are yet other phenomena which Tillich terms "characteristics" of estrangement. One is what he calls "the separation of dynamics from form." (II, 64) By this he means the loss of the proper balance between the principles of dynamism and structure or order. Another involves experiencing as "evil" the basic features of "finitude" (e.g., death, guilt, suffering): "The transformation of essential finitude into existential evil is a general characteristic of the state of estrangement." (II, 68) And yet another involves "the separation of individualization from participation." (II, 66) Here Tillich would seem to have in mind the loss of the ability to exist simultaneously as a genuine individual and in community with others.

Given that these phenomena too are "characteristics" of estrangement, its construal in terms of an existence-essence disparity implies that descriptions of the proper balance between "dynamics" and "form," the proper way of viewing the features of finitude, and the unity of "individualization" and "participation" must also be included in the characterization of man's essential nature. The result is a conception of man's essence that is very complex indeed—so much so, in fact, that it hardly seems tenable.

No conception of such complexity would be required if either the construal of estrangement in terms of a disparity between existence and essence were to be abandoned, or the number and variety of phenomena regarded as "character-istics" of it were to be reduced. The first alternative would seem to be ruled out for Tillich; for this way of conceiving of "estrangement" is too basic to his entire discussion to be abandoned so long as other alternatives remain. The second alternative, on the other hand, would not appear to be at-tended by any great internal inconvenience. Tillich's own occasional references to the phenomena in question as "mani-festations" or "expressions" of estrangement suggest at least some willingness on his part to move in this direction. One or the other of these modifications is necessary, however, if the problem of commitment to an implausibly complex con-ception of man's essence is to be avoided.

The adoption of the second alternative would also have the advantage of at least partially mitigating another difficulty. Tillich's language indicates that he does not consider the above phenomena to constitute so many distinct *types* of estrangement, which may individually be designated as such even if none of the others are present. By terming them char-acteristics of "estrangement generally," he implies that it is appropriate to use the term only if all of them are present. It is not at all difficult, however, to imagine cases in which some are present, but others are not. Unbelief and *hubris*, for ex-ample, would seem quite compatible with maintenance of a proper balance between "dynamics and form," and with both "individualization" and "participation." Tillich does seem to want to be able to speak of "estrangement" in any case in which unbelief, *hubris*, and concupiscence are to be found. For this to be possible, it is necessary that only these phe-nomena (and those—if any—which invariably accompany them) be regarded as characteristics or constituents of "es-trangement generally." Otherwise, cases in which these and only these are present would not constitute cases of es-trangement.

The basic problem is not entirely eliminated, however,

even if attention is confined to these three alone; for the occurrence of any one of them need not be accompanied by that of the others. Unbelief is quite compatible with acknowledgment of one's finitude, and need not be accompanied by concupiscence, which Tillich conceives as "the unlimited desire to draw the whole of reality into one's self." (II, 52) And since the latter is defined solely in terms of a "desire" (with no mention of one's estimation of one's ability to satisfy it), while *hubris* is to be understood in terms of a failure to acknowledge one's limitations, these phenomena too can occur independently of each other. The problem becomes even greater when one recalls Tillich's rather explicit suggestions that estrangement is to be conceived in terms of the loss of one's "essential freedom" (II, 78–79), and in terms of the loss of one's "essential goodness." (II, 59–60) For it is far from obvious that these losses are necessarily associated with or reducible to either each other or unbelief, *hubris*, and concupiscence.

Tillich, once again, does not present these phenomena as so many different and distinct *types* of estrangement. Rather, he takes them to constitute one and the same estrangement. As a result, quite a few things must go wrong simultaneously if the use of the term is to be appropriate. He seems to think they always do; so he does not consider the problem which arises when—as in fact appears possible—they do not.

An indication of how he might deal with this problem is to be found in the fact that he quite clearly wants to be able to speak of "estrangement" whenever one of these phenomena in particular occurs—namely, unbelief. Unbelief would appear to be the real heart of the matter, the other phenomena mentioned being consequences of it which are supposedly present when it is present, and absent when it is absent. If the status of the latter as constituents of estrangement is not primitive, however, but rather derives from their purported (though questionable) association with unbelief, it would follow that this alone is the truly fundamental and definitive characteristic of estrangement for Tillich. This may very well be a point he would be quite willing to allow. Unfortunately, instead of making it clearly himself, he says many things which obscure the issue, and seem to support a variety of rather different interpretations.

Estrangement and Unity with God

At first glance, it may seem odd of Tillich to conceive of "estrangement" in terms of an existence-essence disparity, and at the same time in terms of a loss or lack of unity between the individual and God. For this may appear to involve a curious neglect of the seemingly obvious distinction between the traditional conception of "estrangement from God" and the Hegelian conception of "estrangement (or alienation) from one's self." It becomes at least comprehensible, however, when one recalls that for Hegel, man's essential nature is to be conceived (in part) in terms of universality, and thus of unity with the social substance; and that, therefore, where estrangement from the social substance exists, there also exists a disparity between one's actual condition and one's essential nature. The same sort of connection exists for Tillich; only for him, "unity with God" replaces unity with the social substance. Thus he writes, "essential humanity includes the union of God and man." (II, 94)

This seems clear enough, as long as one is content to talk in such very general terms. But here too, very substantial problems are encountered, as soon as one raises the question of how the "union of God and man" of which Tillich speaks is to be understood. In particular, some of his remarks presuppose the possibility of distinguishing between God and man, as has traditionally been done; whereas others seem not merely to characterize man's essential nature in terms of union with God, but rather to *identify* man's essential nature and God.

Remarks of the first sort are not difficult to find. For example, Tillich characterizes "sin" as "the state of estrangement from that to which one belongs—God, one's self, one's world." (II, 46) Again, he suggests that the Law of the Old Testament "shows to man his essential nature, his true relationship to God, other men, and himself." (II, 81) And he asserts: "Man is estranged from the ground of his being [i.e., God], from other beings, and from himself." (II, 44) In all of these passages, "God" and man's (essential) "self" are mentioned separately; and the general impression created is that the two are quite distinct.

On the other hand, there are central passages in which the two appear to be identified. For example, after using the expression "essential manhood," Tillich says: "One could also speak of essential God-manhood, in order to indicate the divine presence in essential manhood; but this is redundant. . . ." (II, 94) And rather than confining himself to speaking relatively unambiguously of man's estrangement from "the ground of being" (i.e., God) on the one hand, and from "his true (or essential) being" on the other, he often refers to man as "estranged" from "the ground of *his* being"— a phrase which can be interpreted in either way. By using this phrase, he seems to be suggesting that the above distinction is no real distinction, and that man is estranged from one and the same thing in both cases.

The same conclusion emerges when one considers his remarks about man's "center." One's initial tendency is to interpret his references to man's "estrangement from God in the center of his being" (e.g., II, 48), as though his point were simply that man is "estranged from God" not just superficially, but rather deep inside. In point of fact, however, much more is involved than this. Tillich uses the term "center" to refer to the ordering and unifying focal point of the "self." Since the term "self" can be used to refer both to the way a person actually is and to his essential nature, one's "personal center" will fail to coincide with one's "essential center," just in the event that a disparity exists between one's actual condition and one's essential nature. And when one's "personal center" fails to coincide with one's "essential center," Tillich considers it appropriate to speak of "estrangement," just as he does when the above-mentioned disparity exists. Nor is this unreasonable, since the same point is being made in both cases.

Tillich further states that Jesus "is not estranged from the ground of his being. There are no traces of . . . the removal of his personal center from the divine center which is the subject of his infinite concern." (II, 126) Two points emerge from this passage. First, since "the divine center" mentioned is said to be "the subject of [Jesus'] infinite concern," it is

clear that when Tillich uses the former expression he is referring to God. His remarks elsewhere concerning man's relation
to "the divine center," therefore, are also presumably to be understood as concerning man's relation to God. Secondly, since
Jesus' "personal center" is said to be at one with "the divine
center," and since—as the one in whom "estrangement is
conquered" (II, 135)—his "personal center" coincides with
his "essential center," it follows that there is an intimate connection between the notions of man's "essential center" and
"the divine center," or God. And this connection would appear to be one of identity. For after stating, "In estrangement, man is outside the divine center to which his own
center essentially belongs," Tillich goes on to refer to "man's
turning away from the divine center" as a case of man's "leaving his essential center." (II, 49–50)

This identification of God and man's essential being (or
of "Godhood" and "essential-manhood"), and the identification of "estrangement from God" and "estrangement from
man's essential nature" which it entails, might not be considered unfortunate in themselves. And there may be something to be said for his attempt to retain traditional ways of
speaking while radically reinterpreting the notion of God.
But the traditional ways of speaking about God have implications which are often at variance with the proposed rein-
terpretations; and as a consequence, Tillich appears to be
employing several different conceptions of God at once. Indeed, this may be more than an appearance. For there is a
danger, in employing traditional ways of speaking, of lapsing
into traditional ways of thinking; and this is a danger to which
Tillich is far from immune. As has been observed, there are a
significant number of passages in which Tillich's language
requires that God and man's essential being be conceived as
distinct. As a result, no single unambiguous answer to the
question of precisely what "estrangement" involves emerges
from his discussion.

Even if these passages are ignored, however, the answer
which does emerge is not very illuminating. It will be recalled that Tillich's formal characterization of "estrangement"
is in terms of a disparity between actual condition and essential nature; and that "unbelief," or the lack of unity with

God, is the phenomenon in terms of which he would have this estrangement be more concretely understood. But now it turns out that this lack of unity with God consists precisely in a disparity between man's actual being and his essential being! A great deal of ground seems to have been covered; but in fact we know little more than we did at the outset.

To be sure, the use of such terms as "God," "divine," and "ultimate" serves to paint the notion of man's essential nature in more lively colors. But this may not be such a good thing. Nothing is really gained in terms of conceptual content; and terms like these have associations which tend to lead the unwary and the traditionally-minded astray. In particular, the tendency to associate the term "God" with a supernatural being distinct from man and the world is strong. If the retention of traditional language resulted in significant conceptual gains, taking this risk might be justifiable. It is far from evident, however, that it does.

The Origin and Overcoming of Estrangement

In conclusion, notice must be taken of a number of seeming contradictions in Tillich's discussion of estrangement, which appear not to bother him—indeed, he affirms several of them explicitly—but which should give even the sympathetic reader pause. The first occurs in connection with the question of whether the state of estrangement is or is not to be understood as a disparity which develops out of a prior state of unity or harmony of existence and essence. Tillich explicitly disavows the idea of any such idyllic "once upon a time" (II, 29), and asserts upon numerous occasions that the disparity between essence and existence characterizes "the human situation universally." (E.g., II, 36, 45, 74) Yet in spite of this apparently categorical rejection of the idea of an initial period of identity of existence and essence, he constantly uses language which would be appropriate only if an initial identity were presupposed.

"Love," for example, is termed the striving for the "reunion" of what is separated—in the context, existence and essence. (II, 47) "Reunion," however, presupposes "union." Again, Tillich asserts: "In the state of estrangement, the relation to the ultimate power of being is lost." (II, 68) But one cannot have "lost" what one has never *had*. And perhaps most importantly, Tillich constantly speaks of "the transition from essence to existence." Thus while he explicitly rejects the idea of an initial period in human history or in the life of the individual in which there was or is no estrangement, the language he uses often suggests just such an idea. He may not actually hold contradictory views on the matter; but his language makes it seem as though he does, and certainly is misleading.

More seriously, Tillich explicitly holds the individual responsible for his estrangement; yet he equally explicitly traces it to the nature of human existence in general. In addition to the passages cited above, there occur a number of others in which the former position is asserted. For example, "the individual act of existential estrangement" is termed "an act of freedom." (II, 38) Similarly, Tillich speaks of the "element of personal responsibility in one's estrangement." (II, 46) Toward the end of Volume II, he frequently associates the notion of estrangement with the notion of "human guilt." (E.g., II, 170, 178) And in the same vein, he introduces the volume with the statement: "The question implied in human estrangement is directed toward the answer: forgiveness." (II, 15)

On the other hand, passages are everywhere to be found in which estrangement is held to be a necessary concomitant of human existence as such—and thereby, one would think, something for which the individual is *not* to be held responsible. It is said to characterize "the human situation universally," not because it simply so happens that all men exercise the same fateful option, but rather because to exist is to be estranged. "The transition from essence to existence is the original fact. . . . It ontologically precedes everything that happens in time and space. It sets the conditions of spatial and temporal existence." (II, 36) Or, more concisely stated, "Actualized creation and estranged existence are identical." (II, 44) Under these circumstances, it is difficult to see where the responsibility of the individual could lie. Indeed, Tillich explicitly rejects the view that "each individual could always either contradict or not contradict his essential nature." (II, 41)

Here he is neither simply using misleading and inappropriate language, nor unwittingly contradicting himself. He openly asserts that *both* of the above ways of viewing estrangement are correct: One "must simultaneously acknowledge the tragic universality of estrangement and man's personal responsibility for it." (II, 39) The acknowledgment of both simultaneously may pose no problem for those accustomed to performing a similar feat in connection with the traditional Christian conception of "original sin," to which Tillich's concept of estrangement is admittedly and obviously related. To the uninitiated mind, however, he appears to be proposing the acceptance of views which exclude each other. For both to be true would be every bit as mysterious as theologians traditionally have acknowledged original sin to be.

Quite as mysterious is Tillich's subsequent suggestion that estrangement may be overcome after all, in spite of its "tragic universality." While holding that "no act within the context of existential estrangement can overcome existential estrangement" (II, 78), he contends that it can be overcome through "grace." "Grace . . . does what freedom under the conditions of existence cannot do, namely, it reunites the estranged." (II, 79) If man "accepts . . . the divine offer of reconciliation" (II, 170), he is enabled to participate in "the New Being," which is to be conceived in terms of characteristics which are "the opposite of those of estrangement."[7] And if one does so, Tillich states quite clearly, one's estrangement is overcome. "To experience the New Being in Jesus as the Christ means to experience the power in him which *has conquered* existential estrangement in himself and *in everyone who participates in him*." (II, 125; emphasis added.)

If "everyone who participates in [Jesus as the Christ]" has overcome his estrangement, however, and if such participation is a real possibility, we would seem to be confronted with another contradiction. For the view that there can be (and presumably are) such people would appear to contradict the view that "actualized creation and estranged existence are identical." (II, 44) If, as he claims, estrangement is "always

---

[7] "The characteristics of the New Being are the opposite of those of estrangement, namely, faith instead of unbelief, surrender instead of *hubris*, love instead of concupiscence." (II, 177)

present" (III, 355), and "sets the conditions of spatial and temporal existence" (II, 36), it is not easy to imagine how anyone who continues to exist in space and time can reach a state of "Being" the characteristics of which are "the opposite of those of estrangement." If "grace" actually "reunites the estranged," there is no longer any disparity between existence and essence of the person who receives it. The suggestion that this can and does happen, however, is difficult to square with the view that this disparity is "the universal destiny of existence." (II, 38) Here again, it is quite clear that Tillich's affirmation of both positions is not inadvertent; for in the space of a single sentence he refers to "the universality of existential estrangement and the uniqueness of the victory over estrangement." (II, 129)

In short, Tillich's conception of estrangement is developed in a way that commits him to seeming contradictions. The notion of the possibility of a disparity between one's actual condition and one's essential nature, and the use of the term "estrangement" to refer to it, are reasonable enough. Even if a satisfactory explication of man's essential nature is given, however, the tenability of any associated conception of estrangement will be questionable, as long as the appearance of contradiction in its development persists.

IV. *Aliénation* in Sartre's Major Works

Sartre uses the term *aliénation* very differently than Heidegger and Tillich use its German and English counterparts. In fact, he uses it in two different ways in his two principal philosophical works, both of which (in relation to Heidegger and Tillich) are quite distinctive. Neither, however, is radically new. The conception of alienation to be found in his *Critique of Dialectical Reason* (12) is obviously and admittedly Marxian; while that to be found in *Being and Nothingness* (11) is similar to one previously developed by Edmund Husserl. Very briefly, in the *Critique* the term is used in connection with the emergence of the individual's own self-objectification as something alien and hostile to him; while in *Being and Nothingness* it is used in connection with the individual's experience of himself as an object (rather than pure subject), through the mediation of another individual. The latter is Sartre's only non-Marxist, and therefore distinctively "existential," use of the term; and it is a very technical one, quite unrelated to anything most people have in mind when they associate the term with existentialism.

Husserl, *Ent-fremdung*, and Self-Perception

While Husserl's discussion of *Ent-fremdung*[8] is not of very great significance in the context of his own thought, an awareness of it facilitates an understanding of Sartre's use of the term *aliénation* in *Being and Nothingness*. Sartre does not refer explicitly to Husserl's discussion; but it is plausible to assume his familiarity with it, in view of the striking similarity between their uses of the terms, and the fact that he was a close student of Husserl's in the years prior to his writing of this work.

The passage from Husserl in question occurs in *The Crisis of the European Sciences and Transcendental Phenomenology*. (7)[9] At one point in it he is concerned with the phenomenon of *Einfühlung*—a sympathetic "perception of an Other, of another 'I,' [as a] for-itself-I, as I am." Through such sympathetic perception, "an 'other' 'I' comes into existence for me, as co-present with me, and with a kind of self-evidence which is obviously completely other than that of 'sensuous perception.'" (7, 189) This is how Husserl deals with the problem of the detection of the existence of "other minds." The fact that others have the same subject-character for themselves as I do for myself is not something to be *inferred* (e.g., by an argument from the similarity of my "sensuous perceptions" of myself and of the other, and from the fact that in my own case these are given together with my

8 Husserl's hyphenation.

9 As of this writing, this work as such has not yet been translated into English (citations in English are my translations). The original lecture on which it was based has been translated—it is included in the volume *Phenomenology and the Crisis of Philosophy* (6)—but the relevant material does not appear in it.

existence as a subject). Rather, this fact is self-evidently *given* through the phenomenon of *Einfühlung*.

One result, in Husserl's view, is what he calls "my alienation [*Ent-fremdung*]." (7, 189) Others are revealed to me as subjects for themselves through *Einfühlung*; but they are also given to me in "sensuous perception" as *objects*. They thus have both a subject-character and an object-character for me. And as I come to realize that others are subjects for themselves as I am for myself, I am compelled to recognize that in their eyes I have an object-character as well as a subject-character, just as they do for me. Moreover, I must acknowledge that their view of me has as much validity as does mine of them. The other person thus serves as a kind of mirror, in which I perceive that I am not wholly subject, but rather also have the character of an object. Here I experience myself as something "other," something "alien" to me in my subjectivity. In short, I experience "my alien-ation."

Aliénation in *Being and Nothingness*

In Sartre's *Being and Nothingness*, the term *aliénation* is used in connection with a similar experience. Sartre's point of departure is not the phenomenon of *Einfühlung*, the suggestion of community with the other which this term suggests being quite foreign to this work. He introduces the term in connection with another phenomenon, which however lends itself to the same purpose: "the Look of the Other."

When I experience the Other's Look—Sartre's classical example is that of being surprised by another while peeking through a keyhole (11, 259 ff.)—Sartre feels that there can be no question for me of his nature; I can no longer seriously entertain the hypothesis that the Other is nothing more than an object. One can use Husserl's words to convey Sartre's point: I become aware "of another 'I,' [as a] for-itself-I, as I am." And in "the act of being-looked-at" by what I recognize to be another being with the character of a subject (another "I"), I experience what Sartre terms "the alienation of myself." (11, 263)

> In the shock that seizes me when I apprehend the Other's Look . . . I experience a subtle alienation of all

my possibilities, which are now associated with objects of the world, far from me in the midst of the world. (11, 264–65)

In Sartre's view, I am not merely an object, a thing among other things. Rather, my nature is to be conceived in terms of *freedom*. Thus it is my possibilities, and not simply my determinate characteristics, which are definitive of my existence. The Other, however, Looking at me, sees only my determinate characteristics. To him, while he is observing me in this way, I appear as an object, rather than a free subject. "Of course I *am* still my possibilities. . . . But at the same time, the Look alienates them from me." (11, 263) For "my presence, insofar as it is a present grasped by another as my present, has an outside"; and it is only this objective outside that he sees. (11, 267) And perceiving this, I now experience myself as having a dimension of objectivity. Indeed, Sartre suggests that it is only under these circumstances that my awareness of my objectivity emerges: "The Other's Look [is] the necessary condition of my objectivity. . . ." (11, 269)

As in the case of Husserl, my recognition of the subject-character of the Other thus involves the experience of myself as I appear to him. It is as an object that I appear to him, when he Looks at me; and so it is as an object that I now experience myself. The object-self which I experience, however, is a self which seems "alien" to me; for it is radically different from the selfhood I experience when I consider myself simply as subject, as I do when I am confronted merely with a variety of objects.

My natural tendency, according to Sartre, is to be repulsed by this "alien Me," and to try to tear myself away from the relation to the Other which reveals it to me, in an attempt to avoid acknowledging it. "But as I choose myself as a tearing away from the Other, I assume and recognize as mine this alienated Me." (11, 285) For in my very protest that *that* Me is not the *real* Me, I am acknowledging that at least to a certain extent it *is* me. And try though I may, I cannot rid myself of this "alien Me" which I discover in the Look of the Other, and reconstitute myself as pure subjectivity. The Look "constitutes me as an irremediable object." Even when the

Other is no longer present, I cannot escape this "dimension of being-alienated." (11, 412)

It is, above all, the body which is the focus of this alienation; and this is quite logical, since it is first and foremost my
body upon which the Other fixes when he Looks at me.
Sartre considers the body to have three "dimensions of being."
He distinguishes between (1) my body as it is "lived" by me,
i.e., as the subjectively experienced "center" of perception and
action; (2) my body as it is "utilized and known" by the
Other, i.e., as it exists for someone else, an object which has
various observable and utilizable properties as do other objects; and (3) my body as it is experienced *by me as* "a body
known by the other." (11, 351)

It is the third of these dimensions in connection with
which Sartre speaks of "alienation." My body, when I experience it as something "known by the other," is something
"alien" to me; for it is radically different from my body as I
subjectively experience it. Sartre illustrates his meaning very
vividly by means of the example of a medical examination:

> I apprehend . . . the doctor as listening to the sounds
> of my body, feeling my body with his body, and immedi-
> ately what was designated as something lived becomes
> designated as a *thing outside my subjectivity*, in the midst
> of a world which is not mine. My body is designated as
> alienated. (11, 353)[10]

In recognizing that it is as an object that my body exists
for the Other, I experience it as something "alien" to me in
"my subjectivity." It is mine and yet not mine—me and yet
not me, an "alien Me." And it is precisely because of this
double relation in which I stand to my body—of identity in
one respect and nonidentity in another—that Sartre speaks of
its alienation as "the alienation of myself." For if I were not
also identical with this body which I here experience as
"alien," its alienation would not have this significance.

Thus in *Being and Nothingness*, Sartre employs the term

[10] I have slightly modified Barnes's translation, which preserves
Sartre's compactness of expression at the expense of clarity. It would
help still further to take the liberty of reading "revealed to me" for
"designated."

"alienation" in connection with the phenomenon of one's experience of oneself as one is viewed by another subject—namely, as an object. This experience may have one's body as its primary focus; or it may have as its focus oneself more generally, as an empirical existent endowed (for example) with an empirically determinable psychological character as well as a body. The general point, however, as for Husserl, is that one is, so to speak, robbed of the purity of one's subjectivity through the awareness of one's existence as an object for another who also has the character of a subject; and that one's dimension of objectivity of which one thus becomes aware is something "alien" to one *qua* subject. Husserl would not seem to attach any great importance to this alienation; he merely mentions it in passing. Sartre, on the other hand, considers it to be "a great metaphysical fact," which constitutes an essential part of "the human condition." (11, 374 n.)

For Sartre, in *Being and Nothingness*, each person is separated from others by an unbridgeable chasm; true community is an impossibility. It should be clear, however, that as he uses the term "alienation," it does not refer to this separation. Rather, it refers to a separation which emerges in the context of the individual's experience of *himself*. It involves a relation to others; but it is not a form of alienation *from* others.

Further, his use of the term is quite different from Heidegger's. For while Heidegger might also be said to speak of "the alienation of one's self," the "self" which is spoken of as "alienated" by Sartre is far from identical with Heidegger's "ownmost non-relational potentiality-for-being," or "authentic" selfhood. Even if the "self" termed "alienated" by Sartre is taken to be the subjectively experienced "self" which is suppressed to the extent that one experiences oneself as one is "known by the Other," rather than the "alien" object-self which thus comes to light (Sartre is ambiguous on this point), there is no close parallel with Heidegger. For Sartre does not associate the experience of one's dimension of objectivity with the loss of "authenticity" (or, in his terminology, with existence in "bad faith" or self-deception). Rather, he views it as the discovery of a fundamental fact about one's nature, which must come to light if one's self-knowledge is to be complete.

Moreover, the alienation of which Heidegger speaks does not involve an explicit and painful awareness of the absence of the type of selfhood with which he is concerned. On the contrary, it is one of the characteristics of this alienation that the alienated individual is *blind* to his "ownmost non-relational potentiality-for-being." The alienation described by Sartre, on the other hand, involves just such an awareness of the suppression of the kind of selfhood in question. It thus differs from that discussed by Heidegger with regard to both its object or focus and the type of mental state it involves.

It should be obvious that, while Sartre speaks of "the alienation of one's self," he does not have in mind anything like the traditional and Tillichian notion of self-alienation, construed in terms of a disparity between one's actual condition and one's essential nature. It would not be possible for him consistently to advance such a notion, since he explicitly and emphatically rejects the view that man can be said to have an essential nature with which his actual condition may not correspond. The individual's existence as an object for others may be termed a feature of his actual condition; but it is no less essential a feature of human existence for Sartre than is his subjectivity. The subjective experience of the body and the experience of the body as "known by the Other" thus are said to reveal two of its different but equally basic "ontological dimensions" or "dimensions of being." By characterizing both in these terms, Sartre makes it clear that he does not intend one to be viewed as essential and the other as involving a departure from the essential. The alienation of which he speaks is presented as confronting us not with a disparity to be overcome, but rather with a fact about ourselves to be acknowledged.

In view of the fact that Sartre uses the term in a very Marxian way in his recent *Critique of Dialectical Reason*, the question inevitably arises whether his use of the term in *Being and Nothingness* also reflects a Marxian influence. The answer to this question is negative; there is little resemblance between Marx's concept of alienation and that which Sartre develops in the latter work. It might at first seem questionable whether his use of the term could have undergone such a substantial alteration. This becomes plausible, however, when one considers that seventeen years elapsed between the publication of *Being and Nothingness* (1943) and of his *Critique* (1960); and that during this period Sartre underwent what one commentator has called a "radical conversion"[11] from a non-Marxist to a strongly Marxist orientation. He continues to refer to himself as an "existentialist" in his later writings; but a profound transformation of many of his views and concerns occurred in the course of his philosophical reorientation—a transformation which extended to his use of the term "alienation."

The precise nature of this transformation will become clear when his use of the term in his *Critique* is discussed. It is sufficient for the moment simply to compare his conception of alienation in *Being and Nothingness* with Marx's. And it requires but a moment's reflection to see that the phenomena in question in the two cases are very different indeed. In both cases, it is through the mediation of another person that the phenomena in question occur; but here the similarity ends. And this similarity is merely formal; for the *way* in which the other person affects the individual is quite different in the two cases.

For Marx, it is when I surrender my labor to the control and direction of another man in return for wages that my labor and my product become "alien" to me; and it is this, in turn, which results in my "self-alienation," or failure to realize my essential nature. For Sartre, on the other hand, the Other simply Looks at me; our relation has nothing to do with that which obtains between worker and employer. And the "self" which I thereby experience as "alienated" is to be conceived neither in terms of my labor, nor my product, nor my Marxian essential nature (which is realizable only when my labor and my product are truly mine). It does not matter which Sartrean "self" one considers—that which I experience subjectively or that which I experience as "known by the Other"; neither corresponds at all closely to the foci of alienation which Marx discusses.

11 Mary Warnock, in *The Philosophy of Sartre* (16), Chapter 6.

The conception of alienation developed by Sartre in *Being and Nothingness* is thus quite distinctive, and is bound up with a set of considerations very different from those with which other writers who make extensive use of the term have been concerned. And it should be added that, while he himself subsequently ceased to employ the term in this context, it does not follow that this use of it is undesirable or inappropriate. It may plausibly be urged that the kind of experience Sartre describes does not in fact invariably accompany the awareness of being looked at by another person; that it is possible to come to feel relatively at home with the idea of one's dimension of objectivity; and that the alienation of which Sartre speaks thus does not have the status of a "great metaphysical fact," as he suggests it does. Even so, however, the experience in question does appear to be an experience which it is possible to have. It is an interesting one, well worth discussing; and the term "alienation" is capable of functioning usefully in its characterization.

Aliénation in the *Critique of Dialectical Reason*

Sartre's discussion of alienation in his *Critique of Dialectical Reason* (12) is largely unknown to English-speaking readers, principally because the main body of the work has not yet been translated into English. The prefatory essay which accompanies it has appeared in translation, under the title *Search for a Method* (14); and Sartre does speak of "alienation" in this essay (henceforth "*Search*"). His remarks on the subject in it, however, are admittedly sketchy; and they can be misleading if they are not understood in the light of his detailed development of his concept of alienation in the body of the *Critique* itself. Cases of alienation are cited in *Search* which frequently seem far removed from the sort of thing Marx discusses; and this obscures the fact that the conception of alienation with which Sartre is working is basically Marxian.

Near the conclusion of his prefatory essay, Sartre poses a question which he both explicitly acknowledges to be Marx's and takes for his own: "What kind of practical organism is this [i.e., man] which reproduces its life by its work so that its work and ultimately its very reality are alienated; that is, so that they, as something *other*, turn back upon him and determine him?" (*14*, 177)[12] The context in which he now speaks of "alienation" is thus the Marxian context of one's relations to one's productive activity and one's product, and of their implications for one's selfhood. And the Marxian character of his present concept of alienation is quite evident in that he characterizes the object of his study as "the individual, alienated, reified, mystified, as he has been made to be by the division of labor and by exploitation." (*14*, 133) The kind of alienation under consideration here thus is very different from that which he earlier associated with the Look of the Other.

Sartre still holds, as he had previously, that "Man defines himself by his project." (*14*, 150) But he now links the emergence of one's identity with the process of *self-objectification*, precisely as Marx had done, thereby adopting an attitude toward this process very different from his earlier one. "It is perfectly accurate," he states, "to say that man is the product of his product." (*14*, 92) To be sure, he could just as well have said previously, as he now says, that "the realization of the possible necessarily results in the production of an object or an event in the social world; this realization is then our *objectification*." (*14*, 101) In *Being and Nothingness*, however, he had viewed the object thus produced primarily as something which, as "known by the Other," is "alien" to me; and which, from the standpoint of my subjectivity, is transcended and dead from the moment of its appearance. In this earlier work, my objectifications define me only from the standpoint of the Other during my life; and they define me completely only after my death.

In his *Critique*, Sartre takes a significantly different view of the matter: In "objectifying himself," the individual is said to be "producing his life" (*14*, 161), rather than merely leaving a trail of lifeless traces. And Sartre agrees with Marx that "this perpetual production of oneself by work and *praxis* . . . is our peculiar structure." (*14*, 151) It may be that one's objectification "takes on a reality which the agent himself may not know" (*14*, 93–94), and thus becomes something "alien"

---

[12] I have modified Barnes's translation slightly. Cf. *19*, 109.

to him; for Marx too, objectification (in our society) is associated with alienation. But for the Sartre of the *Critique*, as for Marx, self-objectification is an essentially positive phenomenon through which alone one's "life"—one's personality and individuality—can be developed.

Marx had held that when one's potential self-objectification (one's product) and one's potentially self-objectifying activity (one's labor) come under the influence of *another man*, the former becomes "alien and hostile" to one, the latter becomes stultifying and detrimental, and a condition of alienation thus obtains. Sartre takes a similar position: "Each time that the enterprise of a man or of a group of men becomes an object for other men . . . it becomes, for the very people who initiated it, an external object which tends to dominate and to survive them." And he too considers a condition of alienation thus to result. (*14*, 162–63)

To be sure, Sartre's terminology in these passages from *Search* is much more general than Marx's. But no radical departure from Marx is thereby indicated. And when one turns to his discussion of alienation in the *Critique* proper, the similarity of his conception to Marx's is unmistakable. Here, alienation is characterized in a recognizably Marxian way, in terms of "a mediated relation to the other and to objects of labor." (*12*, 154)[13] And Sartre makes it quite clear that, in whatever contexts he may use the term, it is in terms of this basic schema that it is to be understood.

> It is in the concrete and synthetic relation of the agent to the other through the mediation of the thing, and to the thing through the mediation of the other, that we find the basis of all possible alienation. (*12*, 154 n.)

In this important passage, two fundamental Marxian themes are sounded, in rather abstract language. One is that of the reduction of the relations between the agent and others to mere economic relations centering on the thing produced (e.g., those of worker to employer, worker to consumer, worker to co-worker or rival worker), through the

[13] Citations from the *Critique* (*12*) in English are my translations.

reduction of the agent to the level of a mere producer of things. And the second is that of the reduction of the relation of the agent to his product from one in which his product is his free self-objectification, to one in which his product becomes something alien to him, through its subjection to the influence of others.

Like Marx, Sartre goes on to trace this twofold separation —from others and from the product—to a related but more fundamental one. Marx had considered the alienation of *labor*, in which one's "activity" becomes "something alien to him," to be the real heart of the matter.[14] Sartre takes a similar position:

> . . . man has to struggle . . . against his own action insofar as it becomes something other. This primordial type of alienation is manifested through the other forms of alienation, but is . . . that which is their foundation. (12, 202)

Sartre does not by any means follow Marx in every particular. He presents his concept of alienation in his own terms, and goes into many of the issues involved in much greater detail than Marx does. Moreover, he differs with Marx on some important points. For example, he contends that orthodox Marxism is overly "simplistic" in that it fails to recognize "alienation as *necessary*." (12, 373) He thus does not accept Marx's suggestion that the occurrence of alienation is to be explained in terms of the presence of certain eliminable socioeconomic conditions. Rather, he considers it to be an inevitable concomitant of objectification in a world in which there are other men. (Cf. 14, 162–63) To differ with regard to the explanation and necessity of a phenomenon, however, need not be to differ with regard to the general character of the phenomenon itself; and it is not, in the present case.

Sartre does modify Marx's conception of alienation in one important respect. This modification involves a generalization of the terms in which the conception is cast, which makes possible an extension of its application to contexts

14 See pp. 96–97 and 102.

other than that of the labor contract. Thus one of Sartre's principle examples in *Search* is that of a writer, Flaubert, and his novel, *Madame Bovary*. Flaubert's novel is suggested to exemplify "the objectification of the subjective and its alienation" (14, 149) no less than the product of Marx's worker. The same may also be said, for Sartre, of "enterprises" of "groups of men" in the socio-politico-economic sphere. (14, 162)

The relation between the artist and his public is much more subtle and complex than is the relation between the worker and his employer; nor are the two strictly parallel. And the ways in which one's social enterprises are exposed to the influence of others differ from both, and are many and varied. But though the comprehension of the concept is thus broadened considerably by Sartre, and though reference is no longer made to wages, employers, etc., in its explication, it still retains the more fundamental features it has for Marx. In all cases, "objectifications of the subjective" are involved; and these "objectifications" all become alienated to the extent that they become "objects for other men," under whose influence they become "alien" to their creators. Thus Sartre at bottom remains faithful to Marx, while at the same time rendering his concept of alienation more interesting and useful than Marx's by removing certain overly narrow restrictions which Marx builds into his.

It should be observed, however, that while Sartre's use of the term is similar to Marx's as far as it goes, he stops short of using it—as Marx does—to refer to a disparity between one's actual condition and one's essential nature. In his *Critique*, Sartre's debt to the early Marx is great; but he has never abandoned his opposition to the view that man has the sort of ideal essential nature that the notion of such a disparity presupposes. In appropriating the early Marx's concept of alienation, therefore, he sets aside this aspect of it—as indeed Marx himself might well have done, had he continued to speak of "alienation" in his later writings when his emancipation from Hegel was more complete.

Sartre does speak of the alienation of the individual's "very reality" and "life"; but this is not to be understood in essentialist terms. Depending on the context, it refers either to the "alienness" of the individual's self-objectification to him (one of the ways in which Marx himself uses the expression "self-alienation"), or to the fact that the individual's life is not completely his own to the extent that this "alienness" exists. One obviously can imagine a contrasting condition, in which the individual's life *is* completely his own; although Sartre would not appear to consider this a real possibility (otherwise he would not have termed "alienation" *necessary*). Whatever the case may be, however, it would not be possible for him to regard instances of the first sort as involving a disparity between essence and existence. As in the case of Heidegger, such instances can only be characterized legitimately in terms of the (perhaps unavoidable) realization of one possibility and the nonrealization of its imaginable contrary.

Concluding Remarks

The term "alienation" (or, rather, some English or foreign-language equivalent of it) thus is used by certain of the most influential writers commonly termed "existentialists," even though its employment is by no means characteristic of existentialists generally. Those who do use it, however, do not do so uniformly. Heidegger, Tillich, and Sartre all use it differently—both of Sartre's uses of it differing from those of either of the other two. Those who employ it most extensively—Tillich, and the Sartre of the *Critique*—do so in ways which are not peculiar to existentialism, but derive directly from Hegel and Marx. And none of the writers in question uses the term to refer to any of the various phenomena with which the term is most commonly linked, both in popular usage and when existentialism is mentioned: namely, remoteness from other people, antagonism toward the established social order, and a lack of oneness with the world generally. Rather, each uses the term in connection with the "alienness" (in some sense) of some sort or dimension or aspect of "self." In short, it *is* used in existentialist literature, but neither as widely, nor as uniformly, nor as distinctively, nor as voguishly, as is commonly thought.

Philosophical Anthropology:
Arnold Gehlen and Helmuth Plessner

As "philosophical anthropologists," rather than "existential philosophers,"[15] Arnold Gehlen and Helmuth Plessner do not fall within the stated purview of this chapter. Their conceptions of alienation are sufficiently distinctive and interesting, however, to warrant at least a moment's attention. And since they are more closely associated (in time and space, at any rate) with the writers considered in this chapter than with those discussed in any other, this would seem to be the most appropriate place to mention them.

Arnold Gehlen

Gehlen uses the term "alienation" (*Entfremdung*) in his most influential work, *Der Mensch* (3).[16] He devotes relatively little space to it; but it occupies an important position in his analysis of the development of specifically human behavior. He introduces the term in connection with his discussion of a behavioral phenomenon which is said to occur first in children at the age of about one year: the "careful, attentive, and intensely dedicated" repetition of various movements which are to no evident purpose, and which may

[15] Perhaps a word of explanation is necessary; for "philosophical anthropology" is something with which most English-speaking readers will be unacquainted. Like the "existential philosopher," the "philosophical anthropologist" takes man as his object of study. Unlike the former, however, he does not regard the individual's subjective, "lived existence" as a privileged dimension, in terms of which, above all, man's nature is to be understood. Rather, he considers relevant —and, indeed, crucial—such things as man's biological nature and sociocultural life. Gehlen and Plessner may fairly be said to be the dominant figures in the emergence of "philosophical anthropology" as a significant branch of recent European philosophy.

[16] *Der Mensch* (or *Man*) first appeared in 1940. Unfortunately, this very interesting book has not yet been translated into English. Passages cited in English are my translations.

even clearly cause the child some pain. In order to account for this phenomenon, Gehlen assumes that there must be some satisfaction derived from it; and he offers the following suggestion concerning what it might be:

Here, I believe, we are confronted with a fundamental human phenomenon. . . . The pleasant feeling which is the source of such movements is the *feeling of one's activity as one's own*. I do not want to say that we are already dealing with a thinking grasp of these movements; but it is a fact that chance movements together with their consequent sensations can be *taken possession of*, and therewith *undertaken* and *brought about*. I want to avoid saying that the child can assume an "objective" position over against its movements; but through the ensuing sensations it acquires an *alienated feeling of its movements as its own*. (3, 134)

"Alienation" here refers to the achievement of enough distance from one's movements to be able to feel their responsiveness to one's own direction. This feeling is held to be pleasant; and its pleasantness is suggested to explain the behavior in question. Gehlen's reluctance to attribute too much objectivity to the one-year-old child is understandable. He clearly does feel, however, that this behavior presupposes a certain degree of objectivity with regard to the child's own movements. They can be manipulated—"taken possession of," "brought about" deliberately—only if the child's attention ceases to be directed entirely beyond the movements (as in a state of "immediacy"), and instead is focused directly upon them, as something "owned."

It is this alienated feeling of one's activity as one's own which guides the further development of this activity. The astonishing wealth of variable and plastic movements which are developed by man rests upon this presupposition: In order to become conscious and initiable, a movement must sensibly *register*—it must attain an "alienated feeling of mineness," through accompanying actual or anticipated sensations. (3, 134)

Gehlen thus holds that specifically human activity presupposes reflection into oneself, and hence the abrogation of immediacy. Deliberate and purposive activity presupposes that one has acquired the capacity for "conscious and deliberate" movement; and this capacity presupposes an awareness of one's movements as one's own, and as subject to one's own direction. Such awareness involves a degree of distance; and it is precisely this distance to which Gehlen is referring when he speaks of alienation.

This distance should not be confused with that extreme form of disassociation from one's own movements which accompanies certain types of mental disorder. The phenomenon under consideration rather has the character of an "alienated intimacy"; one experiences one's movements as something apart from oneself (one might say, as one's products), without ceasing to feel that they are one's own. Indeed, it is only under these circumstances that they really become one's own; for it is only then that one really takes possession of them.

One can recognize here an old Hegelian theme: One becomes able truly to take possession of that which is immediately one's own only through the attainment of a certain distance from it.[17] Thus Gehlen speaks of "the self-alienation of one's abilities, which is at the same time their appropriation." (3, 145) In employing the term "alienation," Gehlen is characterizing a relation which—while remaining one of unity—is not immediate, but rather involves an element of separation or distance.

Helmuth Plessner

Gehlen uses the term "alienation" in a rather Hegelian way, but employs it in a context far removed from that in which Hegel principally employs it, viz., the relation of the individual to the social substance. Helmuth Plessner, on the other hand, uses it in both a context and a manner reminiscent of Hegel. His conception of alienation is presented in a short essay entitled "With Other Eyes." (10)[18]

[17] See pp. 47 and 58 ff.
[18] In German, "Mit Anderen Augen." As with Gehlen, most of Plessner's work has not yet been translated into English; and this essay is no exception. Passages cited in English are my translations.

Plessner's main point in this essay is that "Distance is necessary in order to be able to perceive" (10, 208); and that "Insightful perception of man and human things is always possible only as Other, with other eyes." (10, 216) He uses the term "alienation" (*Entfremdung*) to refer precisely to the attainment of such "distance" or "otherness," from which standpoint it becomes possible for the first time really to *see* that in which one had been immersed. "One must become alien to the zone of familiarity in order to be able to see it." (10, 207) Otherwise one is so close to it, so at one with it, that one fails to *notice* anything about it. Here again, the term "alienation" is used in connection with a supersession or abrogation of immediacy.

The "zone of familiarity" with which Plessner is concerned is one's cultural environment. This may be seen in the choice of his examples: One "sees with other eyes" when one returns to the place of one's childhood after a period of absence, or when one returns to one's homeland after an extended period abroad. (10, 208) Actual physical absence is not essential, however, as long as one manages in some way to "develop alienated powers, which [enable one to] bring the familiar to expression." (10, 212–13) Plessner has in mind, above all, the poet and the scholar, whose task it is to "grasp the long familiar and obvious in an alienated glance." (10, 208)

> That which in familiarity proceeds implicitly and unnoticed, in alienation becomes explicit and strives toward artistic and methodical expression. . . . Only in the perceptive understanding of one who is alienated is the desired insight into spiritual-human life achieved. (10, 213)

Plessner does not refer to Hegel's conception of a relation of alienation between the individual and the social substance; but there is a striking similarity between it and his own conception of alienation. It should be clear, however, that the alienation of which he speaks is not that of one who experiences his "spiritual-human" environment as something *completely* alien to him. Hegel initially characterizes alienation in these terms, since his initial concern is to portray the exact opposite of the state of immediate unity with the social

substance. The relation to the social substance which Plessner has in mind, on the other hand, has more of the character
of an "alienated intimacy," in Gehlen's phrase. One who
exemplifies alienation as he conceives of it grasps the familiar
"in an alienated glance, and then takes [it] once again into
his heart." (10, 208)[19]

[19] This recalls the third stage in Hegel's developmental sequence,
which succeeds both immediate unity and complete separation—the
stage of *aufgehoben* alienation and re-established, "mediate" unity,
in which the "otherness" of the object of one's attention is still
recognized, but is seen not to be absolute. (See pp. 62 ff.) For Plessner, however, it continues to be appropriate to speak of "alienation"
here; whereas for Hegel, it does not.

7 Alienation:
A General Consideration

The temptation . . . to use [those] words which are most
likely to attract attention and excite belief in the importance
of [one's] subject is almost irresistible.

OGDEN AND RICHARDS,
The Meaning of Meaning

I. Introduction

Sartre has said, in speaking of the term "existentialist": "The
word is now so loosely applied to so many things that it no
longer means anything at all." (8, 289) The same could be
said, with even greater justification, of "alienation." This is
not to deny that the phenomena so designated by those who
use the term are important; on the contrary, many of these
phenomena are of the greatest significance and interest, and
warrant the closest attention. Because the term is employed
in connection with so many different ones, however, it enjoys no special association with any of them. Using the term
"alienation" without explaining any further what one has in
mind communicates little more today than does tapping one's
glass with one's spoon at a banquet; neither does much more
than attract attention.

That this is so is something for which few writers can be
assigned any personal responsibility. While some employ the
term very loosely and widely, its use in the writings of most
is fairly well delimited. But it has become a fetish word, and

people seem to delight in finding ever different uses for it. Hegel found the term helpful, and elevated it to a position of importance in his *Phenomenology*. The young Marx found Hegel's use of it suggestive, and employed it extensively in his early writings. Many recent writers have found Marx's use fascinating, and have been moved to modify it in the light of their own needs and interests. All the excitement has called the attention of many other writers to the term, and has led them to see what they could do with it. The result is the situation indicated above.

It would belabor the obvious to recall the many different phenomena in connection with which the term has been employed, in order to show the absence of any significant factual or conceptual connection between a great many of them. One might still wonder, however, whether the various conceptions of alienation discussed might at least be said to display some sort of *formal* similarity. For though the diversity of conceptions of alienation is undeniable, it might be thought that this diversity is due simply to the diversity of contexts in which the term is employed; and that the term might thus at least specify the same *sort* of relation in each case. In this event, it would at least be possible to identify *some* feature or features common to the use of the term generally.

A number of writers have taken this position, as was observed at the outset. To recall their proposed general analyses, Arnold Kaufman asserts: "To claim that a person is alienated is to claim that his relation to something else has certain features which result in avoidable discontent or loss of satisfaction." (3, 143) Lewis Feuer suggests that "the word 'alienation' [is] used to describe the subjective tone of self-destructive experience," and states: "'Alienation' is used to convey the emotional tone which accompanies any behavior in which the person is compelled to act self-destructively." (2, 132) And Kenneth Keniston says: "Most usages of 'alienation' share the assumption that some relationship or connection that once existed, that is 'natural,' desirable, or good, has been lost." (4, 452)

These analyses, however, are by no means generally valid. It is far from true, for example, that the term as a rule is used in connection with one's "relationship to something *else*," as Kaufman suggests. Marx is greatly disturbed by the alienation of one's labor or productive capacity precisely because it is *not* "something else" in relation to one's self, but rather constitutes one's very life. And neither the "real self" nor the "actual self" of which Horney speaks, nor Heidegger's "ownmost non-relational potentiality-for-being," nor the "self" in Sartre's discussion of alienation in *Being and Nothingness*, nor the essential nature Hegel and Tillich have in mind when they speak of "self-alienation," can be accurately characterized as "something else" in relation to the person who is alienated from one or another of them.

Further, contrary to Kaufman's analysis, there are influential writers for whom alienation need involve *no* "discontent" and *no* awareness of "loss of satisfaction" on the part of those who are termed "alienated." In the case of Fromm, the discontent involved is largely his own, as he surveys "the alienation of modern man," who is often quite content in his deplorable state. Marx represents workers under capitalism as being so "cretinized" by the conditions under which they are compelled to live and work that they often must be awakened from their passive acceptance of them, and to the fact of their alienation. And the disassociations from popular culture and societal values characterized by sociologists in terms of "alienation" are not themselves sources of discontent and loss of satisfaction for many of those thus alienated. Rather, they are often viewed positively by those involved, and are associated with feelings of definite satisfaction. This also bears upon Feuer's analysis; for none of these conceptions of alienation make reference to an "emotional tone" on the part of the alienated individual of the sort he indicates.

It should also be observed, with regard to Feuer's analysis, that even when the term *is* used to refer to the presence of certain negative feelings, these feelings often have nothing to do with any recognition that one is "being compelled to act self-destructively." This would not be an appropriate way to describe feelings of antagonism or indifference toward popular culture, distrust of political leaders, and isolation from other people. And even when the term is used to refer to negative feelings, these feelings are often considered *not* to be "avoidable," contrary to Kaufman's suggestion. The conception of alienation Sartre presents in *Being and Nothingness* is an obvious example. Another is to be found in Fromm, for whom one type of alienation from nature and one type of alienation from others are quite unavoidable. And certain kinds of alienation discussed by sociologists are conceived in such a way that there is nothing the alienated individual can do to avoid them.

Furthermore, many conceptions of alienation do *not* share the assumption that "some relationship . . . that once existed . . . has been lost," to which Kaufman refers. This is not a feature of many of the types of alienation discussed by Fromm, for example; for while he invariably uses the term in connection with the *absence* of (desirable) relationships, these relationships often have never existed previously for the alienated individual, and thus cannot be said to be something he has *lost*. The same holds true of many of the types of alienation discussed by sociologists. And while Heidegger speaks of "alienation" in connection with his concept of "falling," he considers "inauthentic" Dasein to be "fallen" and "alienated" regardless of whether it has ever been "authentic."

Moreover, a number of writers do not even use the term to refer to the *absence* of relationships which they regard as "natural, desirable, or good." The various uses of the term do not have in common any such negative evaluative element, as Keniston suggests they do. Gehlen and Plessner consider the phenomena in connection with which they employ the term to have a very positive significance. And the great majority of Keniston's fellow social scientists at least intend their uses of the term to be free of all evaluative overtones. When Talcott Parsons suggests the idea of an "alienation-conformity" continuum, for example, he does not mean to imply that he considers "conformity" to be a relation that is "natural, desirable or good." Melvin Seeman speaks for most of his colleagues when he explicitly disavows all "critical, polemical [intent]" in using the term "alienation." (9 784)

Feuer claims that "the will to criticize and polemize i . . . the essential intent behind the idea of alienation."

(2, 129)[1] He seems to feel that when he has said this, he has thereby shown the attempt of sociologists to use the term nonevaluatively and unpolemically to be unsound. His only argument would appear to be that Marx and a number of influential recent writers (e.g., Fromm) use it critically and polemically. But these writers have no unique claim upon the term. It was not originally used in this way; for it was with no polemical intent that Hegel used it to characterize a necessary stage in the development of the human spirit, and a process through which (in part) this stage can be surpassed. Writers such as Gehlen and Plessner were using it unpolemically before Fromm began to popularize it. So, in fact, was Sartre; for his concern, in his discussion of alienation in *Being and Nothingness*, is to illuminate an "ontological dimension" of man's nature, not to polemize against it. Thus the sociologists who would have their uses of the term understood unpolemically are not alone. "The will to criticize and polemize" may be the "essential intent" underlying Marx's and Fromm's uses of the term; but it is not the essential intent underlying the use of the term generally. *Their* "idea of alienation" is not "*the* idea of alienation."

II. A Systematic Attempt at Generalization

Kaufman, Keniston, and Feuer all fail in their attempts to provide a formal analysis of "alienation" that would be generally applicable. They do not fail merely because they overlook what is truly common to the various uses of the term. Rather, they fail because there is virtually nothing common even to *most* of its different uses. When confronted with the term, one can be reasonably sure that the matter under consideration is some sort of separation. It would be rash to infer much more, however, until the person using the term

[1] There is an important difference between holding that the term *conveys* a negative attitude on the part of the *speaker* (as Keniston does), and holding that it *refers to* certain negative feelings on the part of those being *spoken about* (as Kaufman does). Feuer affirms both propositions; but it is not clear that he distinguishes between them. This perhaps stems from the fact that he is interested primarily in those who see alienation in *themselves* as well as in others.

has indicated how he wishes to be understood. This becomes clear when one tries to specify any further common features of the use of the term.

Agency of the Separation

As has just been observed, the use of the term is associated with no specific attitude on the part of writers who use it; for it is employed in connection with phenomena which are regarded positively (Gehlen, Plessner), negatively (Marx, Fromm, Horney, Tillich), neutrally (most sociologists), and in various other ways which defy simple description (Hegel, Sartre).

It is also impossible to specify whether the separation is one which the subject can or cannot be considered to have brought about. Fromm would seem to regard a person's "alienation from himself" as something for which he may be held responsible, since he is held to choose the path of conformity when he does take it. The same is true for Heidegger, who places the responsibility for "fleeing" from the possibility of "authentic" existence squarely on the shoulders of the "inauthentic" individual. For Sartre, on the other hand, alienation, in both *Being and Nothingness* and his *Critique*, is something which befalls one through an agency which is emphatically external. And such types of alienation as the feeling of powerlessness and the feeling of the incomprehensibility of sociopolitical events are functions of developments which proceed independently of the subject's own efforts.

Attainability of Opposite Condition

Alasdair MacIntyre correctly observes that "alienation is essentially a contrast concept. We can understand what it is to be alienated only if we can also understand what it is or would be *not* to be alienated." (5, 68) But the term is used by some writers to refer to separations whose opposite conditions can actually be attained, and by others to refer to separations whose opposite conditions cannot. For example, it is purported to be within the power of the individual to overcome a number of the types of alienation of which

Fromm speaks. Where alienation is conceived as the opposite of conformity, conformity is usually considered to be a live option. And Horney clearly feels that the types of alienation she discusses can be overcome. The alienation discussed by Sartre in *Being and Nothingness,* on the other hand, is suggested to be ineliminable; and he terms the type of alienation he discusses in his *Critique* "necessary." Alienation is equally irreversible where it is conceived in terms of a loss of immediate unity, at least for those (like Fromm) who consider a lost immediacy to be irretrievable. Gehlen and Plessner provide other cases in point.

There are also types of alienation whose opposite conditions are attainable, but not through the efforts of the alienated individual alone. Various types of alienation from other people can be overcome only with the cooperation of the others involved. Alienation conceived in terms of feelings of powerlessness may be overcome only through a reorganization of the power structure, which the individual by himself cannot effect. And the forms of alienation of which Marx speaks can only be overcome through a fundamental social and economic reorganization, which can be accomplished (in Marx's view) only when the time is ripe, and only if "workers unite."

In short, while it must be possible to imagine what the opposite condition of any sort of alienation would be like, no particular relation of possibility to this opposite condition is generally associated with the use of the term. And it should be recalled that the opposite condition is not always considered more desirable than the alienation itself.

Development out of Opposite Condition

It is one thing to consider whether, once a condition of alienation exists, the opposite condition is attainable. It is another to consider whether a condition of alienation is to be viewed as having been *preceded by* its opposite condition. In all traditional uses of the term, a transformation of the intimate *into* the alien, or of unity *into* separation, is presupposed; its employment is restricted to cases in which the relevant opposite condition previously existed.

No such restriction, however, is common to the various

uses of the term which have been considered in this study.
Some of the writers discussed do employ the term in such a
way that this feature of its traditional standard usage is pre-
served. These include Hegel, Gehlen, Plessner, Sartre, and
at least to some extent, Marx. But the term is also frequently
used in contexts in which it is clear that no prior, opposite
condition of unity or identity has been lost. Most sociologists
who use the term "alienation" in connection with these feelings do not hesitate to employ it in such cases. Indeed, cases
of this sort commonly constitute the majority of those comprehended by their conceptions of alienation. The same is
true with regard to many of Fromm's types of alienation.
In the context of his discussion, one can be alienated from
others without ever having had the proper relatedness to
them; one need only *lack* it to merit this characterization.
And one can be alienated from oneself without ever having
attained Fromm's ideal of genuine selfhood. Tillich furnishes
an even clearer example; for he very explicitly rejects the
idea of an actual "once upon a time" of this sort, either in
the case of the race or in that of the individual. Thus while
the idea of a transition from the opposite condition is involved in some conceptions of alienation, it is far from being
a feature common to the use of the term generally.

The Subject of the Alienation

Generally speaking, the term is usually employed in connection with the separation of something *from* something.
It is not always used, however, to refer to the separation of
someone from something; the subject of the alienation is not
always a person. In Marx, for example, the point which the
expression "alienated labor" is sometimes used to convey is
that labor in its present forms does not correspond to its essential nature, or purpose and function. Other such uses of
"alienation" occur in the writings of Fromm, who frequently
employs it to characterize a wide range of things other than
man himself: not only work, but also the process of consumption, the modern way of life, friendships, language, thought,
etc. In such cases the separation to which the term refers is
a disparity between the way something is and the way it
should be. In short, it is not a *general* feature of the use

of the term that it is employed to convey the idea of a separation of *a person from* something, even though it often is employed in this way.

The Nature of the Separation

Even if attention is restricted to cases in which the separation involved *is* of this sort, the general nature of this separation is quite different in some cases from what it is in others. In particular, it sometimes consists in a person's *feeling* that something is alien to him; while in other cases it consists in a separation (of a person from something) which is *conceived* to exist, and which he himself may or may not believe exists. In other words, the term "alienation" is used in connection with both subjective states of mind and objectively determined inadequacies, disparities, etc.

The most important and obvious examples of the latter class of uses are those conceptions of "self-alienation" which involve the notion of a disparity between one's actual condition and one's essential nature. Writers who employ the term in this connection have their own criteria for the existence of such a disparity; and they consider the term applicable whenever these criteria are satisfied, regardless of whether the individuals who satisfy them have any awareness of this fact, let alone accept these criteria themselves. Heideggerian alienation provides another example: The alienated individual is blind to his "ownmost non-relational potentiality-for-being," and thus does not himself feel it to be an unrealized potentiality. And for Fromm, one can be alienated from others by lacking the proper form of relatedness to them, without realizing that anything is wanting in one's interpersonal relationships.

For Hegel, on the other hand, the relation of alienation between the individual and the social substance exists only insofar as the individual *experiences* the social substance as something "alien"—only insofar as the social substance is something alien *in his eyes*. Most sociologists who use the term also construe the types of alienation they discuss in terms of the presence of certain feelings. And alienation is conceived by Sartre in *Being and Nothingness* in terms of a kind of self-*awareness*: namely, one in which I *see* myself as the object which I am for the Other.

Thus even when attention is confined to those cases in which the term is used to refer to conditions of separation of men from something, the nature of the separation cannot be further specified even to the extent of indicating whether it consists of a feeling-state or an objective condition. To be sure, in all cases the separations are thought by the writers in question to be significant. But different writers find the separations they are concerned with significant for a great variety of different reasons. Some are considered morally or metaphysically undesirable, others developmentally important; some psychologically harmful, others socially disruptive; some personally unpleasant, others sources of insight. Thus it is not even a general feature of the use of the term that a certain *kind* of significance is attached to the separations it is used to refer to.

Description and Prescription

It would seem, therefore, that virtually nothing is common to the various uses of the term. Two questions therefore arise: (1) In what respects, if any, is this undesirable? (2) Can one presume to do anything more than record this fact and draw out its consequences? That is, do the uses of the term which have been discussed constitute an established "language game," which—as Wittgenstein contends—the philosopher can only "leave . . . as it is"? (10, §124)

With regard to the latter, Wittgenstein's directive may be valid where facts of established usage are concerned. What one is confronted with in the case of "alienation," however, is something like a variety of linguistic experiments and innovations. It is not a fact that *we do* call each of the phenomena so designated a type of "alienation." When we are confronted with one or another of the uses of the term under consideration, there is little point in asking ourselves whether *we would say*—as representative speakers of the language—that it is a standard or nondeviant use of the term, that the phenomenon in question is an actual instance of alienation, etc. And if one resorts to the standard procedures for deciding such questions—consulting dictionaries, conferring with other speakers of the language, etc.—this only shows that one fails to recognize the general linguistic situation with regard to the use of the term. Occurrences of a term can be dealt with in this way only when certain uses of it, or certain rules governing its use, have acquired an established place in the language. In the case of "alienation," however, this point has not yet been reached.

Precisely because we are dealing here with a highly unsettled situation, and not with a set of established conventions of usage, the directive that everything is to be "left as it is" is not strictly applicable. This does not mean, of course, that the ways in which different writers have used the term can simply be ignored. Wittgenstein's companion directive, to "look and see" how a term under investigation actually is used (10, §66), loses none of its validity even in cases of this sort. The first order of business for the philosopher here as elsewhere consists precisely in exploring the ways in which the term actually has been used by those who have made use of it; and any further steps must be grounded upon just such an analysis.

Yet because the uses of the term discussed here do not have the standing of established conventions of usage, each of them need not be considered inviolable. It would constitute no challenge to established usage, therefore, to suggest placing at least some restrictions on the use of the term, even though they might conflict with some of its actual uses—provided, of course, that a case can be made for them. The number of possible nonarbitrary restrictions is not great; but they would have the result that the use of the term "alienation" would convey at least *something* similar in each of its allowable applications.

It is true, as Wittgenstein points out, that we often do quite well with words that have no single strand of meaning running through all of their applications. (Cf. 10, §§66 ff.) This does not mean, however, that the helpfulness of a term might not be increased if its use were to be restricted in such a way that it *did* convey something similar in each instance of its employment. Whether or not such a restriction would have this effect in the case of a particular term depends upon the purposes in relation to which it is employed. In informal discourse, in which precision and rigor are less essential than they are in the various cognitive disciplines, this consideration would appear to count for relatively little. In these disciplines, on the other hand, the helpfulness of terms is, to a much greater degree, a function of their univocality.

The first question raised above was whether or not it is to be viewed as unfortunate that virtually nothing is common to the various uses of the term "alienation." This question receives its answer when one considers in which of these contexts it is meant to function; for it finds its primary employment in discussions which at least aspire to rigor in attempting to shed light upon various problems. Thus the indicated state of affairs is unfortunate indeed. Most writers who use the term are trying to say something philosophically, sociologically, or otherwise analytically significant. If the helpfulness of the term is to be measured in terms of the extent to which it facilitates analysis and communication at this level, therefore, it becomes important for its general use to display at least some degree of regularity. For to the extent that it is impossible to presuppose agreement concerning how the term is to be understood, its use will impede rather than facilitate analysis and communication, and therefore will fail to accomplish its intended purpose.

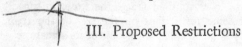

III. Proposed Restrictions

Preliminary Remarks

It thus appears both that some restrictions upon the use of the term are desirable, and that the situation with regard to its current use is sufficiently unsettled to render the proposal of some restrictions legitimate. In proposing such restrictions, it would seem best to treat "self-alienation" (or the use of the term to refer to a disparity between one's actual condition and one's essential or ideal nature) differently from "alienation" used in connection with the separation of the individual from something other than himself. The kinds of restrictions that most naturally suggest themselves in connection with the latter would rule out almost all actual uses of the former; and the peculiar form of the former marks it off from the latter in such a way that one might expect the difference of treatment to be attended by a minimum of confusion.

Several very obvious restrictions, which would be attended by little inconvenience for most writers today, may be applied to both. First, it has been observed that Hegel and Marx speak of "alienation" in connection with acts of surrender as well as conditions of separation. While an act of surrender may be related to a separation, however, either as that which produces it or as something that helps to overcome it, the two are conceptually distinct. To avoid blurring this distinction, it would be well to restrict the use of the term to one or the other. The choice is not difficult to make, since nearly all writers who use the term today do so in connection with separations of one sort or another. The restriction of the use of the term along these lines is thus virtually an accomplished fact.[2]

Next, while certain writers (e.g., Marx and Fromm) speak of a variety of things other than men as "alienated," such uses of the term could be eliminated without any great loss. There is no intrinsic reason why it should not be employed in connection with separations other than those of *men from* something. Nothing substantial is gained where it is so used, however; on the contrary, there would appear to be other, more illuminating ways of characterizing the phenomena in question in most such cases. And it would render the use of the term more informative if one could always know that when it is employed, some separation of a person from something is intended. This restriction would affect more recent writers than would the first, but only a small minority of those who use the term.

Beyond this point a double standard would seem to be indicated for "alienation" from something other than one's

[2] There is no reason, however, why the term should not continue to be employed in legal contexts in connection with the transfer of ownership of property by one person to another. This is a long-established use of the term, which cannot legitimately be challenged. Its existence constitutes no problem, since the "language game" in which it occurs is far removed from those in which the uses of the term under consideration occur.

essential or ideal nature and "self-alienation," if the expressions are to be used in such a way that their respective employments will be relatively consistent, and at the same time are to continue to be used at all as they have been. The proposals immediately following pertain to the former term; "self-alienation" will be considered subsequently.

Alienation from Something Other than Oneself

(1) In its traditional uses, the term "alienation" is only employed in connection with separations which were preceded by the relevant forms of unity. It would be far from arbitrary, therefore, to suggest that its use continue to be restricted in this way. This would only be to respect the basic construction of the term itself. For the grammatical element "-ation" usually serves to indicate process or development,[3] as do the elements "*Ent . . . ung*" in German; and the terms which they form with "alien" and *fremd*, respectively, have the literal meaning of *making* or *becoming* "alien."

There is no good reason to use the terms thus formed in such a way that this literal meaning must be suppressed. Disunities which do not involve the loss of previously existing unities may readily be designated in other ways. If it is considered desirable to use terms formed from "alien" and *fremd* to refer to them, the terms "alienness" and *Fremdheit* are available. Since these terms (not to mention others formed from different roots) are available, the employment of the terms "alienation" and *Entfremdung* in such cases is unwarranted. Moreover, practical considerations count against using the latter terms in such cases; for the result is that the natural way of making an important distinction is lost, and the distinction itself thus tends to become obscured.

While a number of the writers discussed take this consideration into account, others do not. As most sociologists use the term, for example, there is no suggestion of a transformation from a state of unity or identity to one of disunity or distance. If the restriction under consideration were to be implemented, not all instances of, for example, disinterest

---

[3] "*-ation*, the form of the compound suffix *-t-ion* . . . which forms nouns of action from L[atin] p[artici]ples. . . ." —*Oxford Universal Dictionary*.

in or dislike of popular culture, would be considered instances of alienation. Only those that have the character of a *disaffection with* it—i.e., a rejection of it subsequent to an acceptance of it—would be so considered. And not all instances of dislike or distrust of political leaders would be regarded as instances of alienation; rather, the term would be employed only in cases in which people have become *disenchanted* with leaders they once admired or respected.

It may be that sociologists, for the most part, are less *interested* in those cases of such disaffection, disenchantment, disassociation from basic societal values, etc., than they are in the related types of separation generally. But this only means that, given their interests, they have not chosen their terms very carefully. They have used the term "alienation" to characterize phenomena that do not have certain important features which the construction of the term suggests—passing over more appropriate terms, including the term "alienness." As Ogden and Richards observe, "The temptation . . . to use [those] words which are most likely to attract attention and excite belief in the importance of [one's] subject is almost irresistible." (6, 157) It would appear that in the present case this temptation *has* been irresistible, considerations of appropriateness notwithstanding.

(2) It has been remarked that most of the uses of the term fall into two basic groups. The type of situation envisaged is either one in which the individual *experiences* something as "other" or separated from him, or it is one in which the individual is *alleged* to exist in a condition of separation from something, of which he may be unaware. It is possible to speak of an "alienness" in both cases; but the nature of the alienness is quite different. In the first case, *feelings* of alienness are involved; certain things are *apprehended as* separate, or strange, or different, or remote, or indifferent, or incomprehensible, or distasteful, etc., by the individual termed "alienated." In the second case, on the other hand, feelings of this sort are not the issue. The alienness in question is rather the individual's purportedly factual separation from something, which is detected through an objective comparison of his actual state with a conception of what the relevant sort of unity or identity would be like.

While neither general use of the term "alienation" is inherently objectionable, it is hard to imagine a situation more conducive to confusion than one in which the term is allowed to function in both ways. For if the same terminology may be used in both cases, there will be a tendency to blur this important distinction.

Few terms are as well suited to the characterization of the kinds of feelings of otherness in question, as those formed from the root "alien" (or *fremd*). The term "alien" readily comes to mind when one seeks language in which to characterize, for example, the political and economic structure, when it is felt to be inhuman and oppressive; popular culture and societal values, when they are felt to be absurd or unacceptable; one's work, when it is felt to be unrelated to one's interests; and other people, when one feels a lack of community with them. And if a noun is sought to refer to the conditions which exist when these things have come to be viewed in these ways, it is hard to imagine one better suited to this purpose than "alienation."

There is no very great need, on the other hand, to employ the term in connection with the sorts of objectively ascertained separations discussed by different writers. Other expressions are readily available which better convey their meanings than it does. Moreover, if uses of the term in connection with separations from one's essential or ideal nature are excepted, this use of the term is much less common than is its use in connection with the experience of something as "alien." If (as seems desirable) it is to be used in only one of those two ways, therefore, the latter would appear to be indicated.

(3) For a number of writers, "alienation" is a critical and polemical term. They do not speak of *any* sort of separation as an instance or type of alienation. Rather, they employ the term only in connection with separations they consider undesirable, thereby imparting evaluative overtones of a negative sort to it. For other writers, however, it has a purely descriptive function. These writers deny any critical or polemical intent in using it. Their reason for employing it is rather that it provides an accurate and illuminating characterization of the phenomena in which they are interested.

A term cannot be used in both these ways at different times without giving rise to a great deal of confusion and misunderstanding. Descriptive uses can mistakenly be thought to imply criticism, and vice versa. And it becomes possible for a writer to waver uncertainly between description and criticism, or to slip back and forth between them without acknowledging or even recognizing that he is doing so. It thus would appear desirable for the term to be used consistently either one way or the other.

If the restriction previously suggested is adopted, the choice becomes simple. It is primarily in connection with allegedly objectively determinable separations that the term is employed with critical and polemical intent. On the other hand, the term is for the most part used in a nonevaluative way by those who employ it in connection with the occurrence of feelings of "alienness." Here it serves to indicate the existence of such feelings; but it is usually not intended to convey any particular attitude toward them by the writer. The nonevaluative use of the term is thus that which is most consistent with the preceding restriction. To restrict its use in the opposite way, moreover, would render it impossible to speak of a person as "alienated," for example, from the popular culture or the basic values of his society, unless one disapproved of his rejection of them; and this quite clearly would be undesirable.

Of course, if the term were to be used only descriptively and nonevaluatively, this would not put an end to debate concerning the relative desirability of the phenomena so designated and their opposites. One can distinguish between a polemical use of the term, which is understood to *convey* a value commitment, and a nonpolemical use of the term understood to convey no such commitment, *coupled with* an argument or affirmation that the phenomenon under consideration is undesirable. In the latter case, unlike the former, those who do not share the view that the phenomenon is undesirable would still be able to accept its characterization as a type of "alienation"; just as two people can agree on the criteria of nonconformity, yet disagree about whether or not it is undesirable.

The implementation of these restrictions would be helpful; but it would hardly begin to limit the number and variety of uses of the term to the point that it would be meaningful to speak of "the phenomenon of alienation." Sartre at one point suggests that a situation may be said to "involve an alienation" simply by virtue of the fact that it involves an experience of something as "other." (7, 285) The suggested restrictions would further specify merely that the term is applicable only if it is also the case that this experience was preceded by a state in which the object in question was *not* experienced as "other." Even if they were to be generally accepted, therefore, the term "alienation" would continue to be applicable to many of the diverse phenomena—or to modified forms of them—in connection with which the different writers discussed above have used it.

It was argued earlier that the different phenomena to which these writers have applied the term have virtually nothing in common—nothing, that is, except that they all involve a disunity of some sort. The suggested restrictions would have the effect that the phenomena to which the term could be applied *would* have certain common features. But these would be features of a purely *formal* sort. That is, it still would not be the case that the different phenomena in question would have any common substantive features (as do different species of a genus); nor would this necessarily mean that they would display any significant interconnection.

Rather, the situation would be roughly comparable to that which exists in the case of a term like "separation." "Separation" is a very useful term, with many different applications. No one supposes, however, that the term names a specific phenomenon, or that the different phenomena to which it is applicable constitute so many different "modes" or "aspects" or "dimensions" *of* something called "separation," or that they are interrelated in any significant way. It is understood that "separation" is merely a general relational term; that the different phenomena to which it is applicable have in common at most certain purely formal features; and that they are more often than not quite independent of each other. The term "alienation" would have a similar status. Given its breadth of application today, it is incapable of functioning in any other way.

— There would be nothing wrong with this—general relational terms play an important role in language—if it were not for the fact that the term is commonly *thought* to designate some specific set of interrelated phenomena, or even some particular (though possibly multidimensional) phenomenon. As A. J. Ayer observes, "Except where a word is patently ambiguous, it is natural for us to assume that the different situations, or types of situation, to which it applies have a distinctive common feature. For, otherwise, why should we use the same word to refer to them?" (1, 10) It may be, as Wittgenstein argues, that it is wrong to assume this (10, §66), but it does seem to be a fact that people tend to do so. And they tend to assume not merely the presence of common formal features, but of common substantive ones as well. At least, this *is* the tendency in the case of the term "alienation," on the part of both the majority of the writers considered and most of their readers. As long as the term is applied to a wide variety of distinct and independent conditions *and* the view prevails that the different conditions to which it is applied are significantly interrelated, the use of the term is unlikely to contribute to their clear comprehension, and may well have just the opposite effect.

Still, the prevailing view of the matter may change. If it does, and particularly if, in addition, the restrictions suggested above were to be observed, the term would be quite useful; though the spectacular phase of its career would come to an end. There are many things one can experience as "other," feel separated from, view as "alien," or feel "alien" in relation to: for example, the popular culture, basic values, and behavioral norms of one's society; the political system, leaders, events, and issues in one's society; friends and relations, other members of one's society, and other people generally; one's work, and one's products; and things, one's immediate environment, and the natural world as a whole. The term "alienation" could be employed in each such case. A basic condition of its employment, however, would be that an individual would never simply be termed "alienated." Rather, he would only be termed "alienated" *from* something, the nature of which would always be specified. The same would be true of all uses of the term "alienation." People would no longer speak simply of "the phenomenon of alienation"; and one would not speak of "alienation" from society, or from others, or from things, without making it clear precisely how one intends "society" or "others" or "things" to be understood.

Self-alienation

The use of the expression "self-alienation" to refer to a disparity between a person's actual condition and his essential or ideal nature is very obviously "critical and polemical." Further, since such a disparity—if it can exist at all—can exist whether or not the person in question is aware of its existence, it cannot be conceived in terms of that person's *experience* of something as "alien." And finally, since it presumably happens far more often than not that such a disparity was not preceded by the person's temporary realization of his essential or ideal nature, the expression "self-alienation" would be virtually without application if the previous existence of a state of self-realization were made a prerequisite of its employment. Thus none of the restrictions suggested above in connection with the use of the term "alienation" could be applied to "self-alienation," without in effect precluding the use of the expression at all in this connection.

To attempt to preclude its use here would be highhanded, to say the least; and the suppression of it would be undesirable besides. If the time should come when people would cease to find plausible the idea of an essential or ideal nature of man which an individual may or may not realize, the expression so construed would no longer have any utility. As long as people continue to find the idea plausible, however, it will be helpful to have available some way of referring to the latter possibility which is both succinct and transparent to the point intended. The expression "self-alienation" meets these requirements, and has a tradition of use in this connection. It may not be indispensable—other expressions have been employed to a similar purpose—but it is as suitable as any other, and more so than most.

If it is to be used in this connection, however, it is preferable that it not be used in any other. Its utility here is diminished to the extent that it is used to refer to phenomena other than the above-mentioned disparity. It is perhaps necessary that it be left unspecified whether the unrealized "self" is "essential" or "ideal"; for not all writers willing to take a position concerning what man should be, are willing to use explicitly essentialist language. But it is necessary to suppress uses of the expression that refer to something else altogether, if it is not to take in so much that it is incapable of conveying anything at all. The term "self" can be and has been used to refer to a great number of things other than man's essential or ideal nature; and the expression "self-alienation" has been used almost as widely. Hegel and Marx consider the social substance and the product of labor, respectively, to be the objectified "self" of the individual, and thus speak of "self-alienation" in characterizing the separation of the individual from them. Sartre uses the expression in connection with the experience one has of oneself when one sees oneself as the object one is for someone else. Gehlen and Horney provide other cases in point. Considered by themselves, these and other such uses of the expression may have some merit. Their currency, however, would deprive it of the utility it would have if it were used solely to suggest that one is not as one should be. And so employed, its usefulness would be far greater than it ever can be as long as no restrictions are placed on that to which the term "self" in the expression may refer.

A number of those who speak of "alienation" in connection with such a disparity employ the expression "alienation from oneself" (or something similar), rather than "self-alienation"; and some even use the term "alienation" by itself in this context. When Fromm speaks of "the alienation of modern man," for example, he would seem to mean, above all, that "modern man" is not as he should be. If uses of the term "alienation" in other contexts are to be subjected to the restrictions suggested above, however, this is most undesirable. For it is only if uses of the term in this context are clearly set apart from its other uses that it will be possible to avoid confusion concerning whether or not a given occurrence of the term is governed by these restrictions.

Such confusion can easily be avoided if the expression

"*self*-alienation" is always used when a disparity of the sort in question is intended; these restrictions could be understood to apply when the prefix "self-" is absent, and not to apply when it is present. If this convention is not adopted, however, it will be impossible to employ the term in both ways and at the same time to avoid confusion concerning how it is to be understood. The use of expressions such as "alienation from oneself" is less troublesome than is the use of the term "alienation" by itself in this context. But, since no inconvenience attends the use of "self-alienation" in their stead, and since this more compact expression is already set apart by its distinctive form, its employment clearly is to be preferred.

Of course, even if it were to be generally understood to refer to a disparity between what a person is and what he should be, it still would not by itself convey anything specific, either about the precise nature of the person's actual condition, or about the sort of essential or ideal selfhood he purportedly fails to realize. Writers could differ quite considerably with regard to the way in which man's essential or ideal nature is to be conceived, and still refer to those who fail to realize their differing versions of it as "self-alienated." Hegel, Marx, Fromm, Horney, Tillich, and Heidegger all speak of "self-alienation," and in so doing all suggest that those whom they so describe are not as they should be; but they are by no means in agreement about what it is the lack of which makes the expression appropriate.

This is not an undesirable state of affairs—or at least, it is one which must be expected, as long as men differ in their conceptions of what man should be. The expression "self-alienation" can function usefully in all such discussions; it would be completely arbitrary, and futile besides, to attempt to tie it to one particular conception of man's essential nature. It follows, however, that the expression by itself is purely formal, taking on definite meaning only within the context of a specific discussion of how man's nature is to be conceived. Simply to term someone "self-alienated," without indicating how one intends "self" to be understood, would be quite as meaningless as simply to term him "alienated." The only difference between the two cases would be that the use of the prefix "self-" would indicate his failure to be what he should be, rather than his separation from something other than himself.

IV. Basic Issues

Many of the phenomena discussed by the writers considered in this study are very important; and many significant and interesting contentions are advanced in their discussions of these phenomena. This is no less true where the terms "alienation" and "self-alienation" have been employed in ways suggested to be inappropriate or otherwise undesirable, than it is where their employment has been found more satisfactory. This is not to say that all the contentions advanced are valid. The issues raised, however, include many of the most important ones imaginable: They concern man's nature, and his relations to others, his work, his products, his body, God, the natural world, and the culture, values, and institutions of the society in which he lives, to mention only some.

Precisely because of the variety and enormity of these issues, it would be impossible to do justice to them in an entire volume, let alone a few brief pages. Still, it is worth recalling some of the more interesting contentions advanced by writers considered in the course of this study. Some are obviously true, though they are no less significant for that; while others are quite problematical, and some are irreconcilable.

(1) *It is essential to the development of the individual's personality that he have the opportunity to engage in self-directed productive activity, and to give himself an objective embodiment in the world in the form of products which reflect his personality.* This is something on which both Hegel and Marx insist; and echoes of this theme are to be found in such diverse recent writers as Fromm and Sartre. To be deprived of this opportunity, in one way or another, is purportedly to be deprived of the possibility of developing a distinctive personality; though this may or may not be viewed as unfortunate, depending upon one's estimation of the importance of developing one. Such opportunity may be lacking, for example, if one is in a condition of slavery; if physical

need compels one to expend one's energies doing the bidding of someone else; or if one's life is completely regimented by a totalitarian regime. In each case, the result is roughly the same. It is also the same, however, if one has the opportunity but fails to seize upon it. Greed no less than need may induce one to surrender the direction of one's productive activity to someone else; and time and energy can be and often are squandered in activity that is in no sense productive.

(2) *One's work must be such that self-expression is possible in it, if one is to find personal satisfaction and fulfillment in it.* Obviously, this contention is related to the preceding one. It focuses upon the individual's relation to his work, however, rather than simply suggesting that there is a connection between self-realization and self-directed productive activity generally. And it carries the implication that, if one's work is the primary productive activity in which one engages, the nature of one's work directly and significantly affects the extent to which one is able to develop a distinctive personality and achieve personal self-realization. Its validity, however, is not contingent upon that of the previous contention. Even if the latter is questioned, this contention may be taken to make a sound (if rather obvious) point: If a person is unable to express himself in his work, he is bound to view it as an activity devoid of any meaningful relation to him as a person.

(3) *To the extent that one's productive activity, one's products, and one's self come under the control of others, they become alien to him.* This contention is related to both of the preceding ones, in that it stresses the connection between autonomy and identification with what one is, does, and produces. It goes further, however, in several respects. First, and most importantly, it suggests that it is, above all, when one is subject to the control of *other men* that one is unable to find satisfaction and fulfillment in one's work, and to satisfy the conditions of personal self-realization. For when others determine the nature of one's product and direct one's productive activity, the former ceases to be the embodiment of one's personality, and the latter ceases to be its free expression. Secondly, it is suggested that others may even succeed in making a person's own self seem alien to him, through

the power they have of making him see himself as the object he is for them, with the characteristics they ascribe to him. It is in considerable measure beyond his control to determine the way they see him, and the way they see him may differ considerably from the way in which he subjectively sees himself; but though the self they see may thus seem alien to him, he cannot escape the realization that it is him they see. This of course is Sartre's extension of the original Hegelian and Marxian claim made with reference to one's product and productive activity. Acceptance of the latter does not entail acceptance of the former; but the two have in common the suggestion that subjection to the control of other men introduces an element of alienness into one's relation to the objective manifestations of oneself.

(4) *To adopt a purely exploitative orientation toward the natural world is to fail to achieve a proper relation to it.* This contention complements the suggestion, implicit in the reference to productive activity above, that the natural world serves to provide materials through whose transformation the individual achieves personal self-realization. It does this; but the point here is that a proper relation to it is one in which it is not merely viewed in this way. First, one who views it only in this way fails to appreciate the intrinsic aesthetic qualities of natural objects in their natural states. Secondly, such a person forgets that he himself is a part of nature, even though he may be more besides. By regarding nature merely as so much raw material, he loses sight of the fact that he remains subject to its laws; and he fails to develop that feeling of unity with nature which can help reconcile him to this fact, and can also help renew his strength when the pressures of modern life begin to take their toll.

(5) *If one pursues his private self-interest without consideration for the legitimate needs and interests of others, one renders community with them impossible.* This contention suggests the possibility of a relation to other men quite different from that indicated in (3). In that case others were considered with reference to the control they may achieve over the individual; and to the extent that they do achieve it, they have a negative significance for him. Here a positive relation of community with them is acknowledged to be pos-

sible; but it is held to be precluded to the extent that one treats them merely as means to his own private ends, and fails to accord them the sort of respect that he must accord them if they are not to regard him antagonistically. This contention is to some extent the interpersonal parallel of the preceding contention concerning one's relation to the natural world; for those who advance it have in mind, above all, an exploitative relation to others. It differs, however, in that it subsumes relations of competition with and indifference to others as well. It also differs in that it does not advance the thesis that one is not *properly* related to others if he does not exist in community with them. One may of course take this further position; but one need not do so in order to grant the validity of the contention under consideration itself.

(6) *A certain kind of solidarity with others is possible if, and only if, one shares a set of values, beliefs, and practices with them.* This contention differs from the previous one in a number of respects. The kind of solidarity here in question neither entails nor is entailed by the sort of community between men which exists when they respect each other's needs and interests and treat each other with consideration and reverence. The former, unlike the latter, is rather impersonal; since it is simply a function of shared values, beliefs, and practices, it may unite one with others with whom one has no personal contact whatsoever, or toward whom as individuals one feels indifferent and even antagonistic. This is the sort of solidarity one may feel with other citizens of one's country, members of one's social class, or supporters of a common cause. Even if one exists in a relation of community with others in the sense of (5) above, adherence to values, beliefs, and practices different from theirs makes it impossible to feel entirely at one with them. To grant this, of course, is not to commit oneself to the view that the absence of such solidarity is undesirable. One may hold its absence to be either undesirable or desirable, and still allow the contention under consideration to be valid.

(7) *Conformity to sociocultural institutions and the expectations of others involves a substantial limitation of one's individuality.* This is quite obviously true, however one may view the desirability of conformity. For the very notion of

conformity involves the idea of the suppression of the tendency to think and act independently, and of the acceptance of patterns of thinking and acting which do not simply reflect one's idiosyncratic desires and inclinations. "Conformity" is a term which has come to have quite negative associations; but if an expression like "taking one's place in society" is used in its stead, it becomes clear that a considerable part of the education of the individual in any society consists in teaching him to adopt generally accepted patterns of thought and behavior, and to repress any tendencies he may have to think and act contrary to them. And to the extent that his "socialization" is successful, he achieves a sense of that solidarity with others in his society referred to in (6) above; for if he conforms to the same sociocultural institutions they do, he obviously shares a set of values, beliefs, and practices with them. Indeed, such conformity is perhaps the paradigm case of this sort of sharing; and the resulting kind of solidarity is thus that which is foremost in the minds of writers such as Hegel who stress the importance of solidarity with other men.

(8) *One's individuality is not complete unless or until one rejects conformity to sociocultural institutions and to the expectations of others.* This contention is obviously related to the previous one. It implies that individuality is to be conceived, above all, in terms of working out a life style on one's own. And it suggests that, to the extent that one thinks and acts along lines laid down by tradition or other men, one's individuality is not as extensive as it might be. To say this is not to take a position one way or the other concerning the desirability of complete individuality; it is simply to make the rather commonplace observation that individuality and conformity are inversely related. There are of course degrees; a limited conformity is consistent with a limited individuality. Radical individuality, however, is incompatible with any degree of conformity, unless something one has independently resolved upon happens by coincidence to correspond to a commonly accepted value, belief, or practice. It follows, therefore, that to embark upon a path of radical individuality is to lose that solidarity with others which is made possible by the sharing of a set of beliefs, values, and practices, except where such a coincidental correspondence occurs; and since

these coincidences presumably would be rare, it is, for all practical purposes, to forego such solidarity altogether. But it does not follow that all forms of unity with others are thereby precluded. In particular, the sort of community mentioned in (5) above would still remain possible, even though it is by no means entailed by the notion of radical individuality.

(9) *A person is not as he should be to the extent that he does not exist in some sort of unity with others.* This contention and the others to follow all bear upon the question of man's essential or ideal nature. The suggestion here is that man by nature is a social being, and that a person is less than truly human if he fails to achieve any sort of positive relation to other men. This does not necessarily mean that he is untrue to his nature unless he is at one with all mankind; for this contention might also be filled out in terms of a type of unity more limited in scope: e.g., the community mentioned in (5), or the solidarity mentioned in (6). The precise way in which it is filled out will depend upon the way in which one who subscribes to it conceives of the social requirement of man's nature. Stated in this very general form, however, this contention is one with which a considerable number of the writers discussed would agree.

(10) *A person is not as he should be to the extent that he fails to develop a distinctive personality.* On this point there is virtual unanimity among the writers discussed, or at least among those who give any indication of what they take man's essential or ideal nature to involve. If any one of them might seem to be an exception, it would be Hegel; but to attribute a rejection of this contention to Hegel would be to misconstrue him completely. For Hegel holds that a social order in which the individual is denied the opportunity to develop a distinctive personality is very primitive; and that an individual who has not developed a distinctive personality is at a very low level of spiritual life. Profound differences do exist among those discussed, however, with regard to the issue of the importance of individuality relative to that of sociocultural participation. The following contentions give expression to the two basic positions taken on this issue.

(11) *A person is not as he should be if he does not have*

an identity which transcends his distinctive personality, of the sort associated with a significant degree of conformity to the sociocultural life and institutions of his society. The point here is not that distinctiveness of personality is to be suppressed altogether, but rather that it should not be so extensive that it precludes sociocultural participation. It should exist, but only within the limits set by the requirements of such participation in one's particular society. Hegel takes this position on the grounds that universality of thought and action is required by man's essential nature, and is that without which the life of the individual is merely ephemeral and without objective significance; and that such universality is to be attained only through conformity to sociocultural institutions. More generally, this view may be advanced on the grounds that human life is qualitatively different from animal life principally by virtue of its sociocultural component; and that therefore one who rejects sociocultural participation reverts to a subhuman form of existence. Those who would subscribe to this contention could of course differ with regard to the degree of conformity that is desirable, and the degree of individuality that is permissible.

(12) *A person is not as he should be to the extent that his personality is not distinctive, but rather is shaped by impersonal socioeconomic institutions and the expectations of others.* This contention is directly at odds with the preceding one. It is related to (8) above, which suggests individuality and conformity to be inversely related; but it goes further in that it assigns positive value solely to the former, and negative value to any degree of the latter. The ideal of human existence here is conceived in terms of radical individuality. Conformity is held invariably to involve a surrender of individuality, and therefore is regarded as incompatible with the full realization of the human ideal. The suggestion associated with (11), that rejection of sociocultural participation involves reversion to a subhuman form of existence, is emphatically denied. Those who subscribe to (12) are generally willing to allow that one who rejects such participation merely in order to give himself over to the indulgence of his animal appetites does move away from the human ideal, rather than closer to it. But they maintain that radical individuality in-

volves something altogether different than this. It is held to represent a form of existence qualitatively distinct from (and higher than) both sociocultural existence and mere natural or animalistic existence. Sociocultural existence is viewed as but an intermediary stage, without which radical individuality might never have become possible, but which should give way to it once it does.

This by no means exhausts either the issues with which the writers considered in this study are concerned, or the positions they take with reference to them. The interest and significance of these contentions alone, however, indicates the importance of the discussions in which they are advanced. Yet it should be observed that it has been possible to state and explicate these contentions without speaking of "alienation" and "self-alienation" at all. This does not mean that one therefore ought to avoid doing so; but it does suggest that one can well afford to employ the expressions judiciously and sparingly in dealing with these matters. Doing so would be attended by no inconvenience; and it is also the practice most likely to contribute to a clear comprehension of the issues involved.

REFERENCES

Introduction

(1) Feuer, Lewis. "What is Alienation? The Career of a Concept." *New Politics*, Vol. I, No. 3 (Spring 1962), pp. 116–34.

(2) Horowitz, Irving L. "On Alienation and the Social Order," *Philosophy and Phenomenological Research*, Vol. XXVII, No. 2 (December 1966), pp. 230–37.

(3) Katz, Jerrold J. *The Philosophy of Language*. New York: Harper & Row, 1966.

(4) Kaufman, Arnold S. "On Alienation," *Inquiry*, Vol. 8, No. 2 (Summer 1965), pp. 141–65.

(5) Keniston, Kenneth. *The Uncommitted: Alienated Youth in American Society*. New York: Harcourt, Brace & World, 1965.

(6) Wittgenstein, Ludwig. *Philosophical Investigations*. German text with translation by G. E. M. Anscombe. Oxford: Basil Blackwell, 1953.

CHAPTER ONE
The Linguistic and Intellectual Background

(1) Calvin, John. *Commentaries on the Epistles of Paul to the Galatians and Ephesians*. Trans. William Pringle. Edinburgh: The Calvin Translation Society, 1854.

(2) Calvini, Ioannis. *Vini Commentarii in Quatuor Pauli Epistolas*. Geneva: Ioannem Girardum, 1548.

(3) *Dictionnaire alphabétique et analogique de la Langue Française*, ed. Paul Robert. Paris: Presses Universitaires de France, 1953.

(4) *Dictionary of Philosophy and Psychology*, ed. James M. Baldwin. Second Edition. New York: Macmillan, 1911.

(5) Dietz, Philipp. *Wörterbuch zu Dr. Martin Luthers Deutsche Schriften.* Hildesheim: Georg Olms, 1961.

(6) Feuer, Lewis. "What is Alienation? The Career of a Concept." See under References (Introduction).

(7) Gehlen, Arnold. "Über den Ursprung der Freiheit aus der Entfremdung." *Archiv für Rechts- und Sozialphilosophie*, Vol. XL. No. 3 (1952–53), pp. 338–53.

(8) Grimm, Jakob and Wilhelm. *Deutsches Wörterbuch.* Leipzig: S. Hirzel. (The volume containing the entry for *Entfremdung* was published in 1862.)

(9) Grotius, Hugo. *De Jure Belli ac Pacis.* Trans. W. Whewell. London: John W. Parker, 1853.

(10) Hegel, G. W. F. "Differenz des Fichteschen und Schellingschen Systems der Philosophie." *Erste Druckschriften*, ed. Georg Lasson. Leipzig: Felix Meiner, 1928.

(11) ——. *Lectures on the History of Philosophy.* Trans. E. S. Haldane and F. H. Simson. New York: Humanities Press, 1963.

(12) ——. *On Christianity: Early Theological Writings.* Trans. T. M. Knox and Richard Kroner. New York: Harper, 1948. Cf. *Hegels theologische Jugendschriften*, ed. Herman Nohl. Tübingen: J. C. B. Mohr, 1907.

(13) ——. *Schriften zur Politik und Rechtsphilosophie*, ed. Georg Lasson. Leipzig: Felix Meiner, 1923.

(14) Heyne, Moritz. *Deutsche Wörterbuch.* Leipzig: S. Hirzel. (The volume containing the entry for *Entfremdung* was published in 1890.)

(15) Hobbes, Thomas. *Leviathan.* New York: E. P. Dutton, 1950.

(16) Kaufmann, Walter. *Hegel: Reinterpretation, Texts, and Commentary.* New York: Doubleday, 1965.

(17) Klein, Ernst. A *Comprehensive Etymological Diction-*

ary of the English Language. New York: Elsevier, 1966.

(18) Locke, John. "An Essay Concerning the True Original, Extent and End of Civil Government" (or "Second Treatise on Civil Government"). *Social Contract*, ed. Sir Ernest Barker. London: Oxford University Press, 1947.

(19) Lukács, Georg. *Der Junge Hegel und die Probleme der Kapitalistischen Gesellschaft*. Berlin: Aufbau-Verlag, 1948.

(20) *Middle English Dictionary*, ed. Hans Kurath and Sherman M. Kuhn. Ann Arbor: University of Michigan Press. (The section containing the entry for "alienation" was published in 1956.)

(21) *New English Dictionary on Historical Principles*, ed. James A. H. Murray. Oxford: Clarendon Press. (The volume containing the entry for "alienation" was published in 1888.)

(22) Rousseau, Jean-Jacques. "Discourse on the Origin and Foundations of Inequality." *Rousseau: The First and Second Discourses*, ed. Roger D. Masters. New York: St. Martin's, 1964.

(23) ———. "The Social Contract." *Social Contract*, ed. Sir Ernest Barker. London: Oxford University Press, 1947.

(24) Schiller, Friedrich. *On the Aesthetic Education of Man, in a Series of Letters*. Trans. Reginald Snell. New Haven: Yale University Press, 1954.

(25) ———. "Über die ästhetische Erziehung des Menschen." *Werke in Drei Bänden*. Leipzig: Bibliographisches Institut, 1955.

CHAPTER TWO
Hegel's *Phenomenology of Spirit*

(1) Diderot, Denis. *Rameaus Neffe*. Trans. J. W. von Goethe. Leipzig: G. J. Göschen, 1805.

(2) ———. *Rameau's Nephew and Other Works*. Trans. J.

Barzun and R. H. Bowen. New York: Bobbs-Merrill, 1956.

(3) Glockner, Hermann. *Hegel-Lexikon.* Stuttgart: Fr. Frommann, 1935.

(4) Hegel, G. W. F. *Grundlinien der Philosophie des Rechts,* ed. Georg Lasson. Third Edition. Leipzig: Felix Meiner, 1930.

(5) ———. *Phänomenologie des Geistes,* ed. J. Hoffmeister. Sixth Edition. Hamburg: Felix Meiner, 1952.

(6) ———. *Phenomenology of Mind.* Trans. J. B. Baillie. Revised Second Edition. New York: Macmillan, 1949.

(7) ———. *Philosophy of Right.* Trans. T. M. Knox. Oxford: Clarendon, 1942.

(8) ———. *Reason in History.* Trans. Robert S. Hartman. New York: Liberal Arts, 1953.

(9) ———. *Vorlesungen über die Philosophie der Geschichte,* ed. Hermann Glockner. Stuttgart: Fr. Frommann, 1928.

(10) Kaufmann, Walter. *Hegel: Reinterpretation, Texts, and Commentary.* See under References (Chapter One).

(11) Keniston, Kenneth. *The Uncommitted: Alienated Youth in American Society.* New York: Harcourt, Brace & World, 1965.

(12) Marx, Karl. *Early Writings,* ed. and trans. T. B. Bottomore. New York: McGraw-Hill, 1963.

CHAPTER THREE
Marx's Early Writings

(1) Feuerbach, Ludwig. *The Essence of Christianity.* Trans. George Eliot (Marian Evans). New York: Harper & Row, 1957.

(2) ———. *Vorlesungen über das Wesen der Religion,* ed. Wilhelm Bolin. Stuttgart: Fr. Frommann, 1908.

(3) ———. *Das Wesen des Christentums,* ed. Wilhelm Bolin. Stuttgart: Fr. Frommann, 1903.

(4) Hegel, G. W. F. *Grundlinien der Philosophie des Rechts.* See under References (Chapter Two).

(5) ——. *Phänomenologie des Geistes*. See under References (Chapter Two).

(6) ——. *Phenomenology of Mind*. See under References (Chapter Two).

(7) ——. *Philosophy of Right*. See under References (Chapter Two).

(8) Hook, Sidney. *From Hegel to Marx*. Ann Arbor: University of Michigan Press, 1962.

(9) Marx, Karl. *Early Writings*, ed. and trans. T. B. Bottomore. New York: McGraw-Hill, 1963.

(10) ——. *Frühe Schriften*, ed. Hans-Joachim Lieber and Peter Furth. Vol. I. Stuttgart: Cotta, 1962.

(11) ——, and Friedrich Engels. *The Communist Manifesto*, ed. Samuel Beer. New York: Appleton-Century-Crofts, 1955.

(12) ——. *The German Ideology*, Parts I & III, ed. R. Pascal. New York: International Publishers, 1963.

(13) Tucker, Robert C. *Philosophy and Myth in Karl Marx*. Cambridge: Cambridge University Press, 1964.

CHAPTER FOUR

Erich Fromm and Karen Horney

(1) Becker, Benjamin J. "Alienation and the Group Analytic Process," *The American Journal of Psychoanalysis*, Vol. XXI, No. 2 (1961), pp. 273–76.

(2) ——. "Relatedness and Alienation in Group Psychoanalysis," *The American Journal of Psychoanalysis*, Vol. XVIII, No. 2 (1958), pp. 150–57.

(3) DeRosis, Louis E. "Alienation and Group Psychoanalysis," *The American Journal of Psychoanalysis*, Vol. XXI, No. 2 (1961), pp. 263–72.

(4) Fromm, Erich. *Beyond the Chains of Illusion*. New York: Pocket Books, 1962.

(5) ——. *Escape from Freedom*. New York: Avon Books, 1941. Originally published by Holt, Rinehart & Winston.

(6) ——. *Marx's Concept of Man*. New York: Frederick Ungar, 1961.

(7) ——. *The Sane Society*. New York: Fawcett Premier Books, 1955. Originally published by Holt, Rinehart & Winston.

(8) Horney, Karen. *Neurosis and Human Growth*. New York: W. W. Norton, 1950.

(9) ——. *New Ways in Psychoanalysis*. New York: W. W. Norton, 1939.

(10) ——. *Our Inner Conflicts*. New York: W. W. Norton, 1945.

(11) Kelman, Harold. "Alienation: Its Historical and Therapeutic Context," *The American Journal of Psychoanalysis*, Vol. XXI, No. 2 (1961), pp. 198–206.

(12) Martin, Alexander Reid. "Self-Alienation and the Loss of Leisure," *The American Journal of Psychoanalysis*, Vol. XXI, No. 2 (1961), pp. 156–65.

(13) Rubins, Jack L. "The Self-Concept, Identity, and Alienation from Self," *The American Journal of Psychoanalysis*, Vol. XXI, No. 2 (1961), pp. 132–43.

(14) ——. "The Self-Idealizing and Self-Alienating Process During Late Adolescence," *The American Journal of Psychoanalysis*, Vol. XXV, No. 1 (1965), pp. 27–38.

(15) Schachtel, Ernest G. "On Alienated Concepts of Identity," *The American Journal of Psychoanalysis*, Vol. XXI, No. 2 (1961), pp. 120–30.

(16) Vollmerhausen, Joseph W. "Alienation in the Light of Karen Horney's Theory of Neurosis," *The American Journal of Psychoanalysis*, Vol. XXI, No. 2 (1961), pp. 144–51.

(17) Weiss, Frederick A. "Self-Alienation: Dynamics and Therapy," *The American Journal of Psychoanalysis*, Vol. XXI, No. 2 (1961), pp. 207–18.

(18) Wenkart, Antonia. "Regaining Identity through Relatedness," *The American Journal of Psychoanalysis*, Vol. XXI, No. 2 (1961), pp. 227–33.

CHAPTER FIVE
The Sociological Literature

(1) Aiken, Michael, and Hage, Jerald. "Organizational Alienation: A Comparative Analysis," *American Sociological Review*, Vol. 31, No. 4 (August 1966), pp. 497–507.

(2) Blauner, Robert. *Alienation and Freedom*. Chicago: University of Chicago Press, 1964.

(3) Bullough, Bonnie. "Alienation in the Ghetto," *American Journal of Sociology*, Vol. 72, No. 5 (March 1967), pp. 469–78.

(4) Clark, John P. "Measuring Alienation Within a Social System," *American Sociological Review*, Vol. 24, No. 6 (December 1959), pp. 849–52.

(5) Clinard, Marshall B. "The Theoretical Implications of Anomie and Deviant Behavior," in *Anomie and Deviant Behavior: A Discussion and Critique*, ed. M. B. Clinard. New York: Free Press, 1964. Pp. 1–57.

(6) Dean, Dwight G. "Alienation and Political Apathy," *Social Forces*, Vol. 38, No. 3 (March 1960), pp. 185–89.

(7) ——. "Alienation: Its Meaning and Measurement," *American Sociological Review*, Vol. 26, No. 5 (October 1961), pp. 753–58.

(8) Durkheim, Émile. *Suicide: A Study in Sociology*. Trans. John A. Spaulding and George Simpson, ed. George Simpson. Glencoe, Ill.: Free Press, 1951.

(9) Gerson, Walter. "Alienation in Mass Society: Some Causes and Responses," *Sociology and Social Research*, Vol. 49, No. 2 (January 1965), pp. 143–52.

(10) Hajda, Jan. "Alienation and Integration of Student Intellectuals," *American Sociological Review*, Vol. 26, No. 5 (October 1961), pp. 758–77.

(11) Horton, John. "The Dehumanization of Anomie and Alienation: A Problem in the Ideology of Sociology," *British Journal of Sociology*, Vol. XV, No. 4 (December 1964), pp. 283–300.

(12) ———, and Thompson, Wayne. "Powerlessness and Political Negativism: A Study of Defeated Local Ref-
erendums," *American Journal of Sociology*, Vol.
LXVII, No. 5 (March 1962), pp. 485–93.

(13) Keniston, Kenneth. *The Uncommitted: Alienated
Youth in American Society*. New York: Harcourt,
Brace & World, 1965.

(14) Levin, Murray. *The Alienated Voter*. New York: Holt,
Rinehart and Winston, 1960.

(15) Lowry, Ritchie. "The Functions of Alienation in Lead-
ership," *Sociology and Social Research*, Vol. 46, No.
4 (July 1962), pp. 426–35.

(16) MacIver, R. M. *The Ramparts We Guard*. New York:
Macmillan, 1950.

(17) McClosky, Herbert, and Schaar, John. "Psychological
Dimensions of Anomy," *American Sociological Review*, Vol. 30, No. 1 (February 1965), pp. 14–40.

(18) McDill, Edward, and Ridley, Jeanne. "Status, Anomia,
Political Alienation, and Political Participation,"
American Journal of Sociology, Vol. LXVIII, No. 2
(September 1962), pp. 205–13.

(19) Merton, Robert K. *Social Theory and Social Structure*,
revised and enlarged edition. Glencoe, Ill.: Free
Press, 1957.

(20) Middleton, Russell. "Alienation, Race, and Education,"
American Sociological Review, Vol. 28, No. 6 (December 1963), pp. 973–77.

(21) Miller, George A. "Professionals in Bureaucracy: Alienation Among Industrial Scientists and Engineers,"
American Sociological Review, Vol. 32, No. 5 (October 1967), pp. 755–68.

(22) Neal, Arthur, and Rettig, Salomon. "Dimensions of
Alienation Among Manual Workers and Non-
Manual Workers," *American Sociological Review*,
Vol. 28, No. 4 (August 1963), pp. 599–608.

(23) ———. "On the Multidimensionality of Alienation,"
American Sociological Review, Vol. 32, No. 1 (February 1967), pp. 54–64.

(24) Nettler, Gwynn. "A Measure of Alienation," *American*

Sociological Review, Vol. 22, No. 6 (December 1957), pp. 670–77.

(25) Nisbet, Robert. *The Quest for Community*. New York: Oxford University Press, 1953.

(26) Parsons, Talcott. *The Social System*. Glencoe, Ill.: Free Press, 1951.

(27) ——, and Shils, Edward. "Values, Motives, and Systems of Action," in *Toward a General Theory of Action*, ed. Parsons and Shils. Cambridge, Mass.: Harvard University Press, 1951. Pp. 47–243.

(28) Putney, Snell, and Middleton, Russell. "Ethical Relativism and Anomia," *American Journal of Sociology*, Vol. LXVII, No. 4 (January 1962), pp. 430–38.

(29) Seeman, Melvin. "Alienation and Social Learning in a Reformatory," *American Journal of Sociology*, Vol. LXIX, No. 3 (November 1963), pp. 270–84.

(30) ——. "On the Meaning of Alienation," *American Sociological Review*, Vol. 24, No. 6 (December 1959), pp. 783–91.

(31) ——. "On the Personal Consequences of Alienation in Work," *American Sociological Review*, Vol. 32, No. 2 (April 1967), pp. 273–85.

(32) ——. "Powerlessness and Knowledge: A Comparative Study of Alienation and Learning," *Sociometry*, Vol. 30, No. 2 (June 1967), pp. 105–23.

(33) ——, and Evans, John. "Alienation and Learning in a Hospital Setting," *American Sociological Review*, Vol. 27, No. 6 (December 1962), pp. 772–82.

(34) Simmons, J. L. "Liberalism, Alienation, and Personal Disturbance," *Sociology and Social Research*, Vol. 49, No. 4 (July 1965), pp. 456–64.

(35) Srole, Leo. "Social Integration and Certain Corollaries: An Exploratory Study," *American Sociological Review*, Vol. 21, No. 6 (December 1956), pp. 709–16.

(36) Struening, Elmer, and Richardson, Arthur. "A Factor Analytic Exploration of the Alienation, Anomia and Authoritarianism Domain," *American Sociological Review*, Vol. 30, No. 5 (October 1965), pp. 768–76.

(37) Thompson, Wayne, and Horton, John. "Political Alien-

ation as a Force in Political Action," *Social Forces*, Vol. 38, No. 3 (March 1960), pp. 190–95.

CHAPTER SIX
Existential Philosophy and Theology

(1) Camus, Albert. "Le Mythe de Sisyphe," in *Essais*, ed. R. Quillot and L. Faucon. Paris: Gallimard, 1965. Pp. 89–211.

(2) ——. *The Stranger*. Trans. S. Gilbert. New York: A. A. Knopf, 1946.

(3) Gehlen, Arnold. *Der Mensch*. Frankfurt a.M.: Athenäum, 1966.

(4) Heidegger, Martin. *Being and Time*. Trans. John Macquarrie and Edward Robinson. New York: Harper, 1962.

(5) ——. *Sein und Zeit*. Tübingen: Max Niemeyer, 1960.

(6) Husserl, Edmund. *Phenomenology and the Crisis of Philosophy*. Trans. Quentin Lauer. New York: Harper, 1965.

(7) ——. *Die Krisis der Europäischen Wissenschaften und die Transcendentale Phänomenologie*. (*Husserliana*, Vol. VI) The Haag: Martinus Nijhoff, 1954.

(8) Jaspers, Karl. *Philosophie*, Vol. II. Berlin: Springer, 1956.

(9) Marcel, Gabriel. *Being and Having*. Trans. A. and C. Black. London: Collins, 1949.

(10) Plessner, Helmuth. "Mit Anderen Augen," in *Zwischen Philosophie und Gesellschaft*. Bern: Francke, 1953. Pp. 204–18.

(11) Sartre, Jean-Paul. *Being and Nothingness*. Trans. Hazel Barnes. New York: Philosophical Library, 1956.

(12) ——. *Critique de la raison dialectique*. Paris: Gallimard, 1960.

(13) ——. *L'Être et le Néant*. Paris: Gallimard, 1943.

(14) ——. *Search for a Method*. Trans. Hazel Barnes. New York: Random House, 1963.

(15) Tillich, Paul. *Systematic Theology*. In three volumes.

Chicago: University of Chicago Press, 1951, 1957, 1963.

(16) Warnock, Mary. *The Philosophy of Sartre*. London: Hutchinson, 1965.

CHAPTER SEVEN
Alienation: A General Consideration

(1) Ayer, A. J. *The Problem of Knowledge*. Baltimore: Penguin Books, 1956.

(2) Feuer, Lewis. "What is Alienation? The Career of a Concept." See under References (Introduction).

(3) Kaufman, Arnold S. "On Alienation." See under References (Introduction).

(4) Keniston, Kenneth. *The Uncommitted*. See under References (Chapter Five).

(5) MacIntyre, Alasdair. "Marxist Mask and Romantic Face," *Encounter*, Vol. XXIV, No. 4 (April 1965), pp. 64–72.

(6) Ogden, C. K., and Richards, I. A. *The Meaning of Meaning*. Fifth edition. London: Routledge & Kegan Paul, 1960.

(7) Sartre, Jean-Paul. *Critique de la raison dialectique*. See under References (Chapter Six).

(8) ———. "Existentialism is a Humanism," in *Existentialism from Dostoevsky to Sartre*, ed. Walter Kaufmann. New York: Meridian Books, 1956. Pp. 287–311.

(9) Seeman, Melvin. "On the Meaning of Alienation." See under References (Chapter Five).

(10) Wittgenstein, Ludwig. *Philosophical Investigations*. See under References (Introduction).

INDEX

Acculturation, 59 n, 186–87

Acquisitiveness. *See* Egoism

Aiken, Michael, 166–67, 169–70

Albee, Edward, xl

Alienatio, alienare, etc., 9–11, 16, 69

Aliénation, aliéner, etc., 9, 18, 206, 215, 226–28, 234

Alienation, traditional and standard uses of term, lix, 9–15, 70–71, 104–5, 180–81, 251, 258; and mental disorder, 10–11, 14, 43 n, 242; from God, 11, 15–16, 44, 76, 220–23; from nature, 126–30, 162, 248, 263, 269; of labor, work, or production, li–lii, 75, 80 n–82 n, 87–88, 96–102, 107–9, 114–16, 119–20, 144–45, 163, 168–73, 202, 233, 235–38, 252, 260, 263, 267–69; of one's product or property, 10, 13, 51–53, 92–97, 108–9, 112–16, 137, 145–46, 235–38, 263, 268–69; interpersonal, 11–14, 44, 102–8, 114, 116, 130–35, 162, 164–68, 171, 180, 185, 202, 231, 239, 248, 251–52, 260, 263–64, 269–70; political, 33–36, 43–62, 66–69, 71, 173–83, 202, 250, 260, 263; self-, 21 n, 24, 30, 32, 43, 50–62, 64–65, 71–72, 77 n, 81, 81 n–82 n, 108–14, 116 n, 129, 137, 148–60, 162, 181–82, 208–42, 247, 250, 252–54, 256, 258, 264–65, 272–74; sociocultural, 33–37, 43–54, 57–60, 63, 66–69, 71, 78, 92, 135–37, 162, 165, 173–200, 202, 239, 242–44, 247, 250, 253, 259–64, 271

Alienness. *See* Strangeness

Allgemeinheit. See Universality

Amos, lv

Anomie, anomia, anomy, 194–98, 201

Anthropology, philosophical, 240

Apathy, 176, 180, 183

Arendt, Hannah, xxi

Aristotle, xxvii, xxxvii

Art and artists, xxxiv, xl, 32–33, 88, 90–91, 238, 243

Aufhebung, 86 n, 116, 244 n

Authenticity. *See* Inauthenticity-authenticity

Ayer, A. J., 263

Baillie, John B., xx, 39 n, 42 n, 43 n, 59 n

Baldwin, James M., 11 n

Beckett, Samuel, xxxvi

Beethoven, Ludwig van, xl

Being and Nothingness (Sartre), 205, 227, 228–35, 247–51, 253–54

Being and Time (Heidegger), 205, 208–13

Beyond the Chains of Illusion (Fromm), 123–48 *passim*

Bible. *See* specific books, figures

Bifurcation. *See Entzweiung; also* Separation

Bildung, 59, 61–63, 66

Blauner, Robert, 171–73

Bottomore, T. B., 74 n, 80 n

Brecht, Bertolt, xviii

Buber, Martin, xviii, xliv, lv

Buddhism, lvi

Calvin, John, 16

Camus, Albert, xxii, 206–7

Capitalism, xlii–xliv, 86, 88, 107, 136, 247. *See also* Civil society; Private property

Christianity. *See* Religion

Civil disobedience, 193

Civil society, 103, 106–8, 110, 115–19. *See also* Capitalism

Clark, John P., 175

Clinard, Marshall, 194 n

Communism, xli–xliv, 85, 99 n, 102–3, 105, 117; and art, xxxix–xl; and Lukács, xix

Communist Manifesto, The (Marx and Engels), xviii, 74–75, 108

Community. *See* society; Social life

Conformity, xl, 57–59, 129, 131–32, 134–35, 137–38, 140, 162, 248, 251, 261–62, 271–72

Creativity, liv, lviii

Critique of Dialectical Reason (Sartre), 205, 226, 233–39, 250–51

Culture, 1, 24–25, 32, 39, 57–59, 72, 113, 118, 135–38, 184–200, 263, 267, 270–71, 273. *See also* Social substance

Dante, xxxvii

Dasein, 209–12, 248

Dean, Dwight G., 165, 177, 193

Dehumanization, 110–11, 133

Dependence. *See* Independence-dependence

Descartes, René, xxxiii–xxxiv

Deutsches Wörterbuch (J. and W. Grimm), 13–14

Dictionary of Philosophy and Psychology (Baldwin), 11

Diderot, Denis, 43 n, 65

"Difference of the Fichtean and Schellingian Systems of Philosophy" (Hegel), 30–33, 39

Discourse on the Origin and Foundations of Inequality (Rousseau), 19

Disparity. *See* Separation

Distance; transcendence, xxvii, 25, 47, 126–27, 130–31, 185, 228–31, 236, 241–44. *See also* Separation

Division of labor, xli, xlii, 110, 171

Dostoevski, Fedor, lvii

Durkheim, Emile, 194, 196

"Economic and Philosophical Manuscripts" (Marx), xviii, xxiii, 73–119 *passim*

Education, xlvii, xlvix. *See also Bildung;* Acculturation

Egoism; egotism, 103–8, 114–18, 134–35, 167, 269–70

Elijah, lv

Engels, Friedrich, xix, xxiii, xlii

En soi–pour soi (Sartre), xxv

Entäusserung, xvii–xxi, 21–23, 46 n, 55, 79–80, 94, 97. *See also* Surrender

Entfremdung, xvii–xxi, 9, 13–15, 21, 23, 25, 31, 38 n, 43 n, 44 n–46 n, 68, 70, 71 n, 73 n, 77 n, 79–81, 94, 98, 205 n, 206, 208, 215, 227–28, 240, 243, 258. *See also* Alienation

Entzweiung, 31–33, 71. *See also* Separation

Ephesians, Epistle to the, 15–16

Escape from Freedom (Fromm), xvii, 123–48 *passim*

Essence, man's. *See* Man

Essence of Christianity, The (Feuerbach), 75, 78 n, 87 n

Estrangement, 11–12, 71 n, 105–6, 205 n, 213–26. *See also* Alienation

Étrangeté, 207

Euripides, xl

Faust (Goethe), xxxv, xxxvi

Fellowship. *See* Social life

Feuer, Lewis, 5, 15, 16 n, 246–49

Feuerbach, Ludwig, l, li, 75–76, 79, 81 n, 87, 89

Fichte, J. G., 21–23, 30, 76

"Fragment of a System" (Hegel), 30, 40, 57

Fremd. See Strangeness

Freud, Sigmund, xxvii, lv–lvi, 157

Friendship. *See* Social life

Fromm, Erich, xvii, xxi–xxii, 2, 3, 121, 123–48, 149, 159–62, 164–65, 201, 212, 247–53, 257, 265–66

Gehlen, Arnold, 240–42, 244, 248–52, 265

German Ideology, The (Marx and Engels), xli–xlii, 74, 99 n

Glockner, Hermann, xvii, 38 n

God, xxv–xxvi, li–lii, 11, 15–16, 44, 75–76, 216, 220–23, 267

Goethe, Johann Wolfgang von, xxxv–xxxvi, xlvi–xlvii, lvii, 4, 43 n

Greed. *See* Egoism

Grotius, Hugo, 16–19, 55, 56 n

Hage, Jerald, 166–67, 169

Hajda, Jan, 165–67

Hamlet (Shakespeare), xxxviii

Hegel, G. W. F., xvii–lvii *passim*, 2–4, 7, 9, 14–16, 20–37, 38–72, 73–86, 89–94, 96–98, 101, 104, 107, 109, 112–14, 116–17, 119–20, 125, 136–39, 142, 146, 163, 181, 184, 190, 198, 205, 212, 214, 215, 220, 239, 242–43, 246–47, 249, 252–53, 257, 265–66, 269, 271, 272; early political essays, 33–37; early "theological" writings, 26–30; essay on Fichte and Schelling, 30–33; his *Phenomenology* (*see Phenomenology of Spirit*)

Hegel-Lexikon (Glockner), xvii, 38 n

Heidegger, Martin, xxi, 205, 208, 226–27, 231–32, 239, 247–48, 250, 253, 266

Heraclitus, xxxi–xxxii, xxxviii

Hesse, Hermann, xxxii, xxxv

Hinduism, lvi

Hobbes, Thomas, 17–18, 55

Hoffmeister, Johannes, xvii

Hook, Sidney, 74

Horney, Karen, 7, 124, 148–60, 161, 201, 247, 250–51, 265–66

Horowitz, Irving, 6

Horton, John, 175–76

Hosea, lv

Hume, David, xxxiii, xxxiv

Husserl, Edmund, 227–28, 231

Inauthenticity–authenticity, 57, 208–14, 231–32, 248, 250

Independence–dependence, 16–18, 46–51, 54–62, 65, 70, 84, 87–88, 94–102, 103, 108–9, 114–15, 139–42, 165, 174–75, 180–81; *see also* Individuality; Production; Surrender

Individuality, 26, 30, 39, 40, 45–46, 48–49, 51–62, 65–67, 82, 84–86, 110, 126, 130, 132, 136 n, 137–41, 149, 153–57, 236, 271–74; *see also* Independence–dependence; Personality; Self; Self-consciousness

"Inevitability of Alienation, The," Introductory Essay, by Walter Kaufmann, xv–lviii; Contents: 1. Historical Per-

Introductory Essay (*cont'd*) spective, xvii–xxiii, 2. Analysis, xxiv–xxvii, 3. Alienated Philosophers, xxix–xxxiv, 4. Literature and Art, xxxiv–xl, 5. Marx's Dream, xl–xliv, 6. "Things Have Never Been Worse," xliv–xlix, 7. Against Marx's Heritage, xlix–liii, 8. A Pluralistic View, li–lviii

Jaspers, Karl, xx–xxii, 206–7
Jeremiah, lv
Jesus, 215, 221–22, 225–26
Joyce, James, xxxvi
Judaism, lv, 118

Kafka, Franz, xl, liii–liv
Kahler, Erich, xxi–xxii
Kant, Immanuel, xxxii–xxxiv, 21, 27–28
Kapital, Das (Marx), li
Katz, Jerrold, 6
Kaufman, Arnold, 5, 246–49
Kaufmann, Walter, 23, 26 n, 34 n, 42 n; Introductory Essay "The Inevitability of Alienation" by, xv–lviii
Kazantzakis, Nikos, xli
Keniston, Kenneth, 5, 59 n, 186–91, 193, 246–49
Kierkegaard, Sören, xx, lviii, 4, 62, 206
Knox, T. M., 42 n, 59 n
Kosinski, Jerzy, xli

Labor; work, l–li, 2, 39, 75, 79–88, 96–102, 109, 116, 119–20, 128, 144, 162–63, 168–73, 235–38, 247, 252, 263, 265, 267–69; *see also* Production
Landshut, Siegfried, xxii
Leibniz, Gottfried Wilhelm von, xxxiii–xxxiv
Leonardo da Vinci, xxxix
Levin, Murray, 174 n, 175–76, 178–79, 181

Literature, alienation in, xxxiv–xxxix, lxi, 207–8, 243–44
Locke, John, 17–18, 56
"Look of the Other" (in Sartre's *Being and Nothingness*), 228–30, 233, 235
Love, 26–28, 130–31, 140–43, 217, 223–24, 225 n
"Love," Fragment on (Hegel), 26–29, 31, 57
Löwith, Karl, xxi
Lowry, Ritchie, 191
Lukács, Georg, xix–xx, xxiii, 22–23
Luther, Martin, 14–16

McClosky, Herbert, 164, 195, 201
McDill, Edward, 176, 196 n
MacIntyre, Alasdair, 250
MacIver, R. M., 195
Man, man's nature, xxiv–xxv, 2, 22–31, 40–43, 45–47, 49–53, 57–58, 60–62, 66–68, 71–72, 75–79, 81–87, 88–91, 105, 108–16, 118, 125–26, 137–38, 142, 149–50, 157–59, 228–35, 238–39, 264–67, 272–74
Marcel, Gabriel, 206–7
Marcuse, Herbert, xx–xxi
Marx, Karl, xvii–xxiii, xxv, xl–xliv, l–li, lvii, 2–4, 7, 9, 24, 53, 62, 64, 71–72, 73–122, 125–26, 128 n, 136, 138–39, 142, 144–45, 162, 165, 167, 169–70, 173, 178, 180–81, 184, 205–7, 212, 233–39, 246–52, 257, 265–67, 269; early writings (FS = *Frühe Schriften*) of, xviii–xx, xxii–xxiii, xxv, xliv, l–liii, 7, 62, 73–122, 123, 163, 184, 246. *See also Communist Manifesto, The*; "Economic and Philosophical Manuscripts"; *German Ideology, The*; *Kapital, Das*; and "On the Jewish Question"

Marx's Concept of Man (Fromm), xxii–xxiii, 123–48 *passim*

Meaninglessness, 163, 171–73, 177–80

Mental disorder. *See* Alienation, and mental disorder

Merton, Robert, 186–88, 190–92, 194–96, 199

Michelangelo, xxxix

Middleton, Russell, 164, 170, 174, 177, 185, 188, 191, 194, 196 n, 199

Miller, George A., 170, 172

Moses, lv

Mozart, Wolfgang Amadeus, xl

Nature, xxx–xxxi, 2, 24–25, 126–30, 263, 267, 269

Neal, Arthur, 161, 174 n, 195–96, 202–3

Need, 86–88, 100–1, 110, 114–19, 268

Nettler, Gwynn, 184–85, 188–89

Neurosis and Human Growth (Horney), 153–59

New Ways in Psychoanalysis (Horney), 149–51, 153–54

Nietzsche, Friedrich, xxxiii–xxxiv, xlvii, liii–liv, lvi, 206

Nisbet, Robert, 161

Nohl, Herman, 26

Normlessness, 192–93, 195–96

Objectification, objectivity, 32, 40, 51–54, 62–64, 84–85, 91–93, 101, 113, 226, 234–38, 267

Oedipus, xxvii

Ogden, C. K., 245, 259

On the Aesthetic Education of Man . . . (Schiller), 23–25, 27–29, 32, 47–48

On Christianity (Hegel). *See* Hegel, early "theological" writings

"On the Jewish Question" (Marx), 80, 118

Orphism, xxx, xxxii, lvi

Otherness, xxvi–xxvii, 38, 49, 62–64, 130–31, 242–43, 262. *See also* Separation; Strangeness

Others, other men, people, 18–20, 26–28, 49, 56, 65, 81, 89–90, 94–100, 102–8, 111, 114, 116, 130–35, 141, 146, 164–68, 176, 180, 185, 227–39, 269–74. *See also* Social life; Alienation, interpersonal

Our Inner Conflicts (Horney), 151–55

Parsons, Talcott, 161–62, 186–87, 248

Pascal, Gabriel, xxxiii–xxxiv

Paul, Saint, lvi, 15–16

Personality, 20, 25, 39, 46–47, 56, 62, 67, 80–81, 82–86, 91, 95–101, 136–37, 169, 221–22, 236, 267–68, 271–74. *See also* Individuality; Self

Phenomenology of Spirit (PG = *Phänomenologie des Geistes*) (Hegel), xvii, xx–xxi, 7, 15, 21–23, 25–27, 29, 31–32, 34, 38–72, 73–74, 78, 79–80, 81 n–82 n, 83, 84–86, 112, 208 n, 246

Philosophical anthropology. *See* Anthropology, philosophical

"Philosophical Manuscripts" (Marx). *See* "Economic and Philosophical Manuscripts"

Philosophy, xv–xvi, 5–6, 30–33, 75–79, 212–13, 240 n, 254–56; "alienated philosophers," Kaufmann on, xxix–xxxiv

Philosophy of Right (Hegel), 7, 14, 41 n, 42, 79–80, 80 n–81 n, 83, 86, 94, 97

Plato, xxvii, xxix–xxxii, xlvii, lvii

Plessner, Helmuth, 240, 242–44, 248–52

Political institutions. *See* State

Popitz, Heinrich, xxii

Popular culture, 184–89, 191, 197, 247, 259

Population explosion, xlix

Possessions. *See* Property; Wealth

Pour soi. See En soi–pour soi

Poverty, xliii, 117. *See also* Need

Powerlessness, 93–99, 163, 173–83, 250–51

Pre-industrial societies, xli

Private property. *See* Property

Product, 84–86, 87, 92–96, 112–13, 145–46, 235–38, 263, 265, 268–69. *See also* Alienation, of one's product; Objectification; Property

Production, 63, 82–88, 92–93, 97–98, 100–2, 107, 109–10, 127–28, 268–69. *See also* Alienation, of labor; Labor; Objectification

Property, 48, 66, 79, 83–86, 109, 116–18, 145–46; private, 17, 85–86, 107, 115–18; traditional and standard uses of "alienation" in connection with, 10, 13–14, 19, 257 n. *See also* Objectification; Product

Pufendorf, Samuel, Freiherr von, 19, 56 n

Putney, Snell, 191, 196

Pythagoras and Pythagoreans, xxxii

Rameau's Nephew (Diderot), 43 n, 65, 65 n

Rank, Otto, xxvii

Reduction, Feuerbach's and Marx's programs of, 75–77, 79

Religion, lv–lvii, 27–29, 32, 44, 49–50, 75–76, 76 n–77 n, 118; theology and theologians, 15–16. *See also* Tillich; specific Biblical books, figures

Relinquishment. *See* Surrender

Rembrandt van Rijn, xl

Renoir, Pierre Auguste, xxxix

Resignation, Hegel and, 36–37

Rettig, Salomon, 161, 174, 195–96, 202–3

Richards, I. A., 245, 259

Richardson, Arthur, 165, 177

Ridley, Jeanne, 176, 196 n

Rilke, Rainer Maria, xxxiv

Rodin, Auguste, xxxix

Roles, 201–4; role-models, 187

Romans, Epistle to the, lvi

Romanticism and Romantics, 57–58, 113, 137

Rousseau, Jean-Jacques, xxxiii–xxxiv, 18–21, 44 n, 55–56, 60

Russell, Bertrand, xxxiii–xxxiv

Sane Society, The (Fromm), xxi, 123–48 *passim*

Sartre, Jean-Paul, xxv, xxxiii–xxxiv, lvii, 2, 205, 214–15, 226–39, 245, 247–54, 262, 265–66, 269

Schaar, John, 164, 195, 201

Schelling, Friedrich von, 21 n, 30

Schiller, Friedrich, xxxiii, 23–25, 28–29, 31–32, 47

Search for a Method (Sartre), 234–36, 238

Seeman, Melvin, 170, 172, 174–75, 177, 185, 191, 194–95, 199, 248

Selbstdarstellung, lv

Self, selfhood, self-realization, xxiv, xxx, xxxi–xxxiii, xxxv, xxxviii, xl, lii, lvii–lviii, 19–21, 26, 29–31, 41, 45–46, 49–68, 70–72, 82–88, 93, 96, 99–102, 104, 108–15, 129, 132–34, 136–44, 149–59, 220–23, 228–39, 247, 264–69, 271–74. *See also* Alienation, self-; Individuality; Personality; Self-consciousness; Spirit; Universality

Self-alienation. *See* Alienation, self-

Self-consciousness, xxvi, xlvi, 22, 25, 27, 29–31, 44–47, 48, 50, 53, 54, 59–60, 62, 78–79, 84, 86–87, 89, 104, 126–30, 132–34, 137, 139–41, 143, 150–57, 162, 165–66, 174–75, 185, 187–88, 194–96, 200–1, 210–11, 216, 228–32, 234, 241–42, 252–53, 259–60, 264, 271–74

Sensuousness, sensuous life, sensibility, 82, 90–91, 110–11, 145

Separation, disparity, disunity, 15–16, 23–33, 36–37, 43–55, 58–62, 64, 68–69, 71, 76, 91–92, 96, 98–101, 103–5, 108–9, 112, 119–20, 127–31, 134–35, 137–38, 142, 147, 155, 157–59, 162, 183, 198, 203, 209, 212–18, 220–23, 226, 230–32, 237–39, 241–44, 249–67, 269–74. See also Alienation; Otherness; Strangeness

Shakespeare, William, xxxviii–xxxix, xlvii

Shils, Edward, 161

Simmel, Georg, xx

Sin, xxxiii, 220–21, 225

Singh, Khushwant, xli

Slavery, slave labor, servitude, 84, 99–100, 110, 268

Social contract theory, 16–21, 44, 55–56, 60–61. See also specific writers

Social life, sociality, fellowship, community, 82, 88–92, 102–8, 110–11, 131–34, 146, 164–68, 269–70, 272. See also Others; Solidarity

Social mobility, xliii

Social substance, 39–47, 49–55, 58–60, 63–64, 66–69, 71, 92, 104, 112–13, 135–38, 184, 190, 220, 242–44, 253, 265

Society, social institutions, xxvi, 2, 18–20, 25, 33–37, 39, 42–43, 55–56, 57–59, 61–62, 66–68, 72, 78, 86, 89–90, 92, 103–4, 106–8, 113, 115–19, 129, 135–38, 173–200, 242–44, 247, 263, 267, 271, 272–73. See also Civil society; Conformity; Culture; Social substance

Socrates, xv, xxx–xxxi

Solidarity, 89–90, 107, 165–66, 270–72. See also Social life

Sophocles, xxxvii–xxxviii

"Species-being," 81–82, 87, 88–89

Spinoza, Baruch, xxxiii–xxxiv

Spirit, spiritual, 22–23, 27, 29–30, 38–42, 49, 51–54, 57, 63–64, 66, 76, 243, 272

"Spirit of Christianity, The" (Hegel), 27–29, 51

Spontaneity, 86–88, 99–100, 137, 138–39, 149–50, 156–57

Srole, Leo, 196–97

State, political institutions, 2, 16–20, 23, 33–37, 39, 52, 57, 60–62, 66–68, 72, 87, 114, 135–38, 173–83, 263, 267. See also Social substance

Strangeness, alienness, xxvi–xxviii, 22, 27–28, 30–33, 36–37, 47–48, 51, 64, 67, 92–93, 96, 99–100, 128, 131–33, 151–59, 165–66, 177–78, 180–81, 184–88, 206–7, 209–11, 228–31, 236–38, 243–44. See also Otherness; Separation

Struening, Elmer, 165, 177

Substance. See Social substance

Surrender, relinquishment, 16–21, 26, 29, 44, 54–62, 68, 70, 80, 91–92, 94, 96–101, 108–9, 114–15, 119–20, 257. See also Entäusserung

Systematic Theology (Tillich), 205, 214–26

Terence, xxvi

Theology. See Religion; specific writers

Thompson, Wayne, 175–76
Tillich, Paul, 2, 205, 214–26, 232, 239, 247, 250, 252, 266
Transcendence. *See* Distance
Tucker, Robert, 74–75, 81 n

Universality, universal, 29, 41–43, 49–53, 56–61, 66–68, 82, 89, 104, 112, 137–38, 220

Van Gogh, Vincent, xxxix
Veräusserung, 14, 80, 94–95, 98–103, 109
Verdummung, xlvii

Verfremdung, xviii

Wages, wage labor, 75, 97, 99, 101, 106–7, 170
Warhol, Andy, xl
Warnock, Mary, 233 n
Wealth, 48, 66, 87–88, 114, 188–89, 192. *See also* Egoism
Weber, Max, xx
Wisdom, John, 38, 64
Wittgenstein, Ludwig, lxi, 3, 5, 254–55, 263
Work. *See* Labor; Production

ANCHOR BOOKS

PHILOSOPHY

AFRICAN RELIGIONS AND PHILOSOPHY—John S. Mbiti, A754

THE ALIENATION OF REASON: A History of Positivist Thought—Leszek Kolakowski; Norbert Guterman, A661

THE AMERICAN TRANSCENDENTALISTS—Perry Miller, ed., A119

AQUINAS: A Collection of Critical Essays—Anthony Kenny, ed., AP8

BASIC WRITINGS ON POLITICS AND PHILOSOPHY—Karl Marx and Friedrich Engels; Lewis S. Feuer, eds., A185

THE BIRTH OF TRAGEDY and THE GENEALOGY OF MORALS—Friedrich Nietzsche; Francis Golffing, trans., A81

BODY AND MIND—Keith Campbell, PP2

THE BROKEN IMAGE: Man, Science and Society—Floyd Matson, A506

COMEDY, "Laughter"—Henri Bergson—"Essay on Comedy" by George Meredith; intro. and supplementary essay by Wylie Sypher, A87

THE COSMOLOGICAL ARGUMENTS: A Spectrum of Opinion—Donald R. Burrill, ed., A586

CRITICAL EXISTENTIALISM—Nicola Abbagnano; Nino Langiulli, trans. and ed., A642

CRITIQUE OF PURE REASON—Immanuel Kant: F. Max Muller, trans., A551

CRITIQUE OF RELIGION AND PHILOSOPHY—Walter Kaufmann, A252

CUSTOM, LAW, AND MORALITY: Conflict and Continuity in Social Behavior—Burton M. Leiser, A669

DESCARTES: A Collection of Critical Essays—Willis Doney, ed., AP5

EITHER/OR, Volume I—Søren Kierkegaard; David F. Swenson and Lillian Marven Swenson, trans., revised with a Foreword by Howard A. Johnson, A181a

EITHER/OR, Volume II—Søren Kierkegaard; Walter Lowrie, trans., revised with a Foreword by Howard A. Johnson, A181b

ESSAYS IN PHILOSOPHICAL PSYCHOLOGY—Donald F. Gustafson, ed., A417

ETHICAL IMPERATIVE—Richard Means, A735

ETHICS AND SOCIETY—Richard T. de George, ed., A512

EVANGELICAL THEOLOGY—Karl Barth, A408

EVOLUTION AND CHRISTIAN HOPE—Ernst Benz, A607

THE FAITH OF A HERETIC—Walter Kaufmann, A336

FIVE STAGES OF GREEK RELIGION—Gilbert Murray, A51

FOUR EXISTENTIALIST THEOLOGIANS: A Reader from the Work of Jacques Maritain, Nicholas Berdyaev, Martin Buber, and Paul Tillich—Will Herberg, ed., A141

FREUD: The Mind of the Moralist—Philip Rieff, A278

FROM HEGEL TO NIETZSCHE: The Revolution in Nineteenth Century Thought—Karl Lowith; David E. Green, trans., A553

FROM SHAKESPEARE TO EXISTENTIALISM—Walter Kaufmann, A213

PHILOSOPHY (cont'd)

FROM STONE AGE TO CHRISTIANITY—W. F. Albright, A100

GUILT: Man and Society—Roger W. Smith, ed., A768

HEGEL: A Reinterpretation—Walter Kaufmann, A528a

HEGEL: Texts and Commentary—Walter Kaufmann, ed. and trans., A528b

HUME: A Collection of Critical Essays—V. C. Chappell, ed., AP2

INDIVIDUALS: An Essay in Descriptive Metaphysics—P. F. Strawson, A364

AN INTRODUCTION TO ETHICS—J. D. Mabbott, A662

AN INTRODUCTION TO LOGIC—David Mitchell, A714

AN INTRODUCTION TO METAPHYSICS—Martin Heidegger; Ralph Manheim, trans., A251

IRRATIONAL MAN—William Barrett, A351

KANT: A Collection of Critical Essays—Robert Paul Wolff, ed., AP4

LOGIC AND LANGUAGE, First and Second Series—A. G. N. Flew, ed., A449

MAIN CURRENTS IN SOCIOLOGICAL THOUGHT, Volume I: Montesquieu, Comte, Marx, Tocqueville, the Sociologists and the Revolution of 1848—Raymond Aron; Richard Howard and Helen Weaver, trans., A600a

MAIN CURRENTS IN SOCIOLOGICAL THOUGHT, Volume II: Durkheim, Pareto, Weber—Raymond Aron, A600b

MAN IN THE MODERN AGE—Karl Jaspers; Eden and Cedar Paul, trans., A101

MARTIN LUTHER: Selections from His Writings—John Dillenberger, ed., A271

MARX IN THE MID-TWENTIETH CENTURY—Gajo Petrović, A584

MARXISM AND EXISTENTIALISM—Walter Odajnyx, A443

THE MARXISM OF JEAN-PAUL SARTRE—Wilfrid Desan, A507

MEMORY—Don Locke, PP3

THE METAPHYSICAL FOUNDATIONS OF MODERN SCIENCE—E. A. Burtt, A41

MILL: A Collection of Critical Essays—J. B. Scheewind, ed., AP7

MODERN DEDUCTIVE LOGIC—Robert J. Ackermann, NP1

MODERN MORAL PHILOSOPHY—W. D. Hudson, NP2

MODERN SCIENCE AND MODERN MAN—James B. Conant, A10

THE OCHRE ROBE—Agehananda Bharati, A776

THE ONTOLOGICAL ARGUMENT FROM ST. ANSELM TO CONTEMPORARY PHILOSOPHERS—Alvin Plantinga, ed., intro. by Richard Taylor, A435

PATTERNS OF ANARCHY: A Collection of Writings on the Anarchist Tradition—Leonard I. Krimerman and Lewis Parry, eds., A501

PERCEIVING, SENSING, AND KNOWING: A Book of Readings from Twentieth-Century Sources on the Philosophy of Perception—Robert J. Swartz, ed., A460

PHENOMENOLOGY: The Philosophy of Edmund Husserl and Its Interpretation—Joseph J. Kockelmans, ed., A585

12Bb

THE PHILOSOPHY OF HISTORY IN OUR TIME—Hans Meyerhoff, ed., A164

THE PHILOSOPHY OF SOCRATES—Gregory Vlastos, ed., AP11

PRAGMATIC PHILOSOPHY—Amelie Rorty, ed., A538

PSYCHE AND SYMBOL—C. G. Jung, A136

RYLE: A Collection of Critical Essays—Oscar P. Wood and George Pitcher, eds., AP10

SELECTIONS FROM THE WRITINGS OF KIERKEGAARD—Lee M. Hollander, trans., revised edition, A210

SOCIAL AND POLITICAL PHILOSOPHY: Readings from Plato to Gandhi—John Somerville and Ronald Santoni, eds., A370

SOCIALIST HUMANISM: An International Symposium—Erich Fromm, ed., A529

SOCRATES: The Man and His Thought—A. E. Taylor, A9

STRUCTURALISM—Jacques Ehrmann, ed., A719

THE SUFIS—Idries Shah, A765

THE TACIT DIMENSION—Michael Polanyi, A540

THE TANTRIC TRADITION—Agehananda Bharati, A745

THE THEORY OF KNOWLEDGE—D. W. Hamlyn, NP3

THE THREE JEWELS: An Introduction to Modern Buddhism—Bhikshu Sangharakshita (Stavira), A763

THREE WAYS OF THOUGHT IN ANCIENT CHINA—Arthur Waley, A75

TRAGEDY AND PHILOSOPHY—Walter Kaufmann, A689

TRUTH—Alan R. White, PP1

UNIVERSALS AND PARTICULARS: Readings in Ontology—Michael J. Loux, ed., A722

WITTGENSTEIN: The Philosophical Investigations—A Collection of Critical Essays—George Pitcher, ed., AP3

WORLD OF THE BUDDHA: A Reader—From the Three Baskets to Modern Zen—Lucien Stryk, ed., A615

WRITINGS OF THE YOUNG MARX ON PHILOSOPHY AND SOCIETY—Loyd D. Easton and Kurt H. Guddat, trans. and eds., A583

ZEN: Poems, Prayers, Sermons, Anecdotes, Interviews—Lucien Stryk and Takashi Ikemoto, eds. and trans., A485

ZEN BUDDHISM: Selected Writings of D. T. Suzuki—William Barrett, ed., A90

ZEN FLESH, ZEN BONES: A Collection of Zen and Pre-Zen Writings—Paul Reps, ed., A233